# UNCHAINED MEMORIES

# Unchained Memories

TRUE STORIES OF
TRAUMATIC MEMORIES,
LOST AND FOUND

## Lenore Terr, M.D.

BasicBooks
*A Division of* HarperCollins*Publishers*

*Designed by Ellen Levine*

Library of Congress Cataloging-in-Publication Data
Terr, Lenore, 1936–
    Unchained memories: true stories of traumatic memories,
lost and found / Lenore Terr.
        p.   cm.
Includes bibliographical references and index.
    ISBN 0–465–08823–6 (cloth)
    ISBN 0–465–09539–9 (paper)
    1. Amnesia—Case studies. 2. Post-traumatic stress disorder—Case
studies. 3. Psychic trauma—Case studies. 4. Recollection (Psychology)—
Case studies. I. Title.
RC552.P67T47 1994
616.85'21—dc20                                          93–40371
                                                            CIP

95 96 97 98 ❖/RRD 9 8 7 6 5 4 3 2 1

To the Family of My Childhood

*Esther Cagen Raiken (1908– ), Samuel Cagen (1909–1982),*
*Barbara Cagen (1941–1972), and Robert Cagen (1945– )*

*"No man and no force can abolish memory."*
—Franklin Delano Roosevelt

# CONTENTS

# PROLOGUE

Sometimes patients lead their doctors to new interests. Two patients have led me that way, both of them women. Number one was the very first psychiatric patient I ever treated—a young woman whose first words to me, following our exchange of names, were "If you don't stop me, I'm going to kill my child." She had been admitted to the inpatient psychiatric unit at the University of Michigan Medical Center. It was September 1962, and I had just begun my residency, having taken a two-month break to have a child of my own. To an inexperienced psychiatrist and a new mother, her words were especially threatening; this was a challenge that I might or might not be able to meet. It was clear to me that the woman meant what she said. But what jarred me almost as much as her words themselves was the fact that up until then nobody had taken her seriously. She had alerted a number of well-trained professionals. Once, she started to drown her little girl—then a toddler—in the bathtub. Thinking better of it, she brought the youngster, who was still coughing and choking, to the emergency room of a local hospital. "Oh, that's O.K.," the doctor told her, after she had tried to confess. "Kids fall all the time in tubs." A year later, she attacked her daughter with a hot teakettle. When she brought the child to the hospital—a different one—the emergency-room personnel had responded, "Accidents happen."

I asked my patient if I could meet her daughter, now three years old, and the mother agreed. As has turned out to be the case throughout my career, I needed to see this story from the child's point of view. I found the little girl to be extraordinarily angry. Her behavior at home had verged on vandalism. I know now that the problem was psychological trauma, but at the time it was hard for me to tell whether this behavior had originally prompted the mother toward murder or whether the mother's actions had forced the child to strike back. After I got to know the mother in treatment, I realized that the original problem lay with the woman herself. But something else had turned up to help me. A University of Colorado research team led by the pediatrician C. Henry Kempe had published a paper in the *Journal of the American Medical Association* on a newly discovered condition they called the battered-child syndrome. The syndrome almost exactly matched the case I now had before me. While the *Journal of the American Medical Association* article stated that battering parents rarely provided histories matching the physical injuries their children suffered, my own patient was more than willing to provide a history. Child abuse was new to doctors, virtually anything she told me and anything I did with her would be new, it seemed. And if I also followed her young daughter—which I did for a couple of years— almost anything the child showed me would be new.

I spread the word at the medical center. If anybody had a case of child abuse, I was willing to consult. In four years I saw ten cases— not many, when one considers the numbers of abused children showing up at hospitals today. I have been studying childhood trauma ever since. The woman improved—at least, during the years I followed her—and her child survived a particularly vulnerable phase of development. It would take several more years, however, before I could feel I really understood what it means to be traumatized as a child.

The second woman who led me to a new interest in psychiatry came to my San Francisco office in the summer of 1990. That woman got me to think about the memories that adults retain or recapture from early traumas. Her name was Eileen Franklin Lipsker, and she had lost the memories of a murder committed by her father, George Franklin—a murder she had witnessed when she was a child of eight. She had retrieved these memories twenty years after the fact, and she came to see me as a forensic, or legal, case. I was a potential witness for the prosecution of her father, and Eileen Franklin Lipsker posed many more questions than answers for me. What happens to the memories of trauma once a child grows up? Why do some of these memories go underground? And if these memories are hidden, what influences do they then exert over a life? I would revisit my own research data on the traumatic memories of children, and I would begin a new study on memory itself. Long-term childhood memory would be a particularly fascinating subject to follow, especially if these memories were traumatic. A history of trauma would make the search easier, setting up an iridescent thread that could be glimpsed in the fabric of memory.

A coincidence helped me tremendously in this regard. A deluge of letters hit my desk in the summer of 1990, in response to my first book, *Too Scared to Cry,* which dealt with the effects of trauma on children. These letters were life stories from total strangers—striking tales of personal childhood histories lost and found. The letter writers had many things to teach me. They showed me what a wide array of defenses exists to keep adults from recalling the horrors they experienced as children. And they showed me what a wide variety of ways there are for these memories to return. The letter writers also showed me that a whole life can be shaped by an old trauma, remembered or not. A woman wrote that she had spent eight years as a cloistered nun—her means of unconsciously repressing memories of sexual abuse she had suffered as a child. A man wrote of being misdiagnosed as schizophrenic; his lost memories had made his behavior entirely incomprehensible to his therapists, who knew nothing of the childhood incidents that led to it. Another man wrote of running a marathon, reviewing his life in the process, and finding a number of old memories that explained not only certain lifelong fears but also his choice of profession. Some of these letters described how old childhood memories had reappeared—through dream watching, poetry writing, painting, keeping journals. Some of the writers had become amateur detectives, asking questions of old friends or family members, checking out back issues of newspapers and area maps. And a few had gone back to their original family homes, in order to see again the places where their memories took root.

I began to realize that I knew something about memories of childhood trauma from three research studies on traumatized children which I had already completed. These studies had revealed certain ways of dealing with childhood trauma that could also be seen in the letters from my adult correspondents. I knew, too, that in the scientific literature on psychology and brain research there was a great deal of information about memory that could be integrated with what we observe in adults who were traumatized as children. Indeed, there was more information than I had thought.

And so this book took form, propelled by a murder case, a number of friendly nudges from letter writers, and some readings through the literature on mind and brain. In February 1992, the American College of Psychiatrists put on its annual four-day meeting. I was the program chair for 1991–92, and it was up to me and my committee to decide on the topic. We chose "Memory" and invited leading biologists, psychologists, developmentalists, and clinicians to speak. We also invited a number of writers to talk about how their childhood memories were reflected in their work; the poet Robert Hass and the biographer Diane Middlebrook came, as did the novelists Linda Sexton, Frank Conroy, and Tobias Wolfe. Elaine Tipton, the prosecutor of *People v. Franklin,* and Eileen Franklin Lipsker, the key witness, spoke at the meeting. Paul Appelbaum, a prominent forensic psychiatrist, discussed the dilemma that returning memories of crime pose to our courts. This book was already taking shape by the time of the College meeting. But at that meeting, it found considerable muscle.

I decided to write this book in short-story style because that format is enjoyable and relatively uncomplicated. I have always loved reading true "short stories" about psychology and medicine—Robert M. Lindner's *The Fifty Minute Hour* and Berton Roueché's *Eleven Blue Men* were longtime favorites of mine. So I have written *Unchained Memories* in that vein—as a collection of stories about people who recalled traumatic episodes from their childhood. It is a book of remembrances—the snippets that people retain from their early years and the crucial events—many times, the lost ones—that these snippets sometimes represent.

These stories illustrate how we forget childhood trauma, and they tell us how and why these memories return. They also illustrate exactly what goes wrong with memory and what parts of a memory sometimes turn false. One story in this book is about an entirely false remembrance. Another—the last tale, "Searching for Corky"— demonstrates that deliberate and conscientious searches for old memories can meet with success. This story is about one of the many strangers who wrote to me in the wake of my first book.

The stories can be read in any order; each one is complete in itself. But I would suggest reading them in sequence, because the scientific information on memory builds throughout the book. I have included a large section of notes at the end—both to give added information to the interested reader and to offer primary sources to the interested professional.

None of the people whose stories appear as chapters in this book were in treatment with me. The "child star," Lua Greene (whose name and other identifying circumstances I disguise), was never interviewed by me; instead, I watched and listened to her being interviewed by others on videotape and audio recordings. I wrote about another subject of a story, Marilyn Van Derbur Atler, based on her TV appearances, her speeches, her sister's observations, and considerable newspaper and magazine coverage. I was fortunate enough to meet personally and to interview six of the people whose memory stories I tell. They saw me because of their involvement in court proceedings in which I appeared as a witness, or because they were willing to grant me an interview. Here I combined what a reporter does with what a psychiatrist does. I write of three of these people—Eileen Franklin Lipsker, Gwen Mitchell, and James Ellroy—without disguising their names, their characteristics, or the names of the people around them. Three others—Patricia Bartlett, Gary Baker, and Ross Harriman—are disguised, including, of course, their names but also including certain identifying details such as their physical appearance, occupation, and place of residence. In their stories, other individuals—for example, the attorneys who worked on their cases—are also disguised. All researchers and mental-health professionals appearing or referred to in these stories, however—with the exception of Eliana Jacob of "The Silver at the Surface of the Water" and Sarah Alliston and Edward Riley, who are disguised in "The Child Star's Tale" for obvious reasons—are presented with their true names and descriptions.

I wish to thank a number of behavioral scientists who advised and aided me as I worked on this project. My team at the American Board of Psychiatry and Neurology Part II examinations—a group of thirty or so distinguished psychiatrists who come four times a year to various centers in the United States to give oral exams to psychiatrists—pointed me to a good deal of the scientific literature and to several of the people who have enriched this book. My Program Committee for the 1992 American College of Psychiatrists meeting—Robert Hales, Stuart Keill, Linda Logsdon, Elizabeth Small, David Spiegel, Stefan

Stein, John Talbott, and Raymond Waggoner, Jr.—did the same. A number of memory psychologists read sections of the book and offered their help: Robert Bjork, Stephen Ceci, Gail Goodman, and Larry Squire, all of whom deserve my thanks. The neuroscientists Tim Tully, Eric Kandel, and Mortimer Mishkin also read sections, something I deeply appreciate. Two lawyers checked my legal information in chapters 1, 2, and 6: Elaine Tipton, an assistant D.A. in San Mateo County, and an Oklahoma lawyer I call "Tom Blackburn." Three psychiatric readers—Robert Michels, Charles Nemeroff, and George Vaillant—read through the entire manuscript and offered their suggestions. My very special kudos to them. Two friends— Rosemary Patton, who teaches and writes on the art of writing, and Evelyn Keitel, who teaches American literature in Kemnitz, Germany—read the first draft.

When the book was ready for the publisher, my editor at Basic Books, Jo Ann Miller, who was a friend long before we ever took on this project together, did a fabulous job of initial editing. Sara Lippincott, for years an editor at *The New Yorker,* did remarkable work on the final edit. My agent, Joy Harris, has been extremely helpful, too. I send each of them my heartfelt thanks.

The Chowchilla schoolbus kidnapping study was funded by the Rosenberg Foundation, and the study of the children's response to the *Challenger* explosion was funded by the William T. Grant Foundation. Time and space to write up those studies were provided to me by the Rockefeller Foundation. My assistant Marsha Bessey typed every word of this book and helped edit it as well. She did this while trying to do all the other things that a busy medical office requires. My special appreciation to her. My husband, Abba, an allergist and immunologist, read the entire manuscript before it was fully developed. My particular thanks to him; he will always be my most trusted adviser and friend.

UNCHAINED MEMORIES

# 1

# Ringside Seats at an Old Murder

California girls don't always play outside, contrary to what the travel posters might have you believe. Young girls in the southern suburbs sport light year-round tans carelessly acquired on walks to and from school, from an occasional afternoon at the neighborhood pool, from a weekend outing at Disneyland or the beach. Most days after school, West Coast girls like young Jessica Lipsker prefer to stay inside, where they can shelter their heads from the cloudless sky, grab a cookie, watch TV, pretend with friends, and draw houses with tied-back curtains and big red doors.

One unusually smog-free January afternoon, Jessica and two other little girls, freshly home from kindergarten, burst into the family room of the Lipskers' house in Canoga Park. One child was blond, one brunette, and the third, Jessica, was in between, with reddish hair. Freckles marched across the little redhead's cheekbones and onto the bridge of her nose. Eileen Franklin Lipsker, Jessica's mother, sat on the couch. The three little girls curled up on the floor near her. Should she read to them? No, she was busy with both hands bottle-feeding Aaron, her one-year-old son. Folksy children's songs sounded from the tape player—"Oats, Peas, Beans, and Barley Grow," and a French song, and one from Italy, and a kids' version of "Yellow Submarine." "You know," Eileen told me many months afterward, when I first met her, "I was bent on being the perfect mother. Perfect mothers play children's music for their children in the afternoon."

Eileen Franklin Lipsker was an exceptionally attentive mother. At the top of her twenty-eight-year-old "wish list" was to be good at mothering. Her own mother, Eileen thought, had not tended to her well. Jessica, who at age five-and-a-half looked and acted like a seven-year-old, gave Eileen great pleasure. Despite her difficult marriage to an older man, Eileen could pride herself on how nicely her children were doing.

Should the girls draw? "Why, yes, of course. Draw." As long as Aaron stayed quiet, Eileen might just let her mind go and enjoy the late January light streaming in through the steeply slanting blinds.

Little Jessica—everyone called her Sica—seemed determined to be a pleasant hostess. She and her friends shared a prized set of markers without a single whine, protest, or grab. The children sat at Eileen's feet, drawing little girls in ravishing dresses—princesses, perhaps. Eileen let her thoughts wander. Sica occasionally glanced up toward the couch, her clear blue eyes shimmering in the afternoon light. Eileen's mind began to drift.

"I was—I mean, for all practical purposes, I was spaced out," she told me later. "I was thinking of nothing. It's—you know—the afternoon, and the kids are home, and it's almost time to start dinner. Just boring, mundane, nonexistent things. And the light is coming in through the slats of the Levolors, and it's warm. Who knows? The temperature? The light? Sometimes something just happens."

For less than a millisecond Eileen may have thought, "Sica looks older, more grown-up today." But she doesn't remember that now. Perhaps her mind was unconsciously prompted by the little splash of freckles, the red hair not quite as fiery as her own. An odd sense of something—What was it?—may have darted in and out of Eileen's mind.

Reddish blond strands of fine, little-girl hair brightened in the sun. Jessica twisted her head to look at her mother. To ask something? Her chin pointed up in inquiry. She looked up and over her shoulder. Her eyes brightened. How odd! The young girl's body remained stationary, while her head pivoted around and up. Now. Now. Mother's and child's eyes met. The girl's eyes so clear, so blue.

And at exactly that moment Eileen Lipsker remembered something. She remembered it as a picture. She could see her redheaded friend Susan Nason looking up, twisting her head, and trying to catch her eye.

Eileen, eight years old, stood outdoors, on a spot a little above the place where her best friend was sitting. It was 1969, twenty years earlier. The sun was beaming directly into Susan's eyes. And Eileen could see that Susan was afraid. Terrified.

The blue of Susan Nason's eyes was the bluest, clearest blue Eileen had ever seen. Suddenly Eileen felt something move to one side. She looked away from those arresting eyes and saw the silhouette of her father. Both of George Franklin's hands were raised high above his head. He was gripping a rock. He steadied himself to bring it down. His target was Susan.

"No!" Eileen felt a scream welling up in her throat. But not a sound disturbed her family room that January day in 1989. The shout stayed trapped in her mind. "A chill ran up me," she told me, months later. "It was so, so intense. And I said to myself a very clear, very loud 'No,' as if I had the power to stop the memory from coming."

But Eileen Franklin Lipsker's buried memory, once it started rising to the surface, could not be stopped. She remembered the feeling of a scream invading her throat. She remembered Susan, just four days short of her ninth birthday, sensing George Franklin's attack and putting up her right hand to stave him off. *Thwack!* Eileen could hear the sound, a sound like a baseball bat swatting an egg—the worst sound of her life. "No!" she yelled inside her head. "I *have* to make this memory stop." Another *thwack.* And then quiet. Blood. Blood everywhere on Susan's head. "Something whitish" along with the blood. And "some hair that was no longer attached to her body." Blood covered Susan's face. Her hand was smashed.

On a quiet winter afternoon in 1989, a suburban housewife's mind almost shorted out with overload. Her heart pounded mercilessly against her chest. The conclusion Eileen Lipsker drew that moment was that she must be insane.

She did not question her memory, though—just its long absence. She could not understand why a real memory had waited in hiding all those years. Later she told me, "I thought to myself, 'If I let this [memory] show, if anyone finds out, if someone sees, if I tell anyone—then, you know, that's it. Goodbye kids.' You know, I lose the kids."

Eileen sat quietly for many minutes that winter afternoon in 1989, watching as the angle of the sunlight shifted through her Levolor blinds. She knew nothing at all about the psychological defense of repression. She could not understand what had just happened. Jessica's young guests eventually went home, and Eileen rose from the couch, put Aaron in his playpen, and started dinner.

Eileen did not realize that certain very important feelings—even entire experiences—can be banished from consciousness only to influence attitudes and behavior, and even, perhaps, to be reclaimed as full memories at some other time. She simply knew that a twenty-year-old memory had invaded her conscious thoughts as she glanced down at her daughter's uplifted chin, tilted head, and blue eyes. She knew that long ago she had witnessed her best friend's murder. And she felt almost destroyed by the power of the revelation.

For months afterward, Eileen told no one about her newfound memories. She tried to force the memories "back into their own little drawer and seal it"; they caused her too much anxiety. They hurt her stomach and gave her palpitations of the heart. But try as she might, Eileen's "drawer" had stuck open. She could no longer forget what she had so successfully forgotten for twenty years.

Eileen and Susan had been friends and schoolmates in Foster City, a suburb of San Francisco about twenty miles south of the city. Eileen knew that Susan had been murdered—she had always known that. But she had not known that she had been there when it happened. She had simply assumed—as had everyone else after Susan's body was discovered off a highway several miles out of town—that it was one of those crimes that most likely would never be solved.

One recollection, however, led to another. Over the next several months, many small bits of Eileen's memory returned. Some were sights, a few were sounds, and some were simply thoughts. Eileen Lipsker found herself inundated with a slow but inevitable memory cascade.

Sometimes when Eileen Lipsker concentrated hard, a new piece of the Nason murder emerged—the image of a tossed child's shoe, for instance. More often, however, the memories floated in as she paced on her treadmill or jogged past her neighbors' yards. She remembered the makeshift grave in which her father had placed Susan. She came to recall a crushed, stoneless, silver child's ring.

Susan Nason and Eileen Franklin had both been teased as children for their red hair and freckles. Eileen remembered how much they loved looking alike. They had become the best of friends. One September afternoon when she was eight years old, Eileen went off with her father to "play hookey" from the usual after-school routine. Eileen didn't even know what "hookey" meant until Dad suggested it that day. Once the memories came back, she could almost hear him say the word in her mind. She and her father spotted Susan playing in an open field near their house. Eileen begged Susan to come along. She is uncertain about whether or not Janice Franklin, her older sister, was with them at that moment. But she came to remember being a threesome in the van—just Susan, Eileen, and Dad.

George Franklin owned an "old hippie van," complete with mattresses in the back and curtains on the windows. He worked as a fireman, and he was often able to take afternoons off. Keeping the curtains drawn, he drove the two little girls out into the country and up past a coastal mountain lake that Eileen had always thought was the prettiest place in the world. But pretty can turn ugly without a seam. George stopped the van. Susan and Eileen played hard, jumping up and down on a pile of mattresses in the back and pretending it was a trampoline. George went outside for a smoke and a beer. Then he came into the back of the van to play, too.

Suddenly George told Eileen to go up front. The child felt strange about this and turned around to peek. She could see white socks and white child-size underwear. She could hear weak cries. The eight-year-old Franklin girl knew that this was a rape. At age twenty-eight, she did not know how she had known it. But she remembered she had been so terrified as she saw her father thrust his body against Susan's that she had rolled herself into a tight little ball in the front seat.

After a time, George Franklin took Susan Nason out of the van. Eileen remembered going out, too. She stood on a mound a little above them, watching. At the very last moment of her life, Susan twisted her head to look up at Eileen. Their eyes met. The light hit Susan's irises, brightening them. "Help me," she must have flashed. But there wasn't a thing Eileen could do. She thinks now that her father must have killed Susan Nason to keep her from talking. But she has no memories of hearing George Franklin explain.

Eileen's memory cascade included some memories from the moments immediately after the killing. When she saw her friend's slumped body and the horrible injuries to Susan's head and hand, she started to run, screaming, for the van. But her father grabbed her from behind, knocking her to the ground. "It's all over now," he said.

George Franklin ordered Eileen to "forget all about this." He said, "No one will ever believe you." Eileen would be "put away" if she talked, because it had been *her* idea for Susan to get into the van. Eileen came to remember that her father had snarled, as she kept on sobbing, "If you don't stop this, then I'll have to kill *you*."

George ordered his eight-year-old to help him pull a mattress out of the van. When Eileen couldn't or wouldn't do it, he became even more furious with her. Taking a small shovel from the back, he walked out of sight. Eileen eventually remembered hearing the shovel strike the ground "down below," in the place where she had last seen Susan. As they drove away, Eileen felt "terrible . . . completely alone." Later, at home, she developed a bad case of the shivers. She was terrified of what she had seen and what her father might do next. Janice Franklin let Eileen sleep in her bed that night. The younger girl trembled all night long.

As an adult, Eileen could not remember how she began to "forget" the murder. In fact, that piece of memory—about the process of losing memory—never did fall into place. But Eileen does know that her repression began on the night of the day Susan Nason was killed. By the time her teacher spoke to the fourth grade about their classmate's disappearance, Eileen could no longer consciously remember what had happened. She grieved for Susan, and she would have no more best friends in childhood.

Although the concept of repressed memory has not been fully experimentally tested and proved, most clinicians accept the theory of repression developed by Sigmund Freud in the 1890s. People repeatedly see evidence of repression in their friends or in themselves. Before Freud, the philosophers Arthur Schopenhauer and Johann Friedrich Herbart wrote of our unwillingness to face circumstances or ideas that injure our interests. Freud went a step further. Based on his work with the physician Josef Breuer on hysteria, he concluded that people actively and deliberately push into unconsciousness memories that bear important and painful emotional meaning. In Eileen Franklin's case, the meaning was loss and threatened annihilation. Freud asserted that, set aside or no, repressed memories influence behavior, thinking, and emotions, and produce mental symptoms. He also came to see that repression as a defense is not only associated with mental illness but characterizes normal psychology as well.

Repression on a small scale is more commonplace than you might think. Here is an example. In the first week of September, a new graduate student at Berkeley forgets to attend his library orientation. "I just forgot," he says. But a little later his story sounds more complex. He recalls a time when three of his classmates in elementary school shot spitballs in the school library and he, wrongly, was thrown out. He has repressed, not forgotten, his appointment in the graduate-school library. The emotional meaning of his earlier humiliation has interfered with his ability to keep the appointment in mind. Although this young man did not have the kind of hideous experience that Eileen Franklin felt impelled to hide from herself, the mechanism is the same. Many memory lapses and recoveries are related to highly meaningful people or events.

Simple forgetting is different from repression. We cannot possibly file away every single thing we experience. We must discard much of the new information we receive. Some material does not fully register and thus does not move well into storage. And some does not last after it has been stored. I cannot now remember the name of last week's substitute newscaster on one of the national morning TV shows—nor, for that matter, can I remember what show it was. I cannot remember the number of my hotel room from a trip a few weeks ago. Except for trivia collectors, most of us shuck off tons of unnecessary information each day. Even the trivia hound rids himself of what he considers unnecessary.

At age eight, Eileen Franklin fully took in and mentally stored a terrible memory, the worst of her life. Then, by means of a coincidence of perceptions (a redheaded daughter's turned head, a look of concern, sunstruck hair, freckles, and blue eyes penetrated by sunlight), Eileen's old memories resurfaced. When she was eight years old, she had watched her best friend's murder. At age twenty-eight, she would come forward to bear witness against her father.

I should come forward at this point, too. I am a child psychiatrist, and from the month I started my training in psychiatry, I have been studying what happens to children who go through terrible events. I have always conducted my research on childhood trauma. Originally I was concerned with how youngsters get through repeated physical batterings at home, then with what children do in their minds as they respond to a single terrible event. One of the early discoveries I made about trauma was that if a normal child goes through just one horrifying event, he will usually remember it clearly. The event will be etched in, like the frieze on an art-deco window. One terrible event in an otherwise nonterrible life stands out in a child's mind.

I talked to a group of kids seven to thirteen months after they had been kidnapped from their school bus in Chowchilla, California, and I interviewed them again four to five years after the kidnapping. Their abductors had driven them around in darkened vans and then buried them alive in a truck trailer lowered below ground level in a rock quarry. And I talked to another group of kids—153 of them— both five weeks and fourteen months after the *Challenger* spacecraft blew up. Every single child in both groups remembered what had happened. It is hard to repress striking events like those.

But as I studied children over the years and took careful notes on about four hundred separate childhood tales of trauma as they were recounted in my psychiatric office, I began to discover that some children do indeed "forget" traumatic experiences. An enormous controversy exists today about whether or not childhood memories can be fully retrieved in adulthood without major distortion—especially when the memories have been repressed for a number of years. The question is, How accurate is a long-buried memory once it resurfaces? Many adults are coming forward today with newly returned memories of an act of negligence, assault, or even murder. Some of them are suing their parents after retrieving incest memories lost for years. And some of them claim to have been eyewitnesses to old murders. Experts in the mental-health professions are coming forward, too, with opinions about the validity of these reclaimed memories. And often their opinions are diametrically opposed.

Eileen Lipsker's behavior in the days to come would heighten the controversy about recovered memories of trauma. Eileen had no idea what repression was all about. And so she did nothing with her memories for months after they came back to her. On some days, she even wished them to disappear again. She knew that what had crashed her mental barriers that afternoon in January felt extremely dangerous and scary. "I had never met anyone who had repressed anything," she told me. "And surely, I thought, my father never murdered Susan or I would have always remembered."

Repression, as opposed to simple forgetting, is such an active process that it is possible to repress the same thing more than once. For example, a thirty-five-year-old attorney I shall call Jeremiah Converse entered psychotherapy for depression, and within weeks had spontaneously retrieved several repressed memories from a series of sexual abuses he had experienced at about the age of six. An adult male had repeatedly sodomized him, Jeremiah said. But it was not clear in his mind whether this was a family member, a teacher, or somebody else. Then one night Jeremiah saw his abuser's face in a dream. He awoke at 3:00 A.M. with an "Aha!" feeling. He then went back to sleep. The next morning Jeremiah completely "forgot" the face he had seen. He remembered his dream but not the man's identity.

For ten months Eileen Lipsker held on to her newly retrieved memories without going to the authorities. During this time, memory after memory came back. She remembered the brand of beer George Franklin drank on the day he murdered Susan Nason and the brand of cigarettes he smoked outside the van. She remembered the trash bin where he dropped his beer can. She remembered the size and shape of the rock he used to kill Susan. Eileen repeatedly questioned the validity of her memories. But they felt "undeniable and indelible" to her. She agonized about what to do next, torn between a sense of urgency and dread of the consequences of her action.

In his psychiatric writings before 1897, Freud postulated that we repress because our memories cause us painful conflict. Sexual abuse in childhood is the conflicted event that accounts for repression, Freud said early in his career. But after 1897 Freud abruptly turned away from real events in the lives of his patients, holding instead that children's fantasies of being seduced and the related internal conflicts these imagined seductions bring are the reason that people repress. In a sense, Freud turned away from the Eileen Franklins of this world when he shifted his position.

No one can say exactly why Freud made this shift—the psychoanalyst Jeffrey Moussaieff Masson has accused Freud of fearing the disapproval of other physicians and psychologists—and Freud himself did not directly indicate the reason for the abandonment of his theory. He would have been right, however, in both his pre- and post-1897 theo-

ries. Repression can be inspired by either internal or external conflict.
But Freud developed his new ideas into the Oedipus complex, transference, dream interpretation, and defense. And his followers came right
along with him. After 1897, until the mid-twentieth century, only the
independent psychiatrist Pierre Janet, in France, and Freud's psychoanalytic disciple Phyllis Greenacre, in New York City, did much thinking or writing about recovered memories of childhood trauma. Janet
believed that the representations of traumatic events were mentally
"dissociated"—set aside from ordinary processes of the mind by losing
their linkages to conscious thought. Greenacre wrote that these experiences were "repressed"—buried under the narrow layer of awareness.
But almost everyone else in post-Freudian psychiatry in the first half of
the twentieth century left real childhood trauma alone.

In midcentury, however, things began to change. The New York
psychiatrist David Levy generated new interest in childhood trauma
by comparing it with the battlefield trauma suffered by soldiers in
the Second World War. By the early 1970s, the Welsh psychiatrist
Gaynor Lacey and the University of Cincinnati child psychiatrist
C. Janet Newman had reported on the psychiatric changes that two
significant natural disasters (the destruction of a school in Wales by a
slag-heap avalanche, and the destruction of several West Virginia
towns by the Buffalo Creek flood) had on a number of children. Lacey
and Newman looked at the children themselves—something new.

What would really be new, I realized in the early 1970s, would be
a study of one relatively large group of normal children who had suffered an almost identical traumatic experience. By following them
over time, we might begin to understand what terrible reality does in
kids' minds. And so, when twenty-six Chowchilla children were kidnapped on July 15, 1976, from their school bus and then returned
twenty-seven hours later physically unharmed, I knew I had my test
case. I hoped that their signs (what they were observed to do) and
symptoms (what they complained of) would define the syndrome of
childhood trauma. In 1977, I interviewed twenty-three of the children, and in 1980 and 1981 I interviewed twenty-five of them,
matching them at that time to a normal control group who lived in
McFarland and Porterville, two Central Valley towns some hundred
miles distant.

I found that every one of the kidnapped children retained detailed,
precise memories of what had happened, even in the later study. Most

of the remembered details closely corresponded to the memories of the other kidnapped children. The Chowchilla memories stood out in sharp light, as if the whole scene had been lit with a magnesium lamp. Nobody repressed. And nobody forgot. The general outline of the Chowchilla children's recollection of events also closely matched what the police and the FBI found. These youngsters were what I would later define as Type I trauma victims—children who had suffered a single traumatic event.

There were great differences in the wholeness of retained memory between the Chowchilla kidnap victims and Eileen Franklin Lipsker. The Chowchilla group consistently remembered everything. Yet Eileen started to repress on the very night of the day she witnessed her best friend's murder. In January 1988, a year before Eileen "saw" the murder memory in her mind, I published a clinical study of twenty particularly young trauma victims who had come to me with police or eyewitness documentations of their ordeals. These children had been traumatized in various ways prior to the age of five. I found that those children who had been repeatedly traumatized could not remember as fully as could those who were traumatized only once. Had Eileen been traumatized more than once?

When Eileen Franklin Lipsker's story began appearing on TV, early in 1990, I became interested in it, not just because her memory story was unusually dramatic but because a belated murder charge is itself an unusual occurrence. After I met her, I realized that Eileen was what I had defined as a Type II trauma victim—a repeatedly traumatized child. She had always remembered, for instance, that her father was an unpredictably violent alcoholic—this she had *not* forgotten. He threw her and his four other children against walls. He punched her and hit much too hard. He beat her severely until she was about eight years old. And then he stopped, though he did not stop manhandling her mother and her brother and sisters. There were times when Eileen felt sure that her mother would be killed before her very eyes. Morever, Mrs. Franklin was hospitalized a couple of times for mental illness. The illness memories, too, might have been frightening. All this would have added up to make Eileen a child well rehearsed in terror—a child prone to losing the memory of an ordeal.

These experiences were probably frequent enough and awful enough, in fact, to have allowed Eileen to develop the knack for automatic repression. By the time she was eight years old, she had no doubt practiced "forgetting" so often that she could repress when she really needed to. Children who go through a number of terrors protect themselves this way. They are able to muster massive defenses against remembering, because this is the only way they can get through a frightening childhood.

When I first heard of the case, I had no idea what other terrible events had taught Eileen to repress so efficiently. There was no hint at this point that she had ever been sexually abused. But one reason for Eileen's sudden recollection was clear, I thought. She had become comfortable in her third decade of life.

In order for a repressed memory to return, there usually is a ground—that is, a general emotional state—and a cue. Comfort after leaving the family home is fertile ground for memory retrieval. Most of us leave home in our twenties. We begin raising our own families. We are continually stimulated to rethink our childhood by the birth and development of our own children.

At the age of twenty-eight, Eileen Lipsker had finally achieved a sense of well-being. She had acquired almost everything she wanted, she told an audience of psychiatrists much, much later—"two smart and pretty children, a lovely house, nice clothes, and a Mercedes of my own in the garage." I think it's probably significant that "a husband" was not part of Eileen's list. But at least Eileen had learned to relax and let up a little. And as Eileen's mind went on idle, so did the powerful inhibitions that had blocked her memories. The murder memory could come forward. The ground was there for memory retrieval. Eileen's brain must have been issuing a stream of "stop" warnings for years, while her terrible memories lay in storage. Then the warning function temporarily went to sleep.

A repressed memory does not come back, however, just because a ground of comfort has been established. Memory retrieval also frequently requires a strong perceptual stimulus—a cue. Sometimes the cue is a context similar to the context in which the memory was originally planted. More often the cue is a swift, strong perception. Occasionally it is a dream.

Memories are often forced out of lockup when states or moods originally connected with the input of the memory are re-created. This is called state-dependent, or mood-dependent, memory. For instance, if a scuba diver learns words while underwater, he can remember these words better in the same environment, when he is wearing his gear and is back underwater. If a person learns material while under the influence of marijuana, he will retrieve the material better under the same influence. The British medical journal *The Lancet* took note of this phenomenon in a November 23, 1991, editorial: "It would not have been adaptive for our hunter-gatherer ancestors if their minds had been occupied with memories of hunting while they were gathering, or with memories of gathering while they were hunting."

But the most powerful impetus for the return of traumatic remembrance is not mood or state but a very simple perception, or cue. A child's freckled face. A twisted head. Looking down. Any of the five senses can do it. It appears that vision is the strongest immediate stimulus to old lost memories, but this does not mean that the other senses fail to operate as memory cues. A madeleine for Proust. The odor of innocence for the killer in Patrick Suskind's novel *Perfume.* In Walker Percy's *The Last Gentleman,* the protagonist, a young man who has suffered from amnesia since his father committed suicide, recovers his memory upon hearing music—the same chamber-music piece by Brahms that had been playing on a phonograph when his father died.

Vision was the perceptual cue that prompted Eileen Franklin Lipsker to recall the Nason murder. Jessica Lipsker looked so much like Susan that you might have thought they were the same child. Photographic blowups of Jessica at five-and-a-half and of Susan at almost nine bring involuntary gasps to those who see the portraits side by side. It is a tribute to the depth of Eileen's repression that she did not react to the similarity between the two little girls until her daughter tilted her head to look directly into the California sun.


By June 1989, six months after her first memory return, Eileen Lipsker felt impelled to tell someone her story. She wondered aloud to Kirk Barrett, a local psychotherapist she had begun seeing about her marriage problems, whether or not it was possible "for a person to have a . . . really horrible memory of something" that had "never [been] remembered before." Barrett assured her that this could indeed happen, and Eileen then spoke of Susan's murder and her father's involvement. Barrett stayed neutral; he told Eileen he couldn't be certain that her memory was real.

She then went to her brother, George Franklin, Jr., with her mem-

ory. George Jr. was so incredulous that Eileen suddenly felt the need
to endow herself with some extra credibility. "I recovered the memory
under hypnosis," she told her brother. Somehow, in Eileen's mind,
this lie was more persuasive than a spontaneous memory return. But
George Jr. remained skeptical, and Eileen then turned to her mother.

Leah Franklin, who had divorced Eileen's father when Eileen was
fourteen, did not respond to the idea of George Franklin as a murderer with any real shock. Leah had spent months in mental hospitals
while her children were growing up, but she entirely recovered upon
leaving George. She eventually remarried, attended law school, and
opened a successful legal practice. George Sr. was very capable of
killing, Leah told Eileen after hearing her tale. It was a wonder that
Leah herself hadn't been killed during the stormy marriage, she said.
But why in the world would Eileen's memory come back so late?
"Hypnosis," Eileen responded, reaching once again for a magic-
sounding source of credibility. Telling her family, Eileen realized, was
getting her nowhere.

Leah would later testify in court that within weeks, or perhaps
months, of the time of the Nason murder, her husband gave her a
bloody shirt to wash. He claimed that the blood came from a painting accident. Then in 1978, nine years after Susan's death, George
Franklin told Leah that he had written his memoirs but had wrapped
them in plastic, sealed them in wax, and buried them somewhere in
San Mateo County. At that point, Leah leapt to a conclusion. "Did
you murder Susan Nason?" she asked George. And he replied, "Why
do you think things like that of me?"

Another member of the Franklin family came to a similar conclusion six years later. In 1984, Janice Franklin went to the Foster City
police to accuse her father of killing Susan. Janice told the police that
she had absolutely no evidence, just "a hunch." She and Eileen later
swore several times under oath that they had not spoken together
about Susan's murder; nevertheless, Janice's suspicions had begun on
the night Susan Nason disappeared. On the evening of the day Susan
disappeared from Foster City, the phone rang in the Franklin house.
George Franklin answered it. The person on the other end of the line
identified himself as a police detective and asked for Janice. Before
she could take the phone, George kicked Janice so hard on the base of
her spine that her back hurt for weeks. Janice interpreted this to
mean that she had better "shut up," and she did.

Kirk Barrett, Eileen's therapist, never attempted to confirm or deny Eileen's murder memories. He saw her for only a few months. He did not hypnotize her, nor was she hypnotized by anyone else. Barrett could not explain the process by which her memories returned. He did tell Eileen, however, that memories go underground because of conflict.

Conflict is the key to repression. Freud believed that the conflict was between the patient's instinctual drives and the patient's fears. Today that scheme still holds, but other, equally important conflicts have been added. You may experience a conflict between the utter helplessness you feel during a terrible event and the way you wish to see yourself—as human and competent. You may also be torn between two images of your parent—as a monster and as a loving adult. Eileen Franklin's repression sprang from both these motives. She wanted desperately to feel human, to exercise some control. And she also wished to love her terrifying father.

Children like Eileen often decide, or at least partly decide, to repress. To start, they temporarily put something painful far from mind. This has been called suppression by most students of defense mechanisms since Freud. Freud's own term for it was *Unterdrückung* (literally, a "pressing under"). Suppression is a temporary and conscious move. The intent is to set the painful issue aside for a while. Theoretically, the suppressor can return to thinking of the predicament at any time. According to the psychiatrist George Vaillant, who is a leading authority on defenses, healthy men and women often use suppression to cope with their conflicts. In fact, it is the most common defense, Dr. Vaillant finds, in high-functioning individuals. Even though psychoanalysis teaches that defenses are always unconscious, Vaillant and others have expanded the theory to include willful, conscious defense.

But in the case of children, suppression is often a way station to repression. Freud called repression *Verdrängung* ("ousting"). The deliberate act of setting a memory aside leads easily to its permanent removal from consciousness. The transition is simple and almost automatic in some youngsters, especially those who are already experienced with trauma. Eileen Franklin appeared to be such a child. By the age of eight, her suppression was no longer a temporary maneuver. It had moved directly on to repression. Without any thinking or planning, Eileen seemed able to put her memories out of consciousness.

"I was my dad's favorite," Eileen told me. "I was the middle one. The ugly one. But he thought I was beautiful and smart." One reason for Eileen's repression of the Nason murder was her father's threat to kill her, but her love for him was an even more compelling reason. Eileen's face glowed in the light of a hundred inner candles as she spoke to me of George Franklin. Dad had told her she was beautiful, before anyone else recognized it.

In mid-November of 1989, ten months after remembering the murder, Eileen blurted out the story to her husband. Barry Lipsker believed her immediately. He required no false assertions of hypnosis. Hadn't they cut off their relationship with her dad a couple of years before, because he had acted so weird around Sica? George Franklin was sexually perverse about kids, Barry said, that much was clear. Barry instinctively grasped another reason for Eileen's retrieval of her repressed memories: she had completely broken with her father. For the first time in her life, Eileen was totally free of him.

When she told Barry her memories, Eileen received a promise from him that he wouldn't do anything about it. Before letting Barry in on her secret, Eileen had consulted with a criminal attorney to find out whether she could report a crime anonymously. He had advised her to make a statement in his office with a court reporter present. The statement would then go to the police. The attorney had agreed to act as a temporary buffer between the police and Eileen. Eileen planned to make her statement as soon as the 1989 holiday season was over.

But Barry Lipsker was an extremely controlling man. At the time they married, he had been far more sophisticated and stable than his young bride, and he thought nothing of running Eileen's life just as he ran his successful computer business. (Trauma victims repeat. Eileen had found an unconscious way to perpetuate the relationship with her overwhelming father.) Without Eileen's knowledge or consent, Barry telephoned the San Mateo County District Attorney's Office, using only his first name. He said that he had information about an old unsolved killing in San Mateo County. Could he give the information without revealing his source? The person who took Barry's phone call, Inspector Charles Etter, encouraged him but made no promises. Etter sensed that this was neither "a nut" nor "a false alarm." "Keep calling," he said. "Call every day." Barry Lipsker took him up on it. He called five more times.

• • •

Elaine Tipton is an assistant district attorney in San Mateo County. On November 17, 1989, she was relaxing on the shores of Hawaii attempting to forget a trying year. That day the telephone rang at the District Attorney's Office and a man calling himself "Barry" alluded to a twenty-year-old unsolved murder in the county. It was the murder of a child, the man said. Elaine Tipton's upsetting, if often rewarding, legal task is to prosecute the killers of children, and this anonymous call signalled the beginning of the most challenging case of her career.

Elaine Tipton specializes in the unthinkable. She stares at police photos of dead or raped children and arranges for evidence to be presented about their clothes, their bodily fluids, their wounds. She is blond, thin, pretty, and seems a bit fragile. If you look past the fragility, you notice a seriousness around the mouth, small lines at the corners of the eyes, and a steadiness in the gray-blue gaze. When you listen to her, you immediately hear how bright, well-organized, and clear she is, and you realize that very little escapes those knowing eyes.

The crime in question occurred on September 22, 1969, when Foster City was a very young town, built on landfill that a man named T. Jack Foster had dumped into San Francisco Bay. Foster City was already so overstuffed with newly arrived children that when Eileen Franklin and Susan Nason moved in, the elementary school consisted of a series of trailers.

On the warm sunny September day that Susan Nason disappeared, the neighbors reported that she had gone around the corner to deliver tennis shoes to one of her fourth-grade classmates. Just around the other corner lived Susan's best friend, Eileen. After returning the tennis shoes, Susan Nason was never again seen in the neighborhood.

The police and the citizens of Foster City conducted a massive hunt for Susan. Neighbors searched their own properties and the public parks for a trace of the child. The police checked and rechecked with anyone who might have seen her. Rumors of an unfamiliar blue station wagon flew about town. But despite everyone's fervent work, no leads developed. As the days and weeks passed, Don and Margaret Nason and their ten-year-old daughter Shirley suffered indescribable agony.

The Nasons and the police received many tips after Susan's disappearance. Well-intentioned psychics phoned, claiming to know the

girl's whereabouts. A man who proved to have no firsthand knowledge of Susan threatened to return each of her fingers, one at a time,
if the Nasons did not deliver $10,000 to a San Francisco address. The
FBI became involved with that one, and the man was quickly put
away.

On December 2, ten long weeks after Susan's disappearance, a
water-district worker found a child's body approximately seven miles
from the place Susan had last been seen. On a trail below a pulloff on
Highway 92, a winding road that leads to the little coastal town of
Half Moon Bay, the man found the remains of a small child hidden
under some loose brush and an old set of bedsprings. The area was
scrubby. The body lay about a mile from the Crystal Springs Reser-
voir, a manmade lake that feeds San Francisco its water.

The corpse had almost entirely decomposed. The police found little more than mummified tissue, bones, and a skull, which had been
severed from the body. There was a large defect in the rear part of the
skull, behind the right ear. The body was still clothed in the blue
print dress that young Susan Nason had been wearing when she disappeared. Near the body were "a small portion of hair" and "a rock
with hair on it." There was a sock on one of the child's feet; the other
sock was on a bush nearby. One shoe lay close to the body; the other
shoe never turned up. The child's teeth were intact, and the question
of identity quickly, though sadly, received its answer.

A small crushed silver ring rested on the middle finger of Susan's
right hand. While Susan's left hand was intact and undamaged, the
right hand was nearly ruined. Predatory animals, it appeared, had
attacked this hand, perhaps because it had been injured at or around
the time of death.

An explanation of what had happened to Susan Nason did not
come, however, with the discovery of her little body. The circumstances of her disappearance and death did not lend themselves to
accurate reconstruction of what might have happened to her. Nobody
saw her leave Foster City. And nobody saw her in the company of
somebody else. Periodically, both the Foster City Police Department
and the San Mateo County Sheriff's Office reopened the investigation.
But no answers evolved, not even hypotheticals. What all those
detectives could not determine had been locked away in two minds—
the mind of the murderer and, as it later became clear, the mind of
his child.

Inspector Charles Etter, who took most of Barry Lipsker's anonymous phone calls, was both patient and intuitive. He had had enough experience to smell reality behind all this anonymity and hedging. He encouraged Barry, trying to give him some of the assurances he sought, yet the San Mateo County District Attorney's Office was in no position to guarantee total anonymity and safety to Barry's wife. Could "Mrs. Barry," as the D.A.'s staff began calling her, come to the phone without naming the murderer? The D.A.'s Office would then search through its files to determine what, if any, record and evidence existed in the case. Based on its assessment, the office would then advise "Mr. and Mrs. Barry" if this case was at all likely to be prosecuted. Then and only then, Inspector Etter said, would "Mrs. Barry" have to break her anonymity and name the killer.

In deciding to report the murder to the authorities, Eileen had weighed her fears for her safety and that of her children, and her love for her father, against what she considered "the right of the Nasons to have this resolved." She had hoped to put off her disclosures until after the holidays, but suddenly in the middle of a call he made on November 20 Barry handed the phone to Eileen, without identifying her. "My wife will talk to you now," he said. The following is an excerpt of the conversation that took place between Eileen and Inspector Etter. This was the first conversation about Susan Nason that Eileen had ever had with anyone in authority: though the two girls had been best friends, no one on the police force had questioned Eileen about Susan at the time Susan disappeared.

Eileen had no idea she was being taped, and she was vigorously cross-examined later on many of the points she made on this tape. One can hear the conflict that led to Eileen's repression; it is still there as she speaks.

EILEEN: Hi.

INSPECTOR: Hello.

EILEEN: Have you figured out what case this is, on your own? [Here Eileen teases and tests a little, a behavior to which she sometimes resorts under stress.]

INSPECTOR: No, we haven't.

EILEEN: O.K., it was in Foster City.

INSPECTOR: Uh-huh.

EILEEN: Her name was Susan Nason.

INSPECTOR: Uh-huh. And how old was Susan when this happened?

EILEEN: Um, eight or nine. I couldn't tell you exactly. . . .

INSPECTOR: All right. Well, why don't you go ahead and tell us what, what happened, and, uh, maybe we'll have some questions after that. Is that O.K.?

EILEEN: Well, I don't know. Why?

INSPECTOR: Well—

EILEEN: Can't you just look [now] and see if there's anything there?

INSPECTOR: Well, I, I don't have access to the [Foster City] records right here, you see.

EILEEN: No, I understand that.

INSPECTOR: As I understood your husband, you were going to tell us what happened at—?

EILEEN: Well, I, yeah. [To her husband] Why did you tell them I was going to give them all the details and everything? I don't want to. [A brief dispute ensues between Eileen and Barry, out of phone reach.] O.K. I was in a car with the person that committed the crime.

INSPECTOR: O.K.

EILEEN: And we picked Susan up. . . . And we went out to the woods. I know that sounds strange. It's like, um, I think it was like out toward Half Moon Bay. That way.

INSPECTOR: All right.

EILEEN: You know, where it starts to get more wooded out there? [Eileen is mistaken here. This murder did not take place in the woods.]

INSPECTOR: Uh-huh.

EILEEN: And, um, the person that committed the crime raped her. [Eileen's voice breaks when she says "raped."] And I was right there when it happened, and um [her voice stays shaky], and um, . . . after that we were all out. Out of the car—

INSPECTOR: Uh-huh.

EILEEN: And um, Susan was sitting down, and I was standing by the car. She was sitting—I, I can't give you an exact distance. I would say like maybe fifteen feet, twenty feet from the car. And she was sitting on, like, a little tiny hill. Or maybe it was a rock. She was sitting on something that was slightly elevated. [It may seem amazing that an old traumatic memory should be so replete with postural and positional details, but this sense of position is one of the last things to leave in repressed traumatic memory and one of the first aspects of the memory to return.] And he, he hit her on the head. [Her voice breaks again.]

INSPECTOR: Uh-huh.

EILEEN: With a rock. [She still sounds shaky.] And she brought her hand up to her head, and he hit her again, and she had a— Blood went everywhere. She had a ring on her hand, and, and he crushed the ring on her hand.

INSPECTOR: Is there anything more you'd like to add at this point?

EILEEN: Uh. I mean, it doesn't— If this goes along with what you find, then I'll talk more. I mean, this isn't real easy for me to discuss. . . .

INSPECTOR: And what was she dressed in? Do you remember?

EILEEN: Let me think a minute, O.K.? It's just so unclear. Because I want to say it was a dress. . . . I don't know. My inclination was that there was a sweater or a jacket that was either lavender or blue. [There was no sweater or jacket.]

INSPECTOR: Uh-huh.

EILEEN: But I can't remember the exact clothes.

INSPECTOR: What did he do then? After hitting Susan?

EILEEN: Um. Well, this part's real fuzzy for me, because I have sort of a half memory of this.

INSPECTOR: Uh-huh.

EILEEN: Of— That he made me help him put something over her. Um, a mattress or something.

INSPECTOR: Did he leave the body there?

EILEEN: Yeah.

INSPECTOR: At the same spot where he had hit her?

EILEEN: Yeah. [Wrong. Eileen later remembered that her father had carried Susan's body over to another place.]

INSPECTOR: O.K., and then what happened?

EILEEN: Well, I was screaming [after Susan was buried], and he pushed—

INSPECTOR: You were screaming?

EILEEN: And he pushed me on the ground and then held me down. And he told me that he would kill me.

INSPECTOR: Uh-huh.

EILEEN: And that no one would ever believe me. And that if anyone ever did believe me, that they would say that I was a part of it.

And that they would put me away, and they would blame me for this. And that he would kill me if I ever talked about it.

INSPECTOR: And how old were you at this time?

EILEEN: I was eight. . . .

INSPECTOR: There is more?

EILEEN: Well, I have more, you know, details. . . . But, you know, a lot of little details that might not mean anything.

INSPECTOR: How did you come to be in his car, to begin with?

EILEEN: Um, because it was a person that I knew.

INSPECTOR: I see. And, it was not unusual for you to be riding in his car?

EILEEN: No.

INSPECTOR: I see. O.K. Is there anything else you'd like to add at this point?. . .

EILEEN: Yes, she *had* to be wearing a dress, actually, because he didn't take her clothes off when he raped her. He just pushed her dress up. [This is "reasoning a memory through." There is a definite mental picture of the rape here, but hardly any mental picture of Susan's clothing. Eileen's reasoning makes it "a dress," not her mental imagery of Susan in certain clothes.]

INSPECTOR: I see. And you witnessed the actual rape?

EILEEN: Yeah. I mean, well, I didn't stand and stare. I mean, I put my head down after a while, but—I saw it. I mean, this was really terrifying for a child, I hope you can realize that.

INSPECTOR: Oh, definitely. Being an adult, and you're talking to adults, do you feel at this point in time that he actually made penetration of the young la— the young girl? [Inspector Etter makes an unfortunate slip here. When people hear that a young girl has been misused sexually, they may fall into terminology such as "woman" or "lady."]

EILEEN: Um, my feeling is no, which is really strange. I don't know why I feel that way. [The reason is Eileen's conflicted love for her father.]

INSPECTOR: Uh-huh.

EILEEN: But he was definitely on top of her, he was definitely doing a, you know, a physical thrust.

INSPECTOR: Uh-huh.

EILEEN: Of a sexual nature. But I can't say that penetration was made. [There was sperm in Susan's vagina.]

> INSPECTOR: Uh-huh. . . . Is there anything else you'd like to add at this point?
>
> EILEEN: No. You must have asked that a million times to people. . . . Do you guys ever trace calls?
>
> INSPECTOR: Well, it's been known to happen, but we haven't traced yours.
>
> EILEEN: O.K.
>
> INSPECTOR: If that's any comfort.
>
> EILEEN: Well, it is—because it's—I'm just really afraid. If the case was mishandled, or because of the amount of time that elapsed between the murder and the discovery of the body, that, you know, any evidence could be washed away by rain or by this or by that. And then there's nothing but my word, and that basically means nothing.

Eileen Franklin was wrong when she felt that her word meant nothing. As the case developed, Eileen's word came to mean everything. Elaine Tipton would find no physical evidence at the murder scene or elsewhere to link George Franklin to the killing. The D.A.'s investigators had located the old Franklin Volkswagen van, but it was absolutely "clean." Even microscopically. No hair, fiber, blood, fingerprint, tire mark—nothing concrete pointed to George Franklin. Only George's daughter, his eyewitness, could provide the necessary words to convict him. But Eileen's words so overwhelmed her that she could hardly say them aloud at first. On the day after she gave her anonymous statement, she became "too choked up and started crying" when Inspector Etter called and asked for the name of Susan's killer. She handed the phone to Barry and asked him to do it. He did.

What was not clear to Elaine Tipton when she first listened to the tapes was the fact that Eileen had not knowingly kept this horrible secret for years from the police. Barry had said, in his first call, "I guess she can't live with it anymore." But this statement was misleading. For twenty years, Eileen had unknowingly kept her memory from herself.

It was not easy for the D.A.'s Office to decide to file criminal charges against George Franklin. Although there is no statute of limitations for murder, Elaine Tipton understood what a difficult task it would be to convict someone of a murder that had occurred twenty years earlier. Trying to locate witnesses, organize the evidence, coordi-

nate the law that existed on the books twenty years ago (because that
law would be the controlling law in this case)—all this would be a
severe prosecutorial handicap. Because the prosecution must prevail
"beyond the shadow of a doubt," the biggest single challenge would
be the issue of Eileen Franklin's repressed memory.

"First and foremost," Elaine told me after the trial was over, "in the
course of jury selection I was going to have to find twelve people who
were willing, able, and ready to accept the concept of repressed memory. They'd have to be ready to understand it and embrace it. They'd
have to be specifically ready to accept the assertion that a child could
witness a horrible event such as the molestation and murder of her
best friend and then have no conscious memory of it for twenty years.
They'd even have to understand that a child's memory is not perfect—that she might make mistakes. It was clear to me that I was
going to have to present powerful psychiatric expert testimony
regarding memory in order to educate the jury. And that's where you
came in. But the nice thing was the last thing. If I had a jury who
could accept the notion of repressed memory, they would very probably believe Eileen Lipsker's testimony—believe in the truth of what
she said she had witnessed. Because, as I came to learn, Eileen is a
very compelling and believable person."

George Franklin, Sr., was arrested and jailed as 1989 moved into
1990. The San Mateo County D.A.'s men found George living out his
retirement in a tiny Sacramento apartment filled to the brim with
child-size dildos, child pornography, and books on incest. George's
horrible hobbies would have so prejudiced his murder trial that any
mention of them was ordered out by preliminary judicial ruling.
When the inspectors arrived at George's apartment and advised him
that they had reopened the investigation of the Susan Nason homicide case, he immediately turned to them with a question: "Have you
talked to my daughter?" George never clarified which of his daughters he meant.

From the first, the Franklin defense team, led by a smart and well-
qualified San Francisco attorney named Douglas Horngrad, set out to
put Eileen Lipsker's "memory" in question. Horngrad charged that
Eileen could have learned everything she knew from newspaper
accounts published at the time of the killing. Very little of the Nason

murder had gone unreported. Eileen could have woven her "memories" from what she read, he proposed, and then, in some hideous scheme to get back at her father or to create fame and fortune for herself, she could have come forward with entirely manufactured "recollections." She had previously lied to her family about her supposed hypnosis, though she later corrected her false statements. She could be lying about everything else. Eileen's memories were far too detailed and corresponded far too well to the preexisting evidence to be believed, Horngrad charged.

Douglas Horngrad was partly right in his argument that details do not guarantee the truth of a memory. And Elaine Tipton, too, was correct in saying that details are often a very convincing aspect of recollection. When children over the age of three endure a single terrible event, they are nearly always able to recount their experience in precise detail. The children I interviewed who had been kidnapped at Chowchilla certainly did. And five to seven weeks after the *Challenger* blew up on January 28, 1986, my research group found that of sixty-two East Coast eight-year-olds and fifteen-year-olds who had watched the morning disaster "live" on TV, and of eleven children who had watched it from the viewing stands at Cape Canaveral, almost every single one could remember the event in full, strongly highlighted detail. In a less involved group—West Coast kids, who had heard about the explosion before seeing it on taped news segments—four out of five remembered what had happened in extraordinarily vivid detail.

But knowing the details about the explosion in space did not protect these children from making mistakes. Within five to seven weeks after the spacecraft disaster, about a third of the young people exposed to it expressed unrealistic ideas regarding what had gone wrong, whether or not any astronauts escaped, and what might come next. Even a year after the shuttle exploded, and after all those TV replays and detailed explanations had been offered, almost a third of the younger children told me at least one unrealistic thing about the accident.

Occasional mistakes aside, however, the memories of striking events last in children's minds. Studies rarely extend to the twenty-year point, when Eileen's memories came back, but fourteen months after the *Challenger* exploded more than four out of five of the children interviewed could still remember enough to recount a personal incident connected with the accident—for instance, what somebody had said at the time, or what they themselves had done.

This means that both general and personally meaningful details can be found in normal childhood memories of a single striking event—and that Eileen's murder memory, once her repression lifted, might have been expected to sound almost as detailed and replete with personal incidents as did the kids' memories in the *Challenger* study. But that study also showed that mistakes can be made even though a memory is detailed and personally revealing. Details do not, in and of themselves, prove a child's story true.

The prosecution won an important victory in a pretrial hearing, on the question of whether or not the defense could bring old newspaper articles into court as a possible explanation for Eileen Lipsker's highly detailed remembrances. Douglas Horngrad and his trial partner Arthur Wachtel contended that Eileen would offer no detail that had not previously been mentioned in a newspaper. The presiding judge, Thomas McGinn Smith, ruled that twenty-year-old newspaper and TV stories could not come into *The People of the State of California v. George Thomas Franklin, Sr.* Eileen had already testified at the arraignment that she had not read any related newspaper accounts, either as a child or as an adult. Elaine Tipton argued that there were too many libraries, and too much microfilm and videotape, for a prosecutor ever to be able to disprove that a witness had had access to some piece of historical information. In order to prove her case, the prosecutor would have to find each and every false detail in the newspapers and then show that Eileen had *not* retained those particular details in her own account. This would be impossible, the judge ruled. The relevance of news articles was insignificant as compared with the potential for prejudice and confusion in the court.

The question of detail, however, did not disappear with Judge Smith's preliminary decision about news accounts. Elaine Tipton was convinced that the details of Eileen's repressed memories were amazingly accurate. Having won the newspaper decision, she built the foundation of her case on the strength of Eileen's remembered details.

Douglas Horngrad veered away from his "too good to be true" defense once the newspaper ruling went against him. He shifted instead to a double-barreled assault on Eileen's credibility, stressing what he considered to be her overabundance of details along with her inconsistencies and mistakes. She had lied about hypnosis. She could lie about everything else. And even if she didn't lie, her memories were false, he contended. Eileen had initially confused the time of day of the murder, for instance, saying on her phone tapes that she met Susan in the morning or early afternoon and that the killing took place in the early afternoon. In so doing, she had shown that her memory was not foolproof, since Susan had disappeared after school. Eileen was confused as to whether her sister Janice was in the van or playing nearby when she and her father noticed Susan and asked her to join them. Janice had no memory of any of this. Eileen originally thought that her father had pulled a mattress out of the van to hide the body. But he most likely did not. Susan's body was found under an old set of bedsprings. Eileen had originally said that George had buried Susan on the spot where he killed her, but she later remembered that he had carried the body several yards away. And it was questionable whether he did much, if any, digging. Eileen later vacationed and traveled alone with her father, even after she had married Barry. Her willingness to go places alone with George Franklin struck his defense team as highly inconsistent with what she had allegedly witnessed and what she alleged George had threatened to do to her.

A myriad of details and a few mistakes are not mutually exclusive, however. Eileen's retrieved memory was not atypical in this respect. When people are extremely stressed, they do not necessarily see everything correctly. Yet they may retain both the correct and incorrect perceptions in impressive detail. Their memory may be both "right" and "wrong" at the same time. Parts are correct, other parts incorrect.

Since 1977, when I began interviewing the Chowchilla children, I have observed the same kind of inconsistencies between precision of remembered detail and correctness of memory that Eileen Lipsker showed. Every single one of the Chowchilla children I talked to could recall the experience in precise, brilliant detail. Yet eight of them misdescribed something about their kidnappers in the early interviews. Whereas three relatively slim young men had been arrested by the police, who found a ransom note in the home of one of them, five of the kidnapped children initially reported to me a "black man," a "bald man," a "lady," an "old man who used his shotgun as a cane to support a missing leg," and "a fat, chubby man." Three other kids told of visual hallucinations: seeing an extra kidnapper in one of the vans; seeing the kidnappers having lunch above the "hole" after the children had been buried in it; and seeing a mobile home inhabited by the kidnappers at the site (none was found). Under the tension of an extreme event, such mistakes are bound to occur. They join the rest of the details, all of which are "remembered."

When I interviewed twenty-five of the children four to five years after the kidnapping, half of them misdescribed, or remembered misperceiving, something originally connected with the ordeal. Three of the eight children who had initially reported misperceptions or hallucinations had given up their mistakes by this time. But another eight kids, seven of whom had reported things right in the first interview, now exhibited faulty memories, describing a new "man with a long nose," a "man with a pillow stuffed into his pants," an additional pair of "girl kidnappers," a brand new "black man," and a "light-blue van."

One might ask: "How can a particular memory be precise, detailed, and at the same time wrong?" This inconsistency comes from the terrible stress and surprise involved in a single trauma. At the first moments of an unanticipated shock, a child easily perceives things incorrectly. A few of these wrong perceptions carry internal meaning. For instance, a Chowchilla girl I shall call Celeste argued with her mother the morning before she was kidnapped. As she and her sister walked out of their house, her sister shouted, "You're the meanest mommy in the world!" Celeste described her kidnapper as a pretty woman of a certain height, weight, hair color, and complexion. If the FBI had put out an all-points bulletin on such a person, Celeste's mother would have been arrested. Celeste's early-morning anger at her mother fed her afternoon misperceptions. But other misperceptions at Chowchilla held no discoverable meaning. A lad I'll call Billy saw a "light-blue van." The police and everyone else involved in the kidnapping knew that the two vans used were white and dark green. I could find no significance to Billy's "light blue." Perhaps it was a simple perceptual mistake that didn't mean much.

Even though Eileen Franklin was a Type II trauma victim, she made the same sort of perceptual mistakes that the Type I Chowchilla victims did, because Susan Nason's murder was her only murder experience. Eileen could repress like a Type II child, but she made murder mistakes like a Type I child. To Inspector Etter, for instance, she had mentioned trees near the murder site, yet there were none. She correctly remembered Susan's white underwear and socks, but she mistakenly thought that her friend had worn a jacket or a sweater. Eileen's misperceptions eventually cleared, but by the time they improved she had already made her statements on the telephone and in a preliminary hearing. She could be challenged with these mistakes at the trial. It was crucial to the prosecution that Eileen not watch TV or read newspaper accounts of her story, in order to avoid memory "enhancement." Despite Eileen's efforts to comply with this directive, Barry Lipsker collected newspaper clippings and arranged for a friend of his to videotape Eileen for the "Today" show. Eileen testified at the trial that she had watched only a few seconds of "Today" and had not read any of Barry's clippings. She was vigorously challenged on this point in court but managed to hold her ground.

Time is another perception that frequently goes "off" in memories of childhood trauma. It went off for Eileen Franklin, too. Eileen claimed in her tapes and preliminary testimony that the killing had happened in the early afternoon and only later corrected herself, saying that it was closer to the dinner hour. A sense of time is a recent evolutionary acquisition, probably the most recent of all. Even though animals mate and migrate at certain times, their time sense relies on instinct, awareness of polarized light, day length, and so forth. In human beings, however, there is a well-developed linear sense of past and future—of sequencing, causality, and of time extending far beyond one's own existence. But this faculty, being new, is extraordinarily vulnerable. Alcohol or drugs damage it. Traumatic states damage it. The confusion increases even more after the trauma is over.

The kidnapped Chowchilla children's hero, "Bob," who along with another boy dug the youngsters out of their buried truck trailer, remembered that it was either dusk or dawn when he first emerged from the "hole." The group actually got out in midafternoon. This chronological mistake was almost the same one that Eileen made. Times of day evade appraisal under terrifying conditions. Children's memory is especially vulnerable to this.

Despite all these misperceptions and mistimings, the stories that traumatized children tell stay very close to the events that they experienced. Their descriptions are fundamentally borne out by other evidence. One must therefore take a returning childhood memory for what it is—a slightly flawed product from an active and developing mind. One must compare it with what the other evidence indicates.

One must rely on good detective work. Good storage of blood and sperm samples helps. One must hope for the corroboration of other eyewitnesses. But one must also leave a little leeway as to what one thinks is "true" and "false."

Repeatedly traumatized children are less likely than singly traumatized ones to make perceptual mistakes about their abusers. As the Cambridge, Massachusetts, psychiatrist Judith Herman says so poignantly in her 1992 book *Trauma and Recovery,* the repeated abuser serves as a concentration-camp guard, a prison keeper. The child sex-abuse victim is "kept" by her violator. The victim cannot escape. This is a crucial difference between what I call Type I (single-event) and Type II (multiple-event) childhood trauma. Type II children do not ordinarily get mixed-up about their nursery-school teacher, their minister, the husband of their day-care operator, the bus driver, Uncle Gerald, or their father—the people with many chances to traumatize them. If the perpetrator commits the crimes without any disguises, the repeatedly traumatized child, when memory returns, almost always knows who did it. As a Type II child who had witnessed and experienced ongoing violence in her family, Eileen Franklin would have had to accomplish an enormous mind-bending trick in order to confuse her own father with someone else who had really killed Susan Nason.

If they are repeatedly traumatized, children can be expected to "forget" much of what happened, however. Holes in memory are created by defensive operations, such as the very common defense of repression. When repression lifts, the memories may come back relatively intact.

This is where I come into the Franklin story. Elaine Tipton needed an expert witness to explain "repression" and the "return of the repressed." She needed someone who understood the mistakes children make at horrible moments in their lives. She particularly wanted a child psychiatrist. She also wanted a researcher.

Repressed memory had caught my interest by then, and I was studying the adult manifestations of childhood trauma. The Chowchilla kids were growing up, and I was staying in touch, awaiting a twenty-year or twenty-five-year follow-up; even though they were Type I victims, I wondered if they would eventually repress parts of their memories. But there were reasons not to testify, too. This case was bound to create controversy and publicity, two factors potentially detrimental to me and to psychiatry. In retrospect, I think what persuaded me to join *People v. Franklin* was the sound of Elaine Tipton's voice. She was totally committed to her eyewitness. Her obvious admiration, as she told me of the risks Eileen Lipsker had taken in coming forward to testify, convinced me to go ahead.

So I said "Yes" to Elaine Tipton. And I went home and told my husband that I must be crazy.

# 2

# Expert Witness for the Prosecution

Every Monday I give myself a present, a day at the Stanford Medical Library. Nobody bothers me at Stanford, because nobody knows me there; I teach at the medical campus of the University of California at San Francisco. On Monday, November 11, 1990, I broke an almost inviolable vow to save Mondays for myself by arranging to spend the afternoon with Elaine Tipton, the prosecutor of *People v. Franklin.* The trial was already well under way, and tomorrow would be my day to take the stand. Eileen Franklin Lipsker had testified for days about her memories of watching her father kill her best friend on an afternoon more than twenty years earlier. I had spent four hours interviewing Eileen the previous summer; I had also reviewed piles of related papers, and had talked with Assistant District Attorney Tipton innumerable times about how Eileen had lost her memory of the Nason murder and retrieved it many years later. On November 12, I could expect to swear my oath in the morning and sit in the witness chair for the entire day, except for the lunch break and a couple of recesses. Elaine came over to Stanford to prepare me.

We met at noon in the Stanford Hospital cafeteria. It was Veterans Day, and the prosecutor was theoretically on holiday. Luckily for me, she was willing to dispense with her day off. I needed the help.

Judge Thomas McGinn Smith had already ruled on what he would and wouldn't allow me to do tomorrow, Elaine told me, fiddling with her small salad. I could speak to the jury only about memory in general. I could give examples from case histories of adults and children to illustrate my points. But I could not speak at any time about Eileen Franklin Lipsker herself. I could not mention those of her signs and symptoms that seemed related to the murder, nor could I offer any opinions about the veracity of her memories. Putting the case together and deciding whether Eileen was telling the truth was a function for the "finders of fact"—the jury. Judge Smith was willing to let me state my general understanding and opinions about repressed memory. But that was all.

"How will I testify without plugging Eileen into her own symptoms and signs?" I asked, somewhat alarmed.

"Because I already know what you highlighted from your psychiatric evaluation of Eileen last summer. Before the jury, I took Eileen through her own presentation of her symptoms and signs. And the jury stayed right with her." Elaine Tipton smiled. Eileen had been a great witness.

Symptoms are the subjective feelings and signs are the objective findings that confirm terrible memories. If a person has endured horrible moments in life, these moments should leave a scar. Without a scar, one has to wonder whether there was an injury at all. In the sessions that summer with Eileen, I had looked for internal confirmations—clusters of symptoms and signs of Eileen's trauma. Though the prosecutor's mandate to me had been mainly to consider Eileen's memory, I felt that I needed also to determine whether her emotions and past behaviors corresponded with these memories. Some of her accompanying symptoms and signs must have been there from the time the memory started—from the very beginning, in other words. Symptoms and signs operate even when a memory is entirely repressed.

My office is the place where I search for symptoms and signs. Everybody who comes to my office, with the exception of those who hate heights, likes the view. We sit twenty-five stories above the Bay, in an art-deco skyscraper. When you stand at the window, you can see the Mark Hopkins and Fairmont hotels, Alcatraz, Tiburon, and Angel Island. If you glance a little over to the right, you see Telegraph Hill and the Transamerica Pyramid. But when you sit down in my office, you see only sky. I like that—a blue-and-white office decorated with blue, blue sky.

When I interview a forensic psychiatric patient—one who will be

going through the legal system—I warn the person first that nothing
we say will be confidential. I try to warn youngsters of this, too,
telling even the two- and three-year-olds that we "won't be secret,"
and that I will be talking about them to a judge, "a person who wears
black robes and decides things." Once I warn the patient about confidentiality, the evaluation process is almost the same as for any other
patient. Somehow the loss of confidentiality does little to deter people from revealing their symptoms and signs.

I found Eileen to be extraordinarily beautiful—slender, with clear,
light-brown eyes, a freckled face, and long, straight, strikingly red
hair. She dressed simply, in bright cotton dresses with long skirts and
modest necklines. Getting the point of a question almost instanta-
neously, she seemed quite capable of the witty one-liner and the effective verbal counterpunch. Those summer days in my office, however,
she spoke largely in paragraphs, and she wept a number of times. She
occasionally put a hand to her abdomen saying, "My ulcer is acting
up." Even though her memories were more than two decades old,
they broke Eileen's voice and made her chin tremble in the telling. I
could also hear her relief as she went on. She seemed to appreciate
being understood.

Eileen is the middle child of five, four girls and a boy, born to
young parents. Her father grew up in Franklin County, Virginia, part
of the founding Franklin family. Her mother came from a respected
Italian family in the Bay Area. Eileen's parents were not at all well
matched, and were drinking and fighting by the time the children
became aware. George Franklin acted sporadically and terrifyingly
violent. Leah gradually withdrew. Several times, for months at a
stretch, Leah was absolutely unavailable to her children. That left the
major care of the Franklin brood to the wildly unpredictable, charis-
matic George.

Eileen was her father's favorite, and he was the person she admired
most. Eileen bragged to other children about the fact that her daddy
worked as a fireman. She loved his hours off. George called Eileen
"Pooh," for Pooh Bear. "He was very handsome, very strong, very
funny, and very smart," she told me. "He was someone I could adore.
He was also a terrible father."

George's special affection for Eileen did not protect her from his
physical attacks. It did not protect her from something even worse. A
few months after Eileen's memory of the Nason murder came back,

she began having memories of incest. The way Eileen remembered it, the family had just moved to Foster City when George first approached her. She was three years old. She wore a pink nightgown she had been given for Christmas. Eileen had no idea what her father did to her at that time. The act itself did not come back with her other memories of the event. The gown and the new house clued her to the general nature of her recollection, but not to the specific happenings.

Placement and clothing memories are frequently connected, as Eileen's were, to children's mental representations of disasters. Of the East Coast children I studied after the *Challenger* blew up, almost nine out of ten could remember their own personal placements at the time of the accident for at least the fourteen months that we conducted the project. On the West Coast, where the youngsters had not witnessed the accident firsthand, almost two-thirds of those interviewed could describe their own placements at the moment they heard about it. Both sets of children remembered their positions so well that they volunteered to go into last year's classrooms and draw me an "X" on the spot. Eileen's memories of her first incestuous experience lined up with this finding. She could well remember being in a new house, though her father's sexual behavior was lost to her conscious memory.

More than one in five of the East Coast children could picture what they had been wearing on the day of the disaster in space. Dress, too, was a vivid part of Eileen's fragmented and very early memory of her father's first sexual approach.

Another memory of sex with George Franklin came back to Eileen a little while after the first one. Once—maybe at age seven or so—as Eileen stood in her Foster City living room, George inserted a finger into her vagina. She winced with pain. She was aware that everyone in the family was milling about. But nobody seemed to see.

The *Challenger* study also offered an analogy to Eileen's awareness of "who else was there" at the time of her trauma. More than a year after the spacecraft explosion, most of the children remembered at least two people who had been nearby. Awareness of the presence of others is a powerful part of traumatic remembrance.

Eileen told me that she became withdrawn at school after Susan Nason disappeared. She began pulling out the hair on one side of her head, creating a big, bleeding bald spot near the crown. Most likely, young Eileen unconsciously set out to duplicate the horrible wound

she had seen on Susan Nason's head. This behavioral reënactment provided internal confirmation for me of the truth of Eileen's memory.
Even though the traumatic event Eileen behaviorally repeated was, at
the time, entirely repressed in her mind, her reënactment demonstrated that the murder memories still lived and carried an influence.

As an adult, Eileen Lipsker had another habit that I thought
related to her murder experience. Whenever she found a child playing
alone in her Canoga Park neighborhood, she took that child home.
Children alone reminded her unconsciously of Susan Nason, who had
been alone when Eileen and George Franklin picked her up.

Eileen spent a great deal of her childhood pretending she could
escape her frightening family. At five, she hid for an entire afternoon
in a kindergarten "nap cubby." She liked to shut herself into closets
and think about children like Pippi Longstocking or the youngsters
of Nancy Brelis's *The Mummy Market,* who could live in perfect comfort without any parents. Her contemporary behaviors were in line
with what she later remembered of the incest that had made her
childhood miserable.

When Eileen turned fourteen, her parents divorced. Things
quickly changed for her. She still loved her father and even went to
live with him for a while. However, she also began making new
friends and stopped pulling out her hair. "I never saw a correlation,"
she told me, alluding to the lost linkage between her improved
adjustment and the Franklin divorce. "But as far as I know, the sexual
abuses ended right around the time my father left."

Eileen paid a price in her adolescence for all that early sex and violence. She became heavily involved in drugs, eventually dropping out
of high school. Drugs are often used by trauma victims in their teens
and young adulthood. By taking a drug that controls the brain, but
by taking it only in small, seemingly manageable amounts, some
adolescents feel that they are reëstablishing their own personal control over the uncontrollable. This does not begin to explain all substance abuse. But childhood trauma certainly is an important factor.
"I probably got to the point where I was a cocaine addict," Eileen
said. "But I gave it up one day without any assistance, so I'm not sure
if I was or not."

After leaving high school without graduating, Eileen, already sexually active and veering toward promiscuity, tried prostitution. "Fortunately, I was arrested after six weeks," she said. "That scared me

into stopping." In certain cases, prostitution, like drugs, may be a behavioral reënactment of old traumatic memories. Eileen had been forced early into sex. Prostitution must have given her the belated chance to control sex, choose it, and even be paid for it.

Eileen's prostitution arrest posed a problem for the Franklin prosecution. As a prosecutor, Elaine Tipton was required by the California Constitution to report to the Franklin defense team previous felonies committed by any of her witnesses. This requirement insures that the accused is provided with a maximum of information to illuminate the case. But Elaine was not required to report all misdemeanors to the defense. There are both laws and court precedents that preclude using past misdemeanors to cast a shadow over a witness's credibility unless the issue of veracity is directly involved in those particular offenses. Elaine took the records of Eileen's misdemeanor prostitution conviction to Judge Smith in chambers. He ruled that "the underlying conduct [inherent to prostitution] does not and would not relate to the credibility of the witness."

Aunt Sue, Eileen's mother's younger sister, actively intervened at the point when Eileen was arrested. She helped Eileen to find "a respectable job" and spent considerable time talking things over with her. "My aunt explained things to me," Eileen told me, looking soft at the thought of Aunt Sue. "These were things that I desperately needed explained. She told me how to run your life, and how one exists in our society, and what rules of conduct there are. No one had ever told me any of this before."

Eileen met Barry Lipsker when she turned twenty-one. Their sixteen-year age difference, almost a whole generation, may have unconsciously suggested to Eileen the generational boundary violations that had plagued her own upbringing. At first, however, the marriage was "a dream come true." Eileen and Barry traveled together "all over the world." They could afford luxuries at home. As time went on, however, Eileen felt tormented inside. "I felt that I was incapable of having a marriage," she told me. "I was not happy. I tried to be the perfect mother, and I probably succeeded. But Barry and I were having a difficult time together. Now I realize that a lot of it has to do with what was inside of me." Eileen had ongoing trouble trusting relationships. Susan Nason had been her last "best friend."

Eileen ended her final session with me by saying how intensely frightened she still was of George Franklin. She feared "what he can do if he comes back and gets close to Sica and Aaron, or"—and this regardless of the fact that he was jailed—"of what he may still be doing" to other children.

I gave Elaine Tipton an oral report of my observations and opinions. I told her that Eileen was suffering important signs and symptoms of childhood trauma. Some of her problems related to the early sexual abuse she was beginning to remember. But others—especially the bloody hair-pulling all through her midchildhood, the current terror of her father, and her need to deliver home any stray child she found in her neighborhood—appeared more directly related to her murder memories. Emotion had everything to do with Eileen's repression. She had suffered from repeated traumas. She had been repeatedly sexually abused and was probably a child witness to murder. Before the murder, she had taught herself to anticipate, to suppress, and then automatically to repress. By the time she was six or seven, Eileen would likely not have had to suppress first, as a mental defense; she probably repressed automatically.

At the Stanford Hospital cafeteria, Elaine Tipton assured me that Eileen had spoken eloquently from the witness stand about her hairpulling. She had also told the jury of childhood hours spent unsuccessfully trying to escape the world of her frightening parents. For the most part, Eileen's post-traumatic symptoms were allowed on the record and into the jury's minds. My psychiatric report had helped Elaine focus her own questioning of Eileen. She had brought out those symptoms and signs we thought were most closely related to the murder.

Elaine was not terribly concerned by Judge Smith's order that I speak of memory only in the general sense. As an attorney representing the interests of the people, Elaine was used to having early judicial rulings go in favor of the defendant. "Don't worry," she said, as we sipped our iced tea. "We'll get you used to hypothetical questions by the end of this afternoon—and anyway, the case has gone well up to now. 'Beyond a reasonable doubt' means that the defense gets most of the breaks. We name our experts early, for instance, and then the defense gets months to plan how to combat them. We don't see who they will use until ten or fifteen minutes before their expert takes the stand." She stood up crisply, busing our table in less than a minute. "O.K., let's get to work."

We spent the rest of the afternoon—at least four, maybe five

hours—drinking endless glasses of iced tea and making plans. Elaine
brought me up to date on the progress of the trial. Leah would soon
be testifying that her husband had had the day off when Susan Nason
was murdered. Eileen's testimony about her recollection of Susan's
wounds had perfectly matched the pathologist's testimony about the
damage on the cadaver's skull. ("It was beautiful," Elaine noted, with
no intended irony.) Eileen's testimony about the rock she had seen in
her father's hands matched the prosecution expert's testimony about
the wounds on Susan's head and the police evidence about the rock
found near Susan's remains. The judge had allowed Elaine to show the
jury photographs of the body—photographs that corresponded to the
word pictures Eileen had earlier offered. And Eileen had testified
about a visit she made to her father in jail—her only visit—in the
course of which she asked him if he had killed Susan. In response,
George Franklin stayed silent and pointed to a sign on the wall
informing prisoners and their visitors that jail conversations might be
monitored.

There had been one wonderful moment for the prosecution during
Eileen's cross-examination. Douglas Horngrad had asked her, almost
rhetorically, "But no one else saw the murder besides you?" "*He* did,"
Eileen snapped in response, her voice taking on the force of a sprung
trap. She turned to face her father, who was seated at the defense table
with his attorneys, spruced up and dressed in a conservative gray suit.
"*He* was there, too."

The low point for the prosecution had yet to come on the day I met
with Elaine Tipton. She had by then presented to the jury a list of
license-plate numbers, including the one on George Franklin's Volkswagen van, supposedly jotted down by the police at the Nason grave
site exactly a year after the killing. A guilty murderer might well
visit a cemetery on the anniversary of his horrible deed. Maybe curiosity, maybe remorse, maybe even glee would drive him there. But
much to Elaine's embarrassment, the list of license-plate numbers
turned out to have been mislabeled by a San Mateo County law-
enforcement official. It was really a list of the cars parked at the
Nason child's funeral. Douglas Horngrad dramatically brought this
point out late in the trial. Of course, he argued, George Franklin
would have come to Susan's funeral service, as a good Foster City
neighbor. There was absolutely nothing incriminating in his being
there.

Over our lukewarm tea, Elaine suggested that in my testimony I draw the link between incestuous sex and "forgetting," showing how repeated traumatic experiences work to enable children to repress. Anticipation encourages defensive memory loss. A little girl, for instance, can actually plan how she will remove her anticipated agonies from mind. After a while, no conscious deliberation is necessary. Everything is automatic.

Eileen's incest memories had come back in a deluge in the few months before the trial. It's not surprising that she was compelled to repress them. Once, for instance, her father anally raped her in the family bathtub. Eileen was somewhere between the ages of three and five. George was holding her in his lap in the tub, Eileen remembered, when Leah walked into the bathroom and demanded to know what he was doing. Somehow George slipped out of his predicament, life went on, and along with so many of her other early terrors Eileen lost the memory.

The Franklin defense team had virtually conceded Eileen's incest, Elaine Tipton told me. The incidents of sexual abuse had already come into the trial, in fact. The defense had admitted these stories into testimony in order to give Eileen a motive for hating her father so much that she would take her revenge by falsely accusing him. But the prosecutor could therefore use the repeated sexual abuse to explain Eileen's repression.

The jury needed an education from me about memory, Elaine said. Their education would help them frame their own opinion regarding the truthfulness of Eileen's memories. Eyewitness evidence is the strongest evidence one can bring into court, but in this case twenty years and the phenomenon of repression had intervened. Memory deteriorates over time. The jury would want to know whether or not repression would make it worse. "Would it?" Elaine asked.

"No," I told her. Memory does not go bad or vague just because it is repressed. And traumatic memories, in particular, do not deteriorate much at all. Nor do the memories of the opposite of trauma— extremely high moments from childhood. Both kinds of memories stay more alive than other kinds of memories.

I explained to Elaine that firsthand traumatic memory, like Eileen's, does not appear to undergo much weakening over time, nor is there a blurring of the general outline of the event. Over a four- to five-year lapse, the kidnapped children of Chowchilla could recall even the details of what had happened to them. And their stories matched. Over time, these children could also still talk about what parts of the kidnapping carried special meaning for them. Moreover, I knew from my own clinical studies of traumatized adults that the memory of a terrible episode, once buried and not discussed with anyone else, also tends to stay intact. A number of adult patients who recalled repressed memories were able to check these events in the back files of their local newspapers. With the exception of some mistaken perceptual details, the memories were remarkably close to the printed accounts.

One man, for example, came to me because he had gradually retrieved a group of repressed memories suggesting that as a child he had been all alone when an earthquake and a flood had forced his relocation. The man felt that he was two or three years old in this newly retrieved memory fragment. He looked up the records of his old community and could find no earthquake and accompanying flood. But he continued to ask his family and friends their recollections, and eventually somebody remembered that the man had had viral meningitis when he was two years old or so, and had required hospitalization. "Where was I?" he asked—there had been no hospital in the town where he grew up. "Over in Millville," he was told. The man checked the Millville newspaper files. There had indeed been an earthquake, when he was almost three, and the Millville River had flooded the town. The hospital had been evacuated. The man's memory, lost and then recovered only in small bits, had been correct.

A few months after she remembered Susan Nason's murder, Eileen began to see herself around the age of seven or eight being raped by a black man with a green-tipped Afro haircut. Her father had brought her to the rapist, and he assisted in the rape by bearing down on her left shoulder and keeping his hand over her mouth to muffle her screams. She remembered that her legs had been restrained, perhaps tied down. She remembered that the genital pain had been so intense that she wanted to flee, screaming, from it. She also remembered her futile struggle and her futile tears. Her body ached, and when she bent down to put on her shoes, her lower abdomen and bottom felt as if they might break. Eileen eventually heard in her mind what the man had said to her father at the very beginning of their crime against her—"She's going to like this, huh, George?" She also remembered that George had answered his friend with a nasty cackle.

But the man who raped Eileen did not take full physical form in her mind for a few more months. She originally saw him as if he were backlit with green spotlights in a disco parlor. His coloring was almost neon. His Afro haircut was striking. Later, after telling this story to Elaine's investigators, Eileen realized that her mental representation of the rapist had come from a Jimi Hendrix poster on the rapist's wall. Because George had pressed her head in that direction, she had stared at the rock star throughout her ordeal. Once Eileen realized how she had fooled herself mentally into seeing Jimi Hendrix, the man who actually raped her came to mind. It was her own godfather. His white face gradually imposed itself onto the memory. This man—her father's buddy and someone Eileen did not know very well—had arranged with George to rape George's daughter. It was a sick gift from a father to a friend. No doubt the rape preceded Susan Nason's murder; Eileen had immediately known what was happening to her friend in the back of her father's van.

Elaine Tipton and I felt satisfied that we understood how Eileen's mental shift from her black Jimi Hendrix rapist to her white godfather had occurred. It was a natural mistake, the kind of perceptual error that is sometimes made the first time something totally unexpected happens. The false detailing does not necessarily make a memory entirely "false." Elaine was confident that she could explain Eileen's mistake without sacrificing her witness's general credibility before the jury.

Elaine wondered aloud whether the jury would want to know where buried memory is actually kept. I told her that the most human part of the brain, our highly developed cerebral cortex (literally, "the brain's bark"), is divided into eight lobes, four on each side. At the front, behind the forehead, are the frontal lobes. Motor actions, inhibitions to impulsive action, speech production, imagination, foresight, social consciousness, symbolic thinking, and calculation are all conducted here. Not only do the frontal lobes house considerable long-term memory, but at the very front (the prefrontal cortex) they handle quick "working memory"—the kind of immediate memory that allows us to follow a first name with the last or to remember someone's profession when we greet them.

Above and behind our ears sit the parietal lobes, areas of the cortex that handle spatial relationships, physical sensations, body awareness, and our memories of such things—in short, our relationships to and awareness of the external environment. Considerable thinking, language comprehension, and word formation also reside in the parietal lobes, and they are involved, along with other parts of the cerebral cortex, in our sense of the passage of time and in representing semantic concepts. The "proper" word and the "proper" context live up there at the sides and toward the back of our brains.

Behind our temples and mastoid bones, and below the frontal and parietal lobes, sit the temporal lobes. Here we process aural sensations, word sense, and some aspects of word production, as well as the postural and righting sensations that are generated in the inner ear and other parts of the body. The hippocampus, at the far interior of each temporal lobe, receives millions of incoming sensations from the various sensory areas of the brain. It and the medial thalamus, a bilateral structure below the cortex, function in transferring memories into long-term storage. They are both part of the limbic system, a group of structures highly involved both in our emotions and in the immediate processing of memory. The limbic system, I told Elaine, insures that our emotions and our memories travel almost together. Hippocampal neurons send out memory signals to a number of long-term memory and associative centers all over the cerebral cortex. Crossovers from one side of the brain to the other are made almost instantly via the corpus callosum, a bundle of fibers which functions like a telephone cable.

At the back center of our heads, above and behind two bony skull projections known as the occiput, rest the occipital lobes of the cortex. Several visual centers in these lobes pick up of millions of separate signals from the retinas of our eyes and relay them—both for making an integrated picture and for memory processing—forward to the "rhinal" area and the hippocampal formations of the temporal lobes. The occipital lobes are involved in language, too—the language of color and of metaphor.

Since all the lobes of the cortex are involved in memory, a memory is not just the picture or the sound that a person once perceived. The memory would encompass, for example, Eileen's bodily attitude at the time she witnessed Susan Nason's murder, her sense of the environment at the place she and her father stopped, her position above Susan, her father's presence, the condition of her internal organs (a clutched stomach, perhaps), the words she thought—in short, almost everything. When Eileen's memory came back, many sensory and thinking pathways, or circuits, that had been connected with her perceptions during the Nason murder reactivated, bringing her the *sensation* of a memory. Marcel Proust was not the only one to feel, smell, taste, hear, see, and relive his experiences of "things past." We all do. Eileen did.

Elaine continued to muse on whether or not we should involve the jury with the brain as well as the mind. Quietly, she tapped a pencil on her long yellow legal pad. My own thoughts began to drift. It was getting late and my tea was turning to water.

In recent years, those experimental cognitive psychologists and neurobiologists who study memory have agreed to divide it into two primary categories: explicit, sometimes called declarative; and implicit, sometimes called nondeclarative. This division is more about *how* we remember than *what* we remember. Declarative, explicit memory proceeds from starting a conscious record—that is, thinking. You read a book, think about it, and remember. Nondeclarative, implicit memory is planted automatically—more or less unconsciously. You copy, over and over, the letters in a book of handwriting styles, until without really thinking you can address invitations in fancy script. You see a number of words flashed for a few seconds on a screen. A half-hour later, you can unscramble these words much quicker than words you never saw flashed before you.

People who have been taught implicitly are unaware of how they were taught. No conscious thought is necessary. People taught this way are eventually able to perform the particular task, but they may not be able to explain just what they are doing. On the other hand, when you teach people explicitly—by showing them a magic trick slowly, for instance—they often learn and remember instantly, and they can put words to what they have been taught.

Dr. Mortimer Mishkin's primate neuroscience laboratory at the National Institute of Mental Health does experiments that shed light on implicit, nondeclarative human recollection. The Mishkin team's "object-discrimination learning tasks" for monkeys lead eventually to habitual patterns of behavior in these animals. In the primate lab, monkeys are presented with pairs of objects, one of which hides a well in which there is food. The animal gets only one choice between objects. A few seconds later, it sees a different pair of objects, one concealing food and the other not. It again gets an all-or-nothing choice. Many more trials quickly follow. After all the pairs have been pre-

sented to the monkey, it gets a twenty-four-hour rest. The monkey then goes through the same procedure the next day. And the next. And the next. In other words, the animal practices, learning just a little bit more each day. He doesn't "think" about it. But the learning accumulates.

If a monkey has had its limbic system removed, it performs every bit as well at these tests as do normal animals. Implicit, nondeclarative memory is apparently processed in parts of the brain entirely separate from the limbic system, where short-term explicit memory is processed. It turns out that the habit memories of monkeys are handled in part inside subcortical structures known as the basal ganglia. If the monkeys' basal ganglia are damaged, it takes the animals twice as long to form their habit patterns.

The cerebral cortex is not a storehouse of habits in monkeys, it appears. It is not necessary, in other words, for a monkey to think in order to remember a habit. Implicit, nondeclarative memories form without benefit of thought in humans, too. After a while, we don't have to think in order to play our violins or whip up an omelet. We just do it.

The mystery that flows from this division of memory—when it comes to traumatized people—is how something taken into memory explicitly eventually behaves so similarly to the memories that are entirely implicit. These lost, no-longer-verbal memories drive action just as effectively as would a conditioning experiment. If someone had asked Eileen Lipsker in 1988 whether she had ever seen a murder, she probably would have responded like H.M., a famous research subject of the 1950s, who because of intractable seizures had to undergo surgical removal of the hippocampal areas of his temporal lobes on both sides of his brain. After his surgery, H.M. could quickly learn explicitly. He was still bright. But he could not transfer what he had learned explicitly into long-term memory. He could be taught to retain things only implicitly. If, after his operation, you had shown H.M. a videotape of someone being "murdered," he would have said when you later asked him about it, "What are you talking about?" If you had asked Eileen before her spontaneous memory retrieval whether she had ever seen a murder, she, too, would have answered, "What are you talking about?" H.M., because he had no hippocampi, had no capacity to retain declarative memories. Eileen Franklin still had the capacity to retain a declarative memory, but she had totally lost the ability to keep it conscious.

The difference between Eileen and H.M. was the intactness of Eileen's long-term memory. Unavailable to retrieval as it was for twenty years, Eileen's murder memory suddenly emerged, fully detailed. The details corresponded to evidence found at the scene. The memory was still verbal. It still included postural and positional senses. It still contained the horrible sound of a bat thwacking an egg. It stimulated the feeling of a scream welling up in the throat. And it contained a great many pictures.

Elaine Tipton woke me out of my reverie by snapping out of her own. We would not, she told me, review the brain for the jury. We would stay entirely with the mind. Tomorrow I should bring in any large-scale clinical studies that had to do with repression. Elaine had found me the work of John Briere, a psychologist at the University of Southern California. Had I found anything else?

In the late 1980s, Dr. Briere surveyed 440 women and 30 men, all of whom claimed to have been sexually abused as children. Of these adults, almost two-thirds said that they had gone through some period of time when they were unable to remember their abuses. Repression, Dr. Briere concluded, was closely associated with childhood abuse.

I told Elaine about a large-scale 1990 study pertinent to Eileen Franklin's repression which was conducted by Nel Draijer, a friend of mine who is a psychologist in Amsterdam. After interviewing more than a thousand randomly selected Dutch women, Nel found that approximately one in six reported having had unwanted sex with a household member sometime during childhood. Of Nel's 164 incest survivors, a quarter had never spoken about the abuses until they were interviewed. Many of these women, like the women in John Briere's sample, had lost their memory of the abuse at some time previous to the study. Much like Eileen Lipsker's memories, these memories had come back spontaneously during the women's adult years. In childhood, these women hadn't talked. Sometime later, they simply didn't remember.

"Not telling" apparently moves toward suppression of thought and eventually to repression. In 1986 the Bay Area sociologist Diana Russell published a random survey of 930 San Francisco women which indicated that about one in six had experienced incest prior to the age of eighteen (approximately the same percentage as in Draijer's Dutch sample). Before reaching adulthood, almost a third of the women experienced unwanted sex with a nonrelative. A quarter of the sexually abused women noted—although this question was not asked—that they had never told anyone about their abuse before responding to the survey. Although "not telling" does not lead directly, every single time, to "not remembering," there does appear to be a correlation between the two.

In the experimental cognitive lab, declarative memories come into the brain through the five senses, go through a process called "brief intake storage," and, if the subject pays attention, are laid down in "speech code" as memories. A little mental practice, or rehearsal, can prolong this experimentally transmitted memory forever. But when rehearsal is prevented in the laboratory, most memory is lost in about thirty seconds. This means that when things are perceived, they may be blocked from entering long-term memory by blocking any attempts on the person's part to think immediately about the material. One can see how rehearsal of a traumatic event might be prevented if a child goes through the event in a fog. But much traumatic memory, like Eileen's, is an exception in this regard. An alert traumatized child does not have to rehearse in order to remember.

I have appeared as an expert witness a couple of dozen times, but the Franklin case was the first in which I was asked to testify entirely in hypotheticals. I found the prospect disconcerting, and I wanted a little rehearsal myself. Elaine Tipton insisted that I use my own words—she would feed me nothing. "Talk about memory," she reminded me, as we wrapped things up. "But do not once talk about Eileen. I mean it. Don't."

"What happens if I slip and say 'Eileen Franklin'? She's all I've been thinking about for weeks," I teased.

"The judge declares a mistrial." Elaine did not even start to smile. "You cannot testify to the ultimate issue of fact before the jury. You cannot render an opinion as to whether or not a witness is telling the truth. Don't mention Eileen by name or get overly close with your analogies. It will prejudice the case."

She picked up her legal pad, now almost entirely filled with questions she intended to ask me the next day, and packed her briefcase. Dinner was being shoveled into the hospital steam tables as we said goodbye.

•   •   •

A person must qualify before the court each time he or she appears as an expert witness. What this means is that you are required to discuss your credentials in an almost shameless fashion the moment you take the stand. You need to establish before the judge and jury your training and experience in the area in which your opinion is being asked. Unlike other witnesses, the expert witness receives the special privileges of stating opinions and of giving the basis for them. The expert therefore must satisfy the court's requirements before offering any testimony about the issues.

While qualifying, the expert must simultaneously make friends with the jury. First impressions are often lasting, yet a witness must invariably spout so many academic degrees, licenses, board certifications, and years in practice that potential friends may be put off. Qualifying as an expert makes it almost impossible to get a decent start with twelve of your peers.

Elaine and I did the nasty deed as efficiently as we could, and then we got down to the important issue of the day, memory. There are at least six basic kinds, I told the jury. I would testify about just one of the memory types, but first I would provide them with an overview of the various clinical memory types as I see them. The first is a function called immediate memory. I wrote the word "immediate" with a big marker on an oversize piece of paper that Elaine Tipton had tacked to an easel. When you begin a sentence, can you finish it? Do you remember why you have walked into a room? Working memory is a subtype of immediate memory, involving quick associations to what is remembered. When you meet one of your co-workers, can you remember your relationship? When you see eggs on a menu, can you remember that you might want to order bacon, too?

The second memory type is "short-term." I wrote this, too, on the easel. What did you have for breakfast yesterday morning? Where were you last weekend? Who phoned yesterday? This type of memory is attacked early in Alzheimer's disease. Neurobiologists and experimental psychologists tend to lump what clinicians call short-term memory with long-term memory, referring to anything more than a few seconds old as "long-term" and to immediate memory as "short-term." But to those who work with patients, there is an important clinical distinction between short- and long-term memory. Elderly people have an easier time retrieving older, more firmly entrenched episodes than they do retrieving newer memories. This is normal. Young people who use street drugs or alcohol, and people of any age with degenerative diseases of the brain, also do not remember recent events well. This is abnormal. Because short-term-memory problems are common first signs of organic disorder, clinicians will cling to the term.

The next four kinds of memory are all long-term. I added the words "knowledge and skills" to the list on the easel. People say, for instance, that once you learn to type you never forget how. The same can be said of such things as riding a bicycle, telling time, writing in cursive, playing the violin. Whereas much of our skill memory carries few, if any, verbal instructions, our knowledge memory is almost entirely semantic. Both, however, are well entrenched. You do not have to review the alphabet, for example, every time you read. If you learn your multiplication tables well, you will retain them as you age. And if you know your history, you will consider art, politics, and economics in a historical context.

"Fourth," I marked in black on the sheet of paper, "comes 'priming.' Once you've skated on roller skates, roller blading isn't beyond imagination. A foray into one foreign land helps you visit another." Priming is often implicit, or nondeclarative.

"Next"—I looked at the jury and glanced back at my large sheet of paper. And then I went totally blank. I could not believe it! I had forgotten my fifth kind of memory.

"And are there any other types of memory?" Elaine asked quietly, a small smile playing at the corner of her mouth.

"I'm blanking on this one," I said. "Let me think for just a second." Elaine, invariably serious in court, suppressed a giggle. The jury began to laugh.

"Well, I'm allowed to ask you this question," Elaine rushed in to save me. "Are you familiar with the concept of associative memory?"

"Oh yes!" I said, "I'm sorry. Associative memory is the kind of memory that you don't even have to think of. [The court stenographer here records "Lots of laughter."] Because much of it is 'conditioning memory.' If you have been conditioned to do something, such as to be mannerly, to open car doors for girls, to curtsy for the Queen—whatever it was you were conditioned to do, you don't have to think about it. You just do it." Like priming, associative memory can be instilled entirely implicitly, and therefore is amenable to animal research. The conditions that create associative memory can be pleasant (rewards) or unpleasant (punishments). After a while, people don't need punishment or reward. They simply do what they were taught to do.

"There is one further type of memory?" Elaine Tipton cued me again, although by now my own memory was back under control.

"Yes," I said, printing another word onto the big sheet of paper. "The kind of memory that is involved in this trial is 'episodic.' This is the remembrance of things that happened in your life: the happy episodes, the sad ones, the miserable things, the scary things, the wonderful things, the grand things—or just plainness. This is the story of your life, and that is episodic memory."

One can see that the events and the people we experience, which are so much a part of us, are only one piece of the broader picture of memory. Yet episodic memory is the piece that psychiatrists deal with most. And it is the part of memory that came forward to plague Eileen Franklin Lipsker one sunny January afternoon. The other kinds of memory are important in diagnostics and treatment planning for patients. But episodic memory is the memory type that figures more than any other in psychotherapy. And episodic memory is also what comes up frequently in the courtroom for a jury's or a judge's consideration.

Elaine Tipton had convinced me that the better I explained the memory process to the jury, the more chance they would have to disabuse themselves of notions such as "important things are not forgotten" or "a child cannot reliably witness a murder." After we outlined the six kinds of memory, she asked me to describe the three processes of memory—perception, storage, and retrieval. She hoped that the jury would put together in their own minds this kind of sequence: Eileen perceived the Nason child's murder through her eyes and ears, her positional and spatial senses, her time sense. She then registered the memory as an immediate one, adding whatever associations that were available at the time. ("I knew it was a rape," for instance.) Immediate memory was consolidated into short-term memory within a few seconds, and then the transfer to Eileen's long-term storage was effected. Various associative pathways became activated. Eileen's eight-year-old understanding of death, for instance, could be brought to bear on what she had seen. Her clutched stomach could be understood in the context of what she just witnessed. As Eileen's murder memories became stored, the unconscious psychological defense of repression was applied to these memories in order to block their retrieval. Eileen's murder memories had "high storage strength"—they had lasted twenty years—but "low retrieval strength": nothing had reminded Eileen of the killing until she looked down at Sica.

Retrieval, in many ways, is far more quirky and unpredictable than is perception or memory storage. If one is alert, one can put into short-term memory a good amount of what one perceives. Considerable short-term memory is then transferred to long-term stores. Our capacity for storage of memories is almost limitless. But retrieval can be unconsciously defended against by a number of psychological maneuvers. Important memories are often lost to consciousness, especially if they are both terrifying and repeated. If the memories are already primed and active, retrieval may become easy; this explains Eileen's memory cascade after her first memories of the Nason murder emerged. But if the memories are heavily defended, as Eileen's were for twenty years, barely a trace of them may show.

Elaine Tipton made sure that I explained why clinical studies of people who have undergone traumatic events are the best way we currently have to understand how these events are perceived, stored, and recollected. It was important that the courtroom "finders of fact" see that there are great differences between the mistakes that a group of kidnapped children will make, or that a raped little girl will make, and the mistakes a college student in a psych lab, for instance, will make after watching a movie of a simulated automobile accident. In getting me to begin talking about experiments on college students, Elaine was anticipating the testimony of the psychologist Elizabeth Loftus, whom she expected to be called for the defense.

Dr. Loftus, an expert on memory from the University of Washington, studies the "wrong things" that people can be made to perceive and later remember. If you equated the responses of Loftus's college students—who saw nonexistent dents in cars, or incorrectly identified road signs at street corners—with the testimony of Eileen Lipsker, you would be forced to conclude that Eileen must have remembered the murder "wrong." In her experiments, Elizabeth Loftus successfully plants "wrong things" into all three phases of memory—perception, storage, and retrieval.

Despite the interesting points in the Loftus research, psychological experiments on university students do not duplicate in any way the clinician's observations. What comes from the memory lab does not apply well to the perceptions, storage, and retrieval of such things as childhood murders, rapes, or kidnappings. Trauma sets up new rules for memory. You can't replicate trauma in an experimental lab. You can't simulate murders without terrorizing your research subjects. Experiments on college students do not simulate clinical instances of trauma. And they have little to do with childhood itself.

Whenever a falsely perceived detail is reported by a person in a Loftus misinformation study, the person is considered to have gotten his memory "wrong," even if he does remember that there was an automobile accident in the movie. The general subject matter of the memory is not the concern in these misinformation studies. What is emphasized is the single mistake. Eileen certainly made enough mistakes to be rated as having a "false" memory by a University of Washington memory researcher. But the question here was, Would the jury believe the central theme of Eileen's memories? Despite her mistakes, did they think that she actually saw her father kill Susan Nason?

The Franklin jury was sophisticated. The foreman was a pediatrician, who had miraculously survived the elimination process that "selects" the jury. A registered nurse sat on the jury, as did other professional people who deal with various psychological issues as part of their work. They actively followed the testimony about how "forgetting" differs from repression. Some even took notes.

To repress is unconsciously and energetically to defend against remembering, I told them. Freud postulated that repression takes a significant amount of unconscious emotional energy—energy that is therefore unavailable for other mental tasks. More recent hypotheses suggest that repression actually releases energy that would otherwise have been tied up. Clinicians find that once repression lifts, individuals become far more symptomatic. They become anxious, depressed, sometimes suicidal, and far more fearful of items suggestive of their traumas. Eileen was certainly far more uncomfortable once her murder memories came back to her. Headaches and a churning stomach became part of her daily life.

Regardless of how much mental energy is bound up or released by repression, however, this defense puts memory totally out of consciousness. The sexual-abuse researcher Linda Meyer Williams surveyed a group of a hundred women, who as girls under twelve had had examinations in the emergency room of a large city hospital because they or their families had reported sexual abuse to the authorities. She found that thirty-eight of the women had no memories of such an incident. Rather than demonstrating reluctance to discuss something personal and perhaps embarrassing, these women seemed completely unable to remember even the emergency-room visit, for which the investigators had records in their hands. This was repression or some other extreme "forgetting" defense in action. These thirty-eight women were probably more comfortable without conscious recollections of whatever had prompted their visits to the emergency room. But they had lost important memories in the course of achieving this comfort.

Elaine wanted to make sure that the jury would be able to distinguish between repression and forgetting, and so I had thought up the story of "Grandma's brooch" when we prepared together at Stanford. "Grandma's brooch" had echoes of Eileen all through it, but it seemed safely hypothetical nonetheless. "Well, let's say you got your grandmother's brooch in an inheritance or something," I posited toward the end of Elaine's direct examination. "And everything was fine between you and your grandmother. And the brooch was nice. You put it in the bottom of a drawer, and twenty years later you have a certain blouse. You say to yourself, 'Oh, I remember I have that brooch in the bottom of the drawer.' And you dig it up, and sure enough, there it is. That's 'forgetting.' This is a memory to which you are not really attached. You know, it's out of mind most of the time. You go to work, do your thing, and then, when you look for the brooch twenty years later, you know just where it is.

"But let's say," I continued, glancing for a moment at the pediatrician, "that your grandmother died a horrible death, and she was wearing the brooch. And the police brought the brooch over with some blood on it. You cleaned off the brooch. You put it in your bottom drawer. You might use what I would consider very active, though unconscious, repression about that brooch. It is connected now in your mind with pain, with trauma, and with fright. And you might not have another memory of that brooch unless somebody bled in front of you, or somebody else had a similar kind of accident, or you saw someone who looked just like your grandmother."

I wanted the jury to see that repression is more active than is simple forgetting—that it is defensive and unconsciously conflicted. But I also wanted them to understand how repressed memory is retrieved—by a visual cue, for instance. I wanted them to remember how much Jessica Lipsker looked like Susan Nason. "And then suddenly the memory of the brooch would come to you," I went on, letting my eyes rest on a nice-looking woman juror in pearls. "It would not be pleasant to think about the brooch. You would know the brooch was down in the bottom drawer. I don't know if you would want to go look at it." I was indirectly alluding here to Eileen Lipsker's ten months of silence after she retrieved her first memories of Susan Nason's murder. It was important to understand why an ordinary person might not take action at once.

"And [forgetting Grandma's brooch] would be an actively repressed memory," I said, glancing back toward Elaine, who stood silently in front of me. "Such a memory would seem as if it weren't there. But then, when you saw somebody bleeding, or you saw somebody who looked just like Grandma, you might have an immediate rush of memory."

Elaine Tipton had covered the point about look-alikes brilliantly before I ever came to court. She had shown the jury enlarged photo portraits of the two little girls, Sica and Susan, side by side. One child's smile seemed to greet the future, while the other's sweetly evoked the past. If I were less reality-bound, I might have believed one to be the reincarnation of the other. Whatever you believed, however, Elaine Tipton's blowups were magic. Anyone could see why Eileen's memories had broken loose with a glance at her own child.

On cross-examination, Douglas Horngrad skipped from point to point, without backing me into the ropes. Defense cross-examination often proceeds in this way, quickly getting to one point and then darting toward the next. (Elaine objected to hardly any of Horngrad's questions, later telling me she didn't think I needed help.) He asked, for instance, about dreams. He had already established that Eileen hadn't had any dreams of the Nason murder over the twenty years during which she repressed. While I acknowledged that dreams are important to trauma, I added that dreams are not always connected to trauma. Children do not necessarily dream about their traumas. Nor, by the time they reach adulthood, do childhood trauma victims necessarily start dreaming. Some people who repress do dream, particularly as their memories begin to come back toward the surface. But many such people do not.

Horngrad also asked whether or not you could look at a person's symptoms without knowing anything about a past trauma and guess the trauma from those clues. Here he implied that therapists overzealously suggest memories to their clients or patients after having observed a few symptoms. He was suggesting (perhaps) that Eileen's therapist, Kirk Barrett, having observed Eileen's symptoms, had come to his own conclusions about what had occurred and had then planted the murder memories in Eileen's mind.

You can't always guess the nature of a trauma from a series of symptoms, but sometimes you can. I answered his question with an anecdote: Several years ago, my husband and I went to the movie *Stand By Me,* and as we watched the scene in which a train suddenly appears behind four boys on a railway trestle I whispered to him, "Whoever made this movie is playing post-traumatic games with me!" We stayed in our seats at the end and watched the credits. The screenplay had been taken from a story called "The Body," by Stephen King. In *Danse Macabre,* King's 1981 book about the horror genre, I found an autobiographical passage that explained the scene to me. When King was four years old, he and another boy were playing on the railroad tracks, and a freight train hit and killed his little friend. The dead boy's severed body parts were brought home in a wicker basket. In his book, King claims not to remember the episode itself but only what his mother told him of it. Nonetheless, it influenced much of his writing. Directly from his work, one can guess his trauma.

A moment later, Douglas Horngrad stepped into a deep hole. He had hoped, through his cross-examination, to imply that the memories suggested by therapists take on lives of their own. Can traumatic stories be suggested? he asked, in far more complicated words than these. Yes, I said, a story can be suggested. But it won't usually create a cluster of symptoms and signs. After the accident at the railroad tracks, Stephen King wandered home alone. He had wet his pants, and for the rest of that day he was mute. Those are both signs. King's mother could not have suggested those behaviors to him, just as someone who tells you that you have tuberculosis cannot alter your chest X rays or your skin tests. I was using Stephen King as a metaphor for people like Eileen. But the metaphor itself had captured the courtroom.

"King was traumatized?" Mr. Horngrad asked, seemingly incredulous.

"Yes," I said. "King can't stop doing what he does." In fact, I had

had a strange experience in Los Angeles three weeks before, and now I found myself telling it to the lawyers, judge, and jury. I was sitting alone in a hotel coffee shop, and I overheard a conversation at the table next to me, where three men were seated. Two of them were telling the third, who had his back to me, to "mitigate the blood." They repeated this strange phrase two or three times. Apparently they wanted the man with his back to me to stop killing people. This man, I decided, was either a killer for hire or a screenwriter.

It was L.A., and within a few seconds I realized that they must be talking about a movie script. The two men doing most of the talking were apparently on the production side, and they kept telling the fellow with his back to me that too many people died whenever he had anything to do with it. "Try a horse or a dog—pet abuse is in," they said. "Have the boy fall off his bicycle." Finally they added, "If we do this film, only one person can die in the whole thing."

"A ruined bike isn't as strong as a death," the writer replied, sticking to his convictions. "Why not kill more people?" he said, and later, "I've got to do it. . . . That's me."

"And then I looked at this person really carefully," I told the court. "It was Stephen King. He was sitting just about in my lap in the coffee shop. . . . A person who has truly been traumatized . . . may not be aware [that his] behavior is linked to the trauma. But it's there, and it has to be repeated."

The two visions I posed to the Franklin jury, thanks to the defense attorney's half-mocking question about traumatic symptoms, were of a little girl pulling out the hair at the top of her head and of a famous adult writer insisting on a lot of death. The twelve people deciding George Franklin's fate needed to know that behaviors, especially if they are trauma-specific, confirm the gist of a memory. Symptoms and signs, plus their underlying memories, become lifelong motifs for people—sometimes lifelong inspirations.

If Douglas Horngrad's questions had been narrow, my answers might have had to be more confined. He might have asked, for instance, "Is it possible for a therapist to guess wrong about a particular traumatic event from someone's symptoms?" And then, perhaps, "Is it possible for a wrong guess to suggest a false memory to a person?" And finally, "Do people who suffer from false memories ever experience a symptom or two?" Given this narrow focus, I would not have thought of Stephen King. My answers would have had to be

"Yes," "Yes," and "Yes." And in this trial, I would have had a tough time trying to point out why Eileen Franklin Lipsker was an exception to my yesses. I was absolutely forbidden to mention her.

After my testimony, the defense brought in its own expert, the Stanford psychiatrist David Spiegel, who studies hypnosis and the defense of dissociation. Childhood dissociation starts with self-hypnosis, he testified, and he posited in court that a child exposed to horrors such as a father-assisted rape and a murder would have had to hypnotize herself and then sequester her mental processes into a separate kind of consciousness in order to handle the traumatic circumstances that she reported. The events that Eileen said she had experienced, Spiegel believed, were so terrible that repression would not have sufficed as a defense. Once she had dissociated, however, she would not have later been able to produce a particularly accurate recollection of the trauma. She would not have been particularly detailed. She would also be highly suggestible as an adult, because those who can self-hypnotize are almost always too easily influenced by others. Eileen's story, in other words, did not hold together, he thought.

Elaine Tipton did not put David Spiegel through a grueling cross-examination. She pushed him to admit that repression was a much more common defense than dissociation. But Dr. Spiegel, who spends much of his clinical time at Stanford consulting on cases involving extreme dissociation, did not think that repression was an important or common defense against psychic trauma. Elaine told me afterward that she opted against challenging him any further—and indeed she cut short her cross-examination. At this point in the trial, she felt that she was far ahead.

As Elaine had anticipated, Elizabeth Loftus eventually also appeared for the defense. She testified that her misinformation experiments served as proof that repressed memory can be changed in the process of intake, storage, or retrieval. But Elaine was ready for Dr. Loftus and on cross-examination quickly received an acknowledgement from her that she was not a clinician and did not ordinarily use children in her research. In any case, Elaine had painstakingly prepared the jury to decide the outcome on the basis of whether or not they believed in the reality of Eileen's repressed memory of a terrible event in childhood. Loftus's testimony spoke to memory but not to childhood or trauma.

It took the jury a relatively short eight hours to reach their verdict. On November 30, 1990, they found George Franklin, Sr., guilty of murder in the first degree. I was amazed. Brilliant as was the prosecution's case, it was difficult to imagine that a jury had experienced no "reasonable doubt." Elaine informally asked several jurors afterward what had led to their decision. She told me that a number of them said my testimony had convinced them. I learned something from that: sometimes hypotheticals are just as compelling as specifics. For concrete thinkers like me, that's a revelation.

I spoke with Eileen Lipsker on the phone a few hours after the jury came in with their verdict. She sounded disappointed and pleased all at once. Both she and I knew that her impossible emotional conflict—the conflict that had caused her to repress for twenty years—would not be resolved with the completion of the trial. Eileen loved her father. And he was an evil man.


On April 2, 1993, Division One of the California Court of Appeal ruled on *People v. Franklin.* In an unpublished opinion, the court upheld the Franklin conviction. Judge Smith had been correct in ruling out any newspaper evidence, the opinion stated. The fundamental prerequisites and constraints governing the admission of evidence apply to the defense as well as to the prosecution. The trial judge had not abused his discretion in limiting this presentation of the defense to test Eileen's credibility. The higher court concluded that newspaper articles of 1969 had "no more than slight or insubstantial probative value." The prosecution would have had to present a huge, confusing amount of false newspaper detail in order to show what Eileen Franklin had *not* incorporated into her memories. Eileen had testified under oath that she did not read the papers. That was enough.

Eileen's prostitution did not have to be disclosed, except to the judge, the higher court also held. Judge Smith had been proper in his ruling that the misdemeanor did not carry with it inherent dishonesty, which would have reflected on Eileen's credibility.

The court also wrote that Elaine Tipton did not act improperly in her prosecution of the case. She did come too close to the facts in one hypothetical question to me: "Doctor, do you have an opinion regarding whether or not a particularly hideous, violent act occurring in a childhood filled with repeated acts of both physical and sexual abuse starting at an early age, involving multiple persons, including a parental figure, involving death threats and fear of retaliation—do you have an opinion as to whether or not such an event could be repressed?" But the error was "harmless." The court also held that testimony presented by Elaine about George Franklin's behavior in jail during Eileen's visit was used wrongly—as a kind of self-incrimination—but it added that the other evidence presented in this trial had lined up so overwhelmingly against George Franklin that here, too, no harm had been done.

The Court of Appeal ruled that my testimony was offered by the prosecutor for a properly stated purpose: "to disabuse the jury of the identified misconception that a child witness to murder would not be able to forget the event only to recall it accurately twenty years later." Eileen Franklin Lipsker's credibility had been subjected to withering assault by the defense, they noted. The prosecutor had properly obtained expert opinion in order to illuminate the phenomenon of repression and the retrieval of memory. On July 15, 1993, the California Supreme Court declined to hear George Franklin's appeal. None of the seven Supreme Court justices voted to hear the case. At this writing, Franklin's attorneys plan to appeal in federal court.

Eileen Lipsker came to visit me a year after the trial. Her children were thriving, but her husband Barry had become chronically ill with various problems related to restricted blood flow to his heart and head. He could no longer work, and he often slept for much of the day. In fact, since it was a Saturday morning and my office was closed, Barry slept on the couch in my waiting room while Eileen came into my consulting room and talked.

In the late summer of 1992, Barry died in his sleep. He was forty-seven years old. The medical examiner ruled that he died of a cardiac arrhythmia. Eileen spent almost an hour trying to revive Barry when she awoke. She accused herself mercilessly of doing CPR all wrong. That, too, makes for bad memories. But Barry's autopsy reassured Eileen in this respect: when she awoke he had already been dead for a couple of hours.

Eileen cannot take refuge any longer in massive repression. She lives with her memories. She talks freely to Sica and Aaron about Barry, despite her painful memories of their problematic marriage, his illness, and his death in bed beside her. And she vividly remembers Barry—both the good and the bad. Eileen sees a psychotherapist these days. Her marriage had improved markedly before Barry died, and she finds that comforting.

Most of Eileen's siblings will have nothing to do with her. They objected when she first came forward to report her memories of their father. And they object to her now. They do not believe her. And they think she has willfully ruined their reputations, their privacy, and their father's remaining years. But the Lipsker family makes up, in part, for that. They completely accept and love Eileen.

One day I saw Eileen Lipsker entirely, completely happy. In February 1992, she and Elaine Tipton came to the Fairmont Hotel ballroom in San Francisco to explain the process of her memory return and her testimony at the trial to the American College of Psychiatrists. Afterward, the psychiatrists, including some of the most distinguished members of the profession in this country, crowded around Eileen. They believed her, they told her. They admired her. They felt intense compassion for her ordeal. At first, Eileen's big light-brown eyes looked doubtful. But along came another psychiatrist, and another, and yet another. With each one of their congratulations, Eileen brightened a bit. And soon she was glowing like the moon.

# 3

# A Drunken Woman at the
# Side of the Road

Winter in California means rain. That's why the hills turn so green in December and the lupine and poppies bloom so spectacularly in March. Winter means drenching rains almost every day for at least a month—you never know which month until well into its middle. Even during the great winter droughts of the 1980s, a visitor might come to San Francisco expecting a sunny February vacation and instead find himself in a gullywasher. We were headlong into one of those big winter storms when a young dark-blond woman found herself in jail.

Jack Lewisell and his California Highway Patrol partner Marty Neal spotted the woman sitting in a bright-red Toyota just off Highway 101, the freeway you take south from San Rafael down through Marin County and over the Golden Gate Bridge into San Francisco. Her car was parked in the dark, at the East Blithedale off-ramp from the north into Mill Valley. It looked out of gas, maybe—broken down, perhaps. There were no blinkers, no flares, no nothing. It was about 8:30 P.M.

The two policemen sloshed through the roadside puddles as quietly as big men can slosh, bearing in mind that neither of them wished to attract attention. A car that looked abandoned might mean a drug deal in the dark. They simultaneously switched on their flashlights and beamed them inside. The woman sat in the driver's seat. Awake and alone. Not a bit surprised at their intrusion. As a matter of fact, she exhibited very little awareness at all. She looked as if she were seventy feet away, although she sat no more than a couple of feet from them.

"Hey, ma'am," Jack Lewisell said, "don't you know it's dangerous to park on a highway shoulder with no lights on, no flares, and no emergency blinkers?"

Silence.

"Miss," Lewisell tried again—a little more quietly now, because the young woman was looking straight through him—"what's your name?"

No answer.

"Let's see your license."

But the woman did not make a move. Nor did she say a word. She just sat there, a zombie doing nothing. Marty Neal walked back to the patrol car to get some flares.

Patrolman Lewisell tried the car door. It was unlocked. He reached in and pulled the woman's keys out of the ignition. Neal had set up his flares and was splashing back to the Toyota. Lewisell beamed his flashlight into the woman's face. "C'mon, get out your driver's license, ma'am." But the young woman did not move her hands or her eyes. "She must be absolutely plastered," Lewisell thought, as he watched a rivulet of rain run down the left side of her skirt. Nothing seemed able to touch her in this state. She did not flex a forefinger.

The woman was maybe thirty, at the most. With a little lipstick and a few tangles combed out of her curly hair, she might have looked like one of those snappy office girls who cross Montgomery Street diagonally at noon with a yogurt and a plastic spoon in their hands. A nice working-girl blazer. Good pumps perched on the accelerator and brake. No wedding ring. Losing patience, Patrolman Lewisell lifted her purse from the floor next to her feet. "I'm going to have to get your I.D. out myself," he said.

"Leave me alone," warned the surprisingly green eyes, suddenly focused. But the woman's lips did not move. "Jeez, what a quiet, sullen drunk," Lewisell muttered to Neal. "She must think that if she breathes on us we'll smell all the cocktail lounges from Larkspur into Mill Valley."

He cleared his throat. "Get out of the car, and put your hands up on the roof."

She lunged at the door handle and tried to pull the door shut. The quick move forced Lewisell back a step. He recovered quickly, catching the door. This woman *had* to be drunk. Nobody else would act so out to lunch. He produced a breathometer kit. "Miss," he said, keeping things as polite as he could, "blow nice 'n easy into this little balloon."

"No," said the emerald eyes.

Marty Neal read from her license, "Her name is Bartlett. She lives on Redwood Drive, in Lucas Valley. I think it's one of those low-lying condo complexes just off the Lucas Valley exit. I'm going back to the patrol car to run a computer check."

Lewisell was left standing in the rain holding a flashlight and a balloon. He put the balloon close to her mouth. She paid him little or no attention. Except for the brief moment when she had tried to shut her door, she seemed to live somewhere else, on some other planet, in some other universe.

"You've come a long way from your valley to Mill Valley, Miss Bartlett," Lewisell said, trying to keep the irritation out of his voice. "Considerable driving. Just blow a nice little kiss into my balloon to finish up your trip." No movement, not even a flicker.

"Hey! Blow! Now! You've got no choice. C'mon. Blow!" The eyes continued to stare straight ahead. "O.K., we obviously can't straight-line-walk you outside in this kind of rain. We have only one other choice. We'll have to book you and get your blood tested in jail."

Marty Neal sloshed back to the Toyota. "She's clean and the vehicle's clean. Not even parking tickets. Need any help?"

"We'd better get her over to the county jail in San Rafael," Lewisell said. "I'm arresting her for driving under the influence. Let's handcuff her and put her into the back of the patrol car. Then we'll get a tow truck for the vehicle."

Suddenly from inside the Toyota came a growl. A tremendous punch landed on Jack Lewisell's stomach. She flew out of her car, nails extended, teeth bared, fists flailing, and feet kicking. The two patrolmen yelled, "You're resisting arrest—you're crazy—you're assaulting police officers!" But she fought them without pause. As Lewisell informed her of her rights, she bit his hand. With the prospect of a tetanus shot tomorrow and perhaps an AIDS test sometime in the future, Lewisell could take no more. He landed a right hook to the Bartlett woman's jaw and relieved her of any sort of consciousness, drunken or otherwise.

They lifted her into their patrol car, handcuffed her, and laid her out on the backseat. Marty Neal remarked that she smelled good, even in the rain. Jack Lewisell disagreed. He said he could smell the liquor on this one from the very first. Miss Bartlett would really be in the soup now. She'd wake up in jail with several charges against her—drunk driving, resisting arrest, and assaulting police officers. She'd probably wind up incarcerated, even though she was a first offender. Come to think of it, the Bartlett woman had not spoken a word through the whole affair. Exactly what was bugging her? Who in the hell did she think she was with that blank stare, the Daughter of Frankenstein? Dracula's girlfriend? Who the hell *was* she anyway?

She awoke at six. Birds chirped outside. She stretched her cramped muscles, fingered a tender spot on her jaw, and located a run in her stocking. She sniffed freshly brewed coffee and maybe an unwashed body or two—an unwashed body? hers?—before opening her eyes to see walls covered with grime and graffiti. There was a window screened with wire mesh near the ceiling. What was this? Jail? And how did she get here? What in the world was this all about?

A woman with spent yellow hair, purple high-heeled boots, and a very, very short leather skirt stared at her from across the room. "This is a cell, isn't it?" she asked this woman, and then, without waiting, "What day is this? What jail?"

The befrizzed blonde came over to her new cellmate's cot. "You musta really tied one on last night, hon. I saw you fight those cops when they brought you in. And man, did you fight the matron! They finally gave up on getting your blood."

"I'm amnesic," she said. She spoke quietly. "I don't remember anything. I haven't been drinking at all. I don't even know my name."

A look of profound skepticism crossed the face of the blonde in the purple boots, but she launched into the requested orientation speech. It was a pleasant change from the usual requests that came her way; few people ever asked Trudy Stapleton to say anything. "We are inside a famous Marin County, California, pit in designer-pink stucco that was dreamed up by the late, great Frank Lloyd Wright," she began. "You came in DUI last night—February fifteenth, doll—and today's the very next day, if you know how to count by your ones. Last night, at about nine, they dropped you on the cot you're lying on now. You were kicking and biting when I first saw you. And you don't look like the kind of kid who usually winds up in fights. More like Sandra Dee than Madonna. My name's Trudy Stapleton, what's y—"

A policeman with a syringe and some rubber tubing opened the cell and waved Trudy out of the way. "Well, well, well," he said to the green-eyed woman, while he tied the tube around her upper arm and dabbed the inside of her elbow with a cotton swab. "Our nice Mill Valley exit drunk has decided to wake up today and donate her blood. My name's Deputy Sheriff Logan and I'm taking it." He inserted the needle and pulled back the plunger as the syringe filled. "Fine cheat you are, young lady. You let us do the test nice and easy now, when anybody would know that your blood alcohol has to be way back down."

"What in the world are you talking about?" Her voice sounded prim to her own ears. "I don't drink at all." This was a bad dream. Maybe blinking could clear it. She blinked.

The needle was out. "Miss Bartlett, you're in big, big trouble. You don't leave this jail until somebody makes bail for you. And your bail will be high."

"I want a lawyer."

"Know one? Have the money?"

"No to both questions." She was angry and ready to be a little rude herself.

"I'll call the Public Defender's Office the minute I get time. Meanwhile, want some coffee?"

"I'll take it black, thank you," she answered. She had no idea how she knew right away what her own personal tastes in coffee were. Her mind was otherwise a blank. But now she knew her name and her marital status; the policeman had clued her in—"Miss Bartlett." In fact, she could expand on his clue—"Miss Patricia Louise Bartlett." And she apparently knew all about amnesia; she had readily identified herself as amnesic. But the only bit of yesterday that she could remember was two men who looked like globs coming out of the rain and threatening her. Did they take her purse?

She could not remember who her friends were, who her employer was, or the names of any relatives who might bail her out. But Patricia knew, without straining, that she liked her coffee with a lightly buttered piece of sourdough toast. She also knew that she didn't drink any alcohol. None. She also knew somehow, from someplace inside herself, that she worked as a secretary. An executive secretary, in fact. Big downtown firm. Law firm? Yes. And deep inside a chamber in her mind she also knew that something like this had happened before. She even realized that the more cues she picked up now, the more quickly her identity would fall back into place. "Let me see my purse," she called after Logan. "And may I have the Marin and San Francisco phone books? Those, too, please."

Patricia Bartlett had awakened in the Marin County Jail to an old-fashioned psychological amnesia. It was "old-fashioned" because the condition was probably more commonly recognized in Freud's 1890s Europe than it is in 1990s America. In fact, it was Freud's studies of amnesic people in the 1890s that impelled him to describe repression as a defense that sets up a barrier between consciousness and what is submerged beneath it. Similar studies led Freud's French contemporary Pierre Janet, whose view of psychiatry was entirely unrelated to Freud's, to define dissociation as a sidewise slippage from consciousness, with a partition between the dissociated event and the mental component that knows and remembers. What had happened was isolated from conscious thought by being compartmentalized, Janet said. Both Freud and Janet studied the same psychological phenomenon—amnesia. Yet in so doing each discovered a different defense against memory. Most likely each would have looked at Patricia Bartlett quite differently.

When Patricia awoke, she did not know who she was or why she was incarcerated. She had lost all episodic memory—the memory of her life events, the people she knew, her personal circumstances. She had no idea who she was, but she still knew how she liked her coffee. She knew how to check her stocking for a run. Her knowledge-and-skills memory, in other words, was intact. Patricia knew how to talk and how to form semantic thoughts in her mind. She could lay down and store new immediate and short-term memories, remembering at nine o'clock that she had had her coffee at eight, and that Logan had promised her a lawyer from the Public Defender's Office. She remembered his name—"Logan." Patricia would have known her multiplication tables, ice-skating skills, or manners, too, if anybody had asked; her priming and associative memory was completely in order.

All Patricia did not know was her own personal past and her own personal identity.

There are several conditions besides the psychological amnesias which cause a person suddenly to lose all episodic memory. And these are conditions that, had they been suspected, might have prompted Logan or the night matron to send for a doctor. Serious head injury, for instance, will usually cause a person to black out or go into a coma. Upon emerging from this period of unconsciousness, the injured person will often exhibit the loss of a number of mental functions, including memory. How did the highway patrolmen or Patricia's jailers know that she had not been hit over the head a short while before she was found? If she had had a concussion, she might have been suffering from retrograde amnesia—the loss of a number of minutes before the injury because of disruptions of transfer from short-term to long-term memory.

Anterograde organic amnesia was another condition that no one at the jail considered. If Patricia Bartlett had taken one of the benzodiazepine tranquilizers or sleeping pills, for instance, she might have shown an inability, for up to a day or two after ingestion of the drug, to put short-term explicit memories into long-term storage. Because of problems with memory transfer, a person with anterograde amnesia might not remember what happened starting close to the time he began drinking, used a certain drug, or took a certain medication. Although most anterograde amnesias are self-limited and relatively mild, long-standing alcohol abuse can lead to serious permanent problems of memory transfer. If Patricia had been this kind of chronic alcoholic, it would have buttressed the case against her. But would she not have needed some immediate help at the side of the road or in jail?

A syndrome called complex partial seizures also causes behaviors resembling the ones Patricia exhibited. Though people in this condition are apparently awake and alert during the electrical discharges that disrupt their brain activity, they are unable to form any coherent memories during their seizures, which may last anywhere from several minutes up to an hour or so. Was Patricia having a seizure in her car? During such a seizure, people may travel somewhere, as Patricia Bartlett did, and they may behave strangely. They may become violent. Afterward they have no idea how they got wherever they are and what they did. An almost invariable sign of this type of seizure is the tendency to repeat certain stereotyped movements, such as tonguing, blinking, or lopsided grimacing. Patricia did not do this. Another diagnostic clue is an abnormal electroencephalogram. Nobody ordered one for her.

Jails and freeway exits, however, are not the places one goes to get emergency medical help. None of Patricia Bartlett's antagonists on the night of February 15 wondered whether she could be suffering from an amnesia, organic or otherwise. It never occurred to Patrolmen Lewisell and Neal to send for a doctor. The matron wanted to put her to bed. Everybody wanted a blood test. As far as anyone who met Patricia Bartlett at the Mill Valley end of her journey was concerned, the woman was faking it. Amnesia? She was just a drunk trying to stay out of jail.


Jane Thacher truly earned her salary. As a member of the Marin County Public Defender team, she fought for her clients in court and, better yet, planned their defense brilliantly before they ever got there. But Jane was beginning to tire. Five years of drunk drivers, thieves, drug users, and child abusers had left an ache in her head and a numbness in her soul. Jane liked criminal law, but she enjoyed it more in the abstract than in the concrete. Much of the criminal work she did was too dirty to be interesting.

Jane went to the Marin County Superior Court on the morning of February 16 to appear in a couple of preliminary hearings. She then walked to her office in the same sprawling county office building, a futuristic fantasy designed by Wright and built after his death. She'd first see an old client and then stop by at the jail, which was also in the building. The office assistant handed her the morning's roster. "Good old Trudy Stapleton again," Jane smiled as she glanced over the list. "When will she quit? Isn't she getting a bit finger-marked?"

"They also hauled in a drunk woman last night, who fought the highway-patrol guys and the matron," the assistant said. "A Patricia Bartlett."

"Hmm. We don't know her from before, do we?" Jane asked.

The assistant shook her head, picked up the phone, and got Deputy Logan on the line for Jane.

"What's the story on the female drunk driver from last night?"

Jane asked. "And does Trudy Stapleton or anybody else need any of our help?"

"Oh, sorry, Jane. I should've called you earlier. Trudy's out. Her pimp brought in a private lawyer. And the drunken lady is pure poison, I would say. Beauty on the outside, beast on the inside. She's a phony. You know, putting on airs like a socialite. She has only twenty bucks in her pocket and a thirty-two-dollar balance in her checkbook. Some socialite! The assistant D.A. handling the case against her, Bill Hewitt, he was down here this morning, and he says he's going to slap her with at least three felony charges."

"Is there anything special you've noticed about this woman besides her sounding high-toned and being cash poor?"

"She's very good-looking," Logan said. "Seriously, Jane, she's saying she doesn't know a thing about herself. Not even her name. Entirely bullshit, all of us think. But then she turns around and asks for her purse and a couple of phone books—as though, you know, she really does need to figure out where she lives, who her friends are, and stuff like that. Maybe she's trying to work out a defense before an attorney even gets to her. But I've never seen a real amnesic in this jail, and it's going on six years."


Today we classify the psychological amnesias—the category into which Patricia Bartlett's amnesia fell—as dissociative disorders. The defense largely responsible is the one that Pierre Janet defined, which involves the loss or alteration of a person's ability to integrate consciousness or identity. Deputy Logan accused Patricia Bartlett of faking either a psychogenic amnesia or a fugue, the only two psychological conditions that account for total amnesias lasting for more than a day or so. Multiple personality (MPD), another dissociative disorder, can theoretically lead to daylong amnesia, but most people with MPD cycle into their alternate personas and back again to the host personality much quicker than that.

A person who uses considerable dissociation does not link up thoughts, behaviors, and emotions. Frequently there is an alteration in the state of consciousness. Such people may forget or ignore pain. They may forget or ignore parts of their own bodies. They may forget or ignore their own personal history. They may forget or ignore themselves altogether. When the police first found Patricia Bartlett, she looked like a zombie. Her state of consciousness must have felt to her like a waking dream, or an absence, or even a "nonbeing." Patricia ignored her run-in with the California Highway Patrol. She ignored her own presence at the Mill Valley exit. And she ignored who she was. At the moment Officers Lewisell and Neal found her, she was exhibiting massive dissociation; she almost perfectly exemplified it, in fact. Sitting at the side of the road in a kind of trance, she perceived far less than the alert person ordinarily does. Very little of what she registered in short-term memory transferred into long-term storage. In her altered state, she had blocked considerable memory-processing at the "front end," where we perceive and transfer, and at the "back end," where we retrieve. She just wasn't there.

Most of us dissociate a little, just as we also repress a little. To dissociate, you have to step aside from feelings, thoughts, or the sense of connectedness. You have to partly turn off the psychological apparatus that fully perceives, registers, and stores memories. Or you may perceive the memories in one state and then fail to retrieve those memories until you are in that same state again. To repress, you have only to block retrieval of something already fully registered and stored. You are alert when you take in the stimuli that you later repress.

Patricia was anything but alert when the two highway patrolmen picked her up at the Mill Valley exit. And many of us are anything but alert as we listen to long, boring speeches, suffer from bad head colds, or take endless rides on trains. Perhaps we even look a bit like Patricia at such times—glazed eyes, unmoving face, and all. Dissociation requires unlocking the gears and coasting a while on neutral. This happens to people during moments of passion, too. One of the Czech novelist Milan Kundera's female characters, for instance, thinks of shopping lists at the height of sex. Will she later remember everything about the sex? Most of us, however, do not dissociate so completely that we cannot feel intense sexual sensations or rage or pain, or do not know who we are or what we once did as children. Our gears never slip that far.

Self-hypnosis is an entry point to the extreme slippages that such people as Patricia Bartlett employ. It is one thing to drift a little, and entirely another to sail off past all pain and anger. The childhood gateway to pathological dissociation is self-hypnosis—counting, focusing on objects such as Venetian blinds or spots on the ceiling, visualizing another place, or repeating certain phrases over and over. Eventually the dissociation comes automatically, with no preliminary forays into autohypnosis. Dissociation is so closely linked to hypnosis, however, that one might define hypnosis as "guided dissociation." Just as deep hypnosis shuts down full perception, registration, and storage of memories, so does massive dissociation.

One person who slipped into massive dissociation—perhaps even deeper than the supposedly "drunk" Patricia Bartlett—was the well-known American poet Anne Sexton. Sexton dissociated so much that she often frightened her family and friends by her silence and unresponsiveness. She apparently depended on a drifting mind or an almost trancelike state to find her metaphors and work into her rhythms. Martin Orne, her first psychiatrist, writes in his introduction to Diane Middlebrook's 1991 biography of the poet that he decided to tape his sessions with her because she often forgot what went on in them. Sometimes she needed to listen to the tapes twice.

Trance and dissociation do not lend themselves to full, detailed remembrance. The cognitive psychologists have demonstrated that you can prevent storage of explicit memories if you block rehearsal for thirty seconds or so after perception. One seven-year-old patient of mine "blocked rehearsal" as he was being thrown against walls and thoroughly beaten by his stepfather. He pictured himself "at a picnic, on Mommy's lap." After a while, he did not have to picture anything at all. He was just "gone." He felt no pain. Could this boy—I will call him Frederick Waters—remember later what had happened to him? His stepfather had been in his life for two years when I met Frederick. Yet the boy could remember only two instances of abuse. Neighbors had called the authorities on a number of occasions, however, to complain about the sounds of someone being beaten. The parents of Frederick's schoolmates had filed child-abuse complaints, because they saw the bruises on his skin. Yet Frederick himself could remember only "two times." Dissociation to another place— "Mommy's lap"—had blocked some of his memory from going into storage. Dissociation had also acted to block retrieval.

As children, many of us spent considerable time with our minds on idle, but this is in no way as extreme as the kind of trance Frederick Waters or Patricia Bartlett employed. "Mind on idle" is very, very mild dissociation. If a teacher spotted one of us indulging in a glassy moment, for instance, she might try a trick—an explosive, "Johnny,

tell me what I just said!" The funny thing was that Johnny was usually not too far gone to comply. Part of him had heard her and had, at
least temporarily, perceived and integrated her message. True, part of
Johnny was already outside at recess, or in some other state of nir-
vana—that's dissociation. But part of Johnny was also still in the
classroom. Just a little bit of dissociation, perhaps. This kind of mental slippage is normal, and you almost always get away with it.

Patricia Bartlett was different from the "Johnnies" all of us knew as
kids. She shared a mechanism with Johnny, but she went much further than he did. If the patrolmen had not picked her up, Patricia
might eventually have wandered into an emergency room, saying that
she was confused. She might have behaved in a disorganized fashion
and even fought. The doctors there probably would have diagnosed
her condition as psychogenic amnesia. They might either have
brought in a psychiatrist to begin working with her or located a relative and sent her home, advising her to wait it out until her memories
came back. There was little to do but wait until Patricia herself could
recapture her life narrative and her sense of identity. A barbiturate
such as Amytal (sodium amytal) or hypnosis might possibly have
speeded up the process, and if these things were available the doctors
might have arranged for a series of hypnotic or Amytal interviews, or
admitted Patricia to a psychiatric ward.

There was another possible scenario here, too. If Patricia had not
run into the highway patrolmen when she did, she might have traveled somewhere, assumed a new name, and taken a new job. This
more purposeful behavior and less obvious anxiety would have
defined her condition as a fugue, a more complex state than simple
amnesia. Patricia would have been aware that she could not remember her past. And for a few weeks she might have remained unde-
tected. Fugue victims travel, interview for jobs, and form new relationships. They can remember their skills. They are the stuff of which
the films of the 1940s were made.

The 1945 film *Love Letters*, starring Jennifer Jones and Joseph Cotten, is typical of this genre. The character played by Jennifer Jones
has a terrible fight with her husband. Her aunt, who is her legal
guardian, rushes to help her and fatally stabs the husband. The aunt
then has a stroke and loses her powers of communication. The Jennifer Jones character becomes massively confused and is arrested. The
shock of her husband's death has induced total amnesia. The young

woman cannot defend herself in court. She is sent to a mental institution, where they tell her that she will recover her memories when she is ready. No one is to remind her of the past. She eventually leaves the institution, still without any old episodic memory, and assumes a new name. She meets Joseph Cotten, and he prevails on her to visit a cottage that he knows is really her old house. Jennifer recovers all her traumatic memories there. Her visit to "the scene of the crime" has freed her of her amnesia.

Moviegoers of the 1940s believed in the reality of this kind of film. The reason for the popularity of such notions is unclear, but it was well known that a number of soldiers suffered from total psychological amnesia during the Second World War, and that they could be helped by being interviewed under the influence of sodium amytal close to the field of battle. The idea was to get the soldier to "abreact" —to retell and refeel the terrifying experience that had created the amnesia in the first place. The disorder was dramatic. The treatment was dramatic. America loved it.

Classic 1940s films teach us several true things about the amnesias. They tell us that amnesics do not benefit from being told their memories but must find these memories for themselves. They tell us that amnesia and fugue have no effect on intelligence: purely psychological amnesias inhibit only episodic-memory functions, and people who suffer these psychological conditions can still do their sums, dress themselves, and acquire new knowledge and skills. We also learn that returning to the place where the memory was lost is a powerful aid to its retrieval. Place, more than anything else, remains attached to highly emotional episodic memory.

But the typical 1940s amnesia films also make a false threat. Amnesia victims are so frail, they say, that you may well "crack" them by asking for their memories. This is movie dramatics—and here we must fade as the music swells.


Jane Thacher journeyed to the Marin County Jail by elevator. She asked Deputy Sheriff Logan for Patricia Bartlett's arrest record, the incident report on her attack on the matron, and the blood test. The blood test had just come in from the lab—Patricia's alcohol level was zero. It seemed highly unlikely that a bout of heavy drinking could have yielded a blood-alcohol level of zero by six o'clock the next morning.

Jane called for Miss Bartlett, and Patricia walked into the interviewing room with considerable poise. Except for the run in her left
stocking, she looked neat enough to be going to work. She enunci-
ated with the sort of midatlantic diction that Jane had heard sarcasti-
cally referred to as Peninsula British. She must be a private-school
product from the Bay Area peninsula, south of Colma. Clearly the
woman was bright. She also sounded mixed-up. She still did not
know where she worked. She had no idea how she got to Mill Valley.
But she did not seem as emotional about her confusion as Jane would
have expected. She looked cool and unruffled, even distant.

There was no question that Patricia Bartlett was not the kind of
drunk Jane was used to defending. No alcohol had been found in her
Toyota. Then, too, drunks reeked of alcohol the next day and frequently shook, sometimes hallucinating or even having a seizure in
jail. Nor did this woman seem tough enough, hard enough, to have
fought with the police. In fact, she struck Jane as rather sweet—kind
of an "old-fashioned girl." The whole thing did not hold together.

Jane recalled a pointer she had picked up from one of her Berkeley
law school professors, a psychiatrist named Bernard Diamond, whose
life's work revolved around criminal behavior and criminal law.
"Amnesia defenses are virtually impossible," Professor Diamond had
said. Amnesia hardly ever served as a successful criminal defense,
unless the alleged perpetrator convincingly demonstrated to the court
earlier bouts of amnesia, starting in childhood or adolescence. Psychogenic amnesias were easy to fake and thus difficult for lawyers to
prove. Juries tended to disbelieve defendants with such stories. They
sounded too much like Gregory Peck in *Spellbound.*

Jane was an excellent attorney, and she enjoyed creating with the
law. She found herself mapping an "impossible" amnesia defense for
Patricia Bartlett. If everything worked out, she would bring the case
to court. She would find a number of character witnesses who
believed Patricia to be a good, reliable person. A psychiatrist would
testify about amnesia and dissociation. Jane would also beat the
bushes to find somebody who knew about an altered state in Patricia's
childhood. But would Patricia Bartlett herself slip and show knowledge of something she should not have known? Would she be found
to have led the life of a trickster? In that case, Jane's "impossible"
defense would be just that.

Jane phoned Professor Diamond at his home. He was retired, she knew, but perhaps he could assess Patricia Bartlett's mental condition and help Jane develop a strategy. Dr. Diamond declined. He was suffering from emphysema. It was winter, and the doctors had advised him not to leave the house. He did know somebody else, however. A friend. Lenore Terr.

Late in the afternoon of February 16, Jane Thacher found Patricia Bartlett the money for bail. In Patricia's address book under the Gs, Jane had discovered an Aunt Gert. Gertrude Demerest proved to be a maiden aunt on the maternal side, who lived south of San Francisco in the beautiful hills of Woodside. She, like Jennifer Jones's aunt in *Love Letters,* had raised her niece from an early age. Aunt Gert knew very little about Patricia's current life, but she was pleased to be back in touch.

Patricia's father, Gertrude Demerest told Jane, had run away when Patricia was two. Nobody ever saw him again. "He must be dead for years now, the way he loved his bourbon," Miss Demerest said. "Unfortunately, my younger sister drank, too." Jane Thacher experienced a bad moment. She knew that alcoholism runs in families. The information that Patricia's father and mother were both alcoholics would not help in court. But Gertrude Demerest must have read the distress on Jane's face. "My niece does not drink," she said emphatically. "Not at all."

Patricia's mother, a nice woman, died in a kitchen fire when Patricia was nine, Aunt Gert told Jane. The child came to live with Miss Demerest and attended private schools after that. Patricia was a quiet and well-behaved girl. Not a terribly eager student, she eventually learned her professional skills at a good secretarial school, in Boston. For the past two years, Patricia had been living in Marin County with a divorced stockbroker named Cameron Simpson. They shared a condominium that Simpson had bought during his marriage. Miss Demerest predicted that unless Patricia had changed the young man drastically over the last year, he would tell her niece that she deserved anything the court meted out. "I'm *not* just being jealous," she added, though Jane had had no such thought.

Aunt Gert wanted to know if it would be all right to post Patricia's bail and bring her home to Woodside. Yes, it was all right. But then Jane issued a warning. "Please do not suggest anything to Patricia while she stays at your house," she said. "It is important that she remember everything on her own."

This injunction reminded Aunt Gert of something else. The same sort of episode had taken place once before. At age nineteen, Patricia had gone off on her own to the school in Boston, but being alone was stressful for her. During Patricia's final shorthand and typing test, she went entirely blank. Couldn't remember a thing she had learned. She got up to leave, and a teacher stopped her and asked her where she was going. She said she was "Sally Burns, from the *Boston Globe*," on her way out to do an interview.

The school director made Patricia attend their summer session. It had been hard to persuade the school not to kick her out altogether. Aunt Gert came to Boston to stay with Patricia for the summer. Her niece passed the test and graduated.

Jane asked Miss Demerest if she would be willing to testify to the episode she had just related. "Of course," she said. Jane Thacher had enrolled her first witness for the "impossible defense."

I entered Patricia Bartlett's life a few days after her Aunt Gert bailed her out of jail. Jane Thacher phoned me to ask if I would like to consult on a highly unusual drunk-driving, assault, and resisting-arrest case. The woman Ms. Thacher was defending had been, as far as she could tell, totally amnesic for about a day.

I told Jane that in my opinion the defenses of repression and dissociation often worked in tandem in a case of psychological amnesia. This is a somewhat unorthodox view; I see fugues and other generalized amnesias as starting with a recent and painful incident that is fully taken in and almost immediately repressed. The person then goes into a trance and begins to dissociate, moving onto another plane of awareness. The incident that engendered the repression may be recovered later, but any incidents that were part of the dissociated trance may be completely forgotten. Or, if remembered, they may be shrouded in a gauzelike haze.

Dissociation is not ordinarily available to a child the very first time he is terrified. We knew very little about Patricia's childhood at this point, but I told Jane Thacher that it usually takes repeated terrors to inspire dissociation. Dissociation takes practice. It often starts in childhood, with small exercises in self-hypnosis. "I am not really here," the child says to himself, as he knows he is about to be frightened and hurt. "I will not feel this pain."

Not every child is able to employ massive dissociation. Not all of us can self-hypnotize, even when we desperately want to. Only some people achieve a true separation of self from pain or terror. "Brad," a twelve-year-old patient of mine, had the knack of moving his thoughts aside. He told me that he had been using a self-taught "mind-clearing trick" for about a year to cope with scary movies. He would think back to a summer afternoon in Corning, New York, where his grandparents lived. Five older boys did wonderful tricks on their bicycles that afternoon. "Mostly at night when I'm going to bed [after one of those scary movies], I'll picture what the guys did on their bikes," Brad told me. "I'll remember it, and it keeps me from having a bad dream. I just knew it would work. Nobody told me how to do it." Brad's technique of deliberate visualization, a step toward dissociation, is one often utilized by hypnotists and hypnotherapists. The boy had used one particular mental picture to separate himself from one particular feared item—scary movies.

Brad's mental pictures would not have been a problem for him if everything else had gone trouble-free in his life. But the year he turned twelve, Brad rode on a train that derailed. He lost a finger and countless nights of sleep. "I still feel the pain," he said three months after his accident, when he first came to see me. "But when I think of the bikes that do tricks, my thought gets rid of the pain. I'm not trying to be a bike champ myself. But when I think of those kids on their bikes, it clears my mind. Since the accident, I do it at least twenty times more than I used to."

Brad's dissociative "trick," once useful, had become far too mind-consuming after his accident. There was no telling whether he would eventually slip automatically into one of his "mind-cleared" states without picturing the bikes at all. His trick handled fear and pain. But the trick also created difficulties in processing incoming material—in handling new input and transferring this into long-term storage. It might well end by interfering with memory retrieval, too. If Brad at age twenty-five attempted to remember the year he was twelve, he might not be able to recall much, if anything. If he had simply repressed his memories—as did Eileen Franklin, the child witness to the Nason murder—then these memories might return later in vivid entirety. But since Brad had begun to dissociate so fully, he would probably retrieve nothing but haze or fragments.

Dissociation is a mechanism that enables a person to quit a place where bad thoughts or events are happening. There is an important exception, however. Researchers into hypnosis tell us that some deeply hypnotized individuals harbor "hidden observers." These people may remember events that occurred in the dissociated state better than do others who use dissociation. Dr. Ernest Hilgard, a Stanford psychologist who specializes in the study of hypnosis, believes that almost half his subjects—most of them undergraduate volunteers— keep a hidden observer present during hypnosis. If, for instance, Hilgard immerses a deeply hypnotized subject's hand in ice water and then tells the subject he or she will feel no discomfort, the person's benumbed hand will rest in the water much longer than would the hand of an unhypnotized subject. If Hilgard then says to the hypnotized person, "Perhaps there is some part of you that is aware of some discomfort" and asks the subject to signal the extent of the pain by moving a finger, the subject often signals considerable pain. In other words, such a subject is still fully aware of bodily sensation, though disengaged from it.

The "hidden observer" is a controversial concept. After all, under hypnosis Dr. Hilgard's subjects may especially want to please him, raising their fingers because he asks them to. Clinically, however, it appears that Ernest Hilgard is right. Some patients do seem to keep hidden observers around, and thus keep tabs on themselves as they dissociate. These patients watched their abuse as children from the ceiling of their childhood bedroom or saw themselves fall from a window at a great distance from the fall. And, of course, there are the "Johnnies"—those kids in the classroom who slip away but can answer the teacher immediately about what she just said. Normal "mind on idle" states probably require a kind of divided consciousness—a hidden observer, in other words. For someone who, like Patricia Bartlett, uses dissociation pathologically and massively, however, the hidden observer may be hard to come by.

When children anticipate disasters and successfully dissociate, they are often "gone." It's difficult to predict how long a hidden observer will stick around to see what happens next. Most of the time, it is too dangerous for the child to "stay." Fortunately, children who have not stayed to watch and take in everything that happens to them can still be helped in treatment. And they can be successfully treated in adulthood, too, although the process is often long and arduous. Helpful as it might be, where memory is concerned, for the dissociater to keep a hidden observer around during childhood, adult cures have been effected without complete remembrances. One does not necessarily need renewed memory for emotional relief.

Had Patricia Bartlett experienced something as a child which made it too dangerous for her to "stay"? I told Jane Thacher that I would interview Patricia for four hours—two in the morning and two in the afternoon—and take her through her memories of childhood. Since her amnesia was so recent, the events that led to her "drunk-driving" incident might be freshly defended against and thus easily accessible to relatively undirected interviewing. Childhood incidents might be tougher to elicit. But I would try. Patricia's legal situation interested me. Like Jane Thacher and Bernard Diamond, I had never seen a good amnesia defense.

And so Patricia Bartlett came to my blue-and-white office above the Bay. It was a week after her strange flight to Mill Valley. She was extremely polite, and immediately wanted to get the pronunciation of my name just right. I smiled and told her how to pronounce it, suggesting that she call me Lenore if she liked. And then I asked for the details of her life before she blanked out—where she had lived, where she had worked, and who had lived with her. I warned her that everything said between us might be used in court.

By now, Patricia had remembered almost everything—including her name and address and the fact that her mother was dead and her father had left home when she was very young. But she commented that there were voids in her memory concerning her life in Marin County with Cameron Simpson. "My boyfriend brought all my clothes over to Aunt Gert's," she almost whispered, brushing aside a quickly gathering tear. Patricia had lived with "Cam" until the day she went to jail, she said, but she was now temporarily staying in Woodside with her aunt. "My aunt is willful and opinionated," she said, "but she took good care of me when I was a child. She's here with me this morning, if you want to meet her."

She suddenly shifted our focus, as I nodded my agreement to meet Aunt Gert. "Do you do marriage counseling? I wish you could fix things for Cam and me. He just won't talk to me. Maybe he'd talk in front of someone else."

I reminded Patricia that she had serious legal problems. We needed to concentrate entirely on those. But I didn't mind hearing a little about Cam. Did she know what had gone wrong?

Patricia's answer sounded incomplete. Like an old sock, her memory had worn thin in a few of the most crucial places. "Something happened between us the evening I was arrested," she said. "I know that, inside of me, but I can't remember. Cam says the relationship is over. He says I must have known I'd have to move out, after the things that went on between us the night I went to jail. But he would not say what happened."

"Do you have your own memories of what happened?"

"No. Hardly any. I mean, Cam says I know every single thing that took place and that I'm trying to manipulate him into telling me the story again so he'll feel guilty."

"What *do* you remember? Try to tell me whatever bits are in your mind, even though not everything you say may stick together or make sense."

"There are several blank spots between about four o'clock in the afternoon and about six the next morning. I remember most of the morning after I woke up in jail. I remember the early afternoon before I went to jail, too. I remember a little from the Mill Valley off-ramp—these two policemen who looked like globs. I'd never recognize them now."

"Go ahead with the beginning," I said, writing as fast as I could.

"Well, it starts this way. On the fifteenth of February, my boss, who is a very busy trial lawyer in the city, had decided to go home. We had just completed a very important business contract, and both of us were relieved. Mr. Johnson said that he'd be going home by midafternoon. I should do the same. Daisy could handle our phones.

"Well, O.K. So I left the office. I thought about shopping at I. Magnin's, but I was too tired and I didn't have any money. Maybe northern Marin would be completely fog-free, and I could be outside sunning myself at our condominium pool by three o'clock if I sped. I'd hurry home—well, it's actually Cameron's place. He made the down payment, but we split the mortgage payments and our expenses fifty-fifty. Please don't say anything about this criminal mess, by the way, to Mr. Johnson. He thinks I'm sick. My Aunt Gertrude told him she's taking care of me in Woodside."

If Patricia's defense won the day, Mr. Johnson would surely read about Jane Thacher's triumph in his *Recorder,* the San Francisco Bay Area attorneys' newspaper. We could not keep this affair to ourselves forever, I said.

Patricia sighed, "I wish this mess would disappear. I wish I could disappear." But Patricia stayed with me both physically and mentally that day. And the day stayed in Patricia's memory. For whatever reason, this day was not one for her to dissociate.

"Let's go back to your going home the afternoon before you were arrested. Picture that it's about three o'clock, and you are driving home. It's still early. Do you put on your bathing suit? Is it indeed warm and sunny outside?" Episodic memory often works like a movie. Sometimes you can see only a few frames. But once you've decided to use them, you can pick others up off the cutting-room floor.

"No. No bathing suit. No pool. But it was warm. Beautiful, in fact. There were a few high clouds up there in the sky, but you wouldn't have guessed that a big storm would come in within the next few hours. When I got home, I became upset. Very, very upset. What was it? I can't quite remember."

"Something was very upsetting, you say. Do you know where you were standing or sitting when you became upset? Was anyone else there?" I was looking for Patricia's associated positional and people memories, because these are the most likely to last after terrible events.

"It was Cameron!" Patricia exclaimed. "He was at home when I got there. And—oh no, it's coming clearer now—he was with that bitch who lives two doors away, Midge Something-or-other. Terrific in a bikini out at the condo pool but, I mean, unprincipled, a gold digger—rotten! I always knew it about her. She was one of those women who never bothers talking to women. You know what I mean?"

Yes, I knew. But we needed to go on. "Tell me what happened with you and Cameron and Midge that afternoon. Were the two of them already there when you got home, or did they come in later? Try to retrace your steps as you come into your condo."

"Mmm. Nobody was in the front hall when I came in. It was quiet. I figured Cam was still at work—you know how West Coast stock-brokers work from six in the morning till about three? He'd be home in an hour or so. I'd leave him a note to look for me at the pool. Maybe I'd catch him coming up the drive, if I sunned myself in the right spot. So that's what I thought, but that's not what happened. Gosh, I can't quite remember."

"You're doing fine, Patricia. You wrote Cam the note?"

"No, I went into the kitchen. It was quiet. I tore some paper off the message roll we keep by the phone. But then I went up to change first. Write later."

"But you say there was no bathing suit ever that day? What happened to your resolve?"

"Mmm. This is a dark spot. Let me retrace my steps again. I let myself into the condo. Quiet. Stopped at the kitchen, tore off the paper, but decided to undress first. Oh, I know! There was no pencil by the message pad, so I had to go upstairs to get one. Cam can be so maddening. He carries off my pencils.

"I walked into the bedroom. Stood at the door. Oh, God! I saw something there. This is really upsetting. God!"

"O.K., Patricia. Try to face what you saw." Patricia looked upset and not at all absent. "This may have something to do with what happened later that evening. You've arrived at the point of standing at the bedroom door. You look into the room. Tell me."

Patricia's color had changed, her California tan as evanescent as some California dreams. But she stayed in her condo bedroom. And her mind stayed there, too. She appeared to be recapturing something repressed. She seemed to have taken in a whole memory. And the whole thing was coming back.

"Cam was with her," she said. "With Midge. In my bed."

"Having sex?"

"No, not all the way. Not legally. No 'penetration,' as people might say. He must have got home a short while before. His suit pants were still on, but his fly was open. Her blouse was off, but her bra was still on. She had nothing over her legs. They were kissing, so they didn't see me. They were starting, I guess. But it was clear, as I stood there, that they had been together before. They seemed *sooo* comfortable."

Patricia took a Kleenex out of her purse and sniffed, but no streaks marred her carefully applied makeup. She wanted to cry—anybody could see that—but she could not commandeer the tears. I said something sympathetic, along the lines of "That must have been horrible for you," and then waited. It did not take long. The event that had precipitated Patricia's bizarre evening now lay exposed.

"So that Midge—that brazen Midge *Morgan,* that's her name!—she faces me. No hand moves down so that she can be a little bit modest. No way. And she says, 'Good! So you know about us. Good, Patricia!

Little Miss American Pie can go away now and have a good cry and get the hell out of here.' And Cam says to her, 'Midge, shut up!' He's zipping himself up and tucking in his shirt. But Midge says to me, 'I like your boyfriend. And he likes me. So go!'"

"What did Cameron do about this?"

"He looked angry—I couldn't tell if it was at her or at me. And he told me, 'Ignore it.' I think he was trying to get a handle on what had just happened. He's always in control, but this time it seemed that his new girlfriend had taken over. Cam and I fought a while later. But I'm not sure how we got to that. It was later. We were alone."

"Go ahead, Patricia. Keep telling me what you remember, even if it isn't all linked up."

"I think I was managing. I sometimes have trouble feeling real about things—and I was having a little trouble that way, but not too much at this point. I figured Cam couldn't truly care for Midge—she's too available. We'd even joked once that some sugar daddy must support her, because she didn't seem to work for a living. Midge kept standing there, mostly undressed. 'Bet you never put out enough. That's why he likes me so much.' 'It's been going on for months, and you've been too dense to notice it.' Stuff like that. While she was talking, Cameron got a big peach-colored beach towel—one that an office friend of mine gave me for my birthday last summer—and he wrapped it around Midge's waist like a sarong. That was too much. *My* towel. I ran out of the room and sat down in the kitchen. I went a little blank. I couldn't stand it any more."

"How long did Midge stay?"

"I have no idea. Time meant nothing. I don't think I moved for five—I don't know, ten—fifteen minutes, an hour. Who knows?" Now the tenor of Patricia's story began to change. Her mental mechanisms sounded much closer to dissociation than to repression. She was reporting a period of "going blank."

"Then, I heard Cam tell Midge to go home," she said. "They'd talk later. She walked up to him at the front door, which I could see from the kitchen, and French-kissed him. I know she wanted me to see that. As for Cameron, he cooperated fully. I closed my eyes. Started to drift. And then I heard Midge singing 'Bye Bye, Miss American Pie' and closing the door."

"Do you remember the rest?"

"God, I don't know." Patricia's color had returned, but her eyes looked encased in plastic wrap. "I guess I tried to talk with Cam. He said that Midge meant absolutely nothing. I was the important one. After—I don't know how long, or what he said—I started believing him. 'Stick with him,' I thought. 'We'll be O.K.' It was like a lullaby. 'Stick with him, stick with him.' I was getting into it. 'We'll be O.K. We'll be O.K. We'll be O.K.'"

Patricia took a deep breath and expelled a long sigh. "Cam knew that I could be lulled into believing him. I don't carry very strong convictions, I guess."

"It sounds as if he was persuading you to forget it—forgive him— to get on with your lives together. And it sounds as if you were persuading yourself to go along."

"He was. I was. That's what I wanted. Oblivion. And a deal from him never to get involved with Midge again—never to do that to me. I wanted him to tell me if he wasn't happy with me. I wanted to get married. And I'd try to be sexier."

"So then?"

"Mmm. I think I know the rest, but I hate to say it."

"Go ahead, Patricia. It *is* rough telling something like this to a stranger."

"Yes. A lot is back. Not everything. While Cam and I are talking, Midge walks back into the house, using a key. A key! I can't believe this. The key to my place. 'Come on,' she says to Cameron. 'I'm all worked up from this afternoon. It's time to unravel a few kinks. Your place or mine?' Brazen. Totally brazen.

"Cam says to me, 'Patricia, I want tonight with Midge. Tomorrow you and I will work out the future. O.K.?' I can't believe this! All my dreams revolve around this one particular guy, and he is ready to walk out with a woman who already feels free to use her own key to the condo. I get some courage from I don't know where, and I say three little words—a question, actually: 'Midge or me?' Cam wheels around. 'Get out, Patricia,' he says, in a voice from the freezer. 'Pack up and get out. I want my freedom and fun. And I don't like being challenged the way you always do.' That wasn't fair at all. I always let things go Cam's way. And then he walks out with Midge."

"What happened next?"

"Here comes total haze. There's hardly anything left." Patricia paused for ten or fifteen seconds. "I think I sat in my chair. Long, maybe. I don't know. I think I wondered if I should phone Cam at

Midge's. Then, too, I think I was saying those words, 'Stick with him. We'll be O.K.' I lose track of everything here. I thought of packing. I must have stopped thinking altogether. I just sort of went blank."

Massive dissociation had set in. After Cameron left, Patricia did what battered wives, young victims of sexual abuse, and victims of war and torture often find helpful. She used repetitive words and phrases—"Stick with him, stick with him, stick with him, we'll be O.K."—to put herself out, to relieve herself of the pain. Patricia appeared to be completely familiar with self-hypnosis. When she had mentally incanted enough, she spent the rest of the time in her condo absolutely blank.

If repression is a burial of memory, dissociation is a sidewise slippage. By her own account, Patricia's sidewise slippage began as she sat in her kitchen and went blank, reciting her litany to herself. Pierre Janet observed that his dissociating patients lost the capacity to integrate their knowledge, emotions, and memory. Dissociation causes traumatic memories to be set aside—set apart from normal consciousness. Bodily responses, emotions, actions, and memories have little or no relationship to one another. Physical pain is missing from physical injuries. Affect is missing from extremely moving events. And memory may be missing altogether, except for fragments.

That is what happened to Patricia. When the patrolmen found her in Mill Valley, she was employing massive dissociation. Nothing was integrated. Patricia eventually remembered her whole fight with Cam—the who, where, what, and why of it. Most likely, that part of the episode had been repressed, or if dissociated it had been set aside with a hidden observer, so that the memory would be intact and available to eventual retrieval.

"What made you take off in your car?" I asked Patricia.

"I never packed," Patricia said. "They found no luggage with me, I've heard. I drove south—maybe to ask for my aunt's help. I have no idea why I turned off at Mill Valley, however. I do have a friend at work, Sarah Schubert, who lives there. In fact, she's the one who gave me the beach towel. I've been at her place before. I may have realized after getting to the Mill Valley exit that I didn't know the way to Sarah's house. Maybe that's why I pulled over. I don't know. Maybe the rain made me stop. Lots of good drivers stop in the rain."

"So what happened next?" I asked, thinking how easy it would be for me to fill in the gaps in Patricia's story. As it was, she had already filled in a few gaps by reasoning and by using what she had recently learned from her attorney. She actually remembered hardly anything about driving to Mill Valley. In her mind, there was barely a snippet of real memory from the car trip.

"These two men—they didn't look like policemen, more like globs—they told me to roll down the window," she went on. "I thought they wanted to rob me or rape me. One of them, the big one, took my handbag. Then it felt like he was trying to suffocate me with some rubber thing. I thought he was a killer. A weirdo. I don't know. I must have fought them. Jane says I did. It seems stupid now, but at the time I must have felt there was no choice. I can't really remember fighting the police. I can't remember anything about being in a police car. I can't remember coming into the jail. I guess I really hurt the matron. I feel bad about that. But Jane tells me she's O.K. now. The next morning, I couldn't remember much of anything at first. I was lost. A little memory came in later, but the part about Cam and Midge didn't come back until just now." Patricia wiped away a small tear.

"Don't try to solve the Cameron problem this very minute," I suggested. "It will take some time and thought. Maybe the two of you can talk together in a few days. What I want you to do right now is to go have some lunch with your aunt. We'll take an hour's break, and then we'll meet again. You've done very well this morning. I still need to know about your childhood. Try to clear your mind of serious worries over the lunch hour, but don't drift off if you can help it. Then we will work very hard in the afternoon."


I spent the lunch hour at my desk, looking like a female version of Rodin's *Thinker with Egg Salad Sandwich and Coffee*. I got through my mail with a quick shuffle and a couple of hastily written replies. For the most part, I mused over Patricia's amnesia. The young woman struck me as sincere. She had certainly responded with a loss of color and later with a glassy-eyed stare, as she attempted to recapture the painful afternoon and evening that had preceded her arrest. Her mother was dead and her father had abandoned them—this she had told me when I wrote down her address, phone number, and next of kin. But that was all the mention Patricia Bartlett had made of her childhood. I needed to hear much, much more.

Dissociation usually requires repetition—the Type II situation of multiple trauma. One event usually is not enough to get serious self-hypnosis going in a child. Abuse and violence at home is the most common setting in which children dissociate. Chronic illness. Alcohol in the family. Both Patricia's parents were alcoholics. She might have practiced putting herself "somewhere else" when her parents got drunk.

Creative children sometimes dissociate as a form of pretend. The mechanics of their dissociations lie in rhythm and dancing, magic and spells, and extraplanetary worlds. In a child's lexicon, "invisibility," for instance, may be another word for "altered states." I thought of a memorable patient, a physically mistreated nine-year-old I'll call Jamie, who had watched his mother shoot his abusive father to death. Jamie thought he could make himself invisible. "I know I can," he told me. "I do it here on earth, and I do it all the time on my planet. You're just going to have to believe me. My friends believe it."

I asked Jamie whether he wanted to demonstrate his invisibility for me, so that I could see how it was done.

"If I turn invisible in front of everybody, they'd take away my powers," he responded.

A few one-time-only traumatic events are so marked by extraordinarily dehumanizing sights and sounds that dissociation takes place in the very first moments, even though the child might not have had any practice. The large group of essays collected by Professor Arata Osada from schoolchildren who survived the bombing of Hiroshima shows that the vast majority of these young witnesses remembered the events of August 6, 1945, with the kind of clear, precise detail that marks the memories of most victims of first-time childhood trauma. The children I interviewed following the Chowchilla school-bus kidnapping retained this kind of clear, brilliantly lit memory of their experiences. But a few of the Hiroshima youngsters wrote about the sense of passing through the atomic bombing in a trance. This is the subjective sense of dissociation. Dissociation makes for fuzzy, unclear recollections or a series of holes in memory. Because the experience of Hiroshima was so dehumanizing and unbelievably horrible, immediate dissociation became possible for a few.

More commonly, however, the child who dissociates easily and frequently is a child who has taught himself through repeated practice how to achieve self-removal. The child does so knowing he has to cope with ongoing terrible events. The writer Virginia Woolf, for instance, spent her childhood practicing dissociation. She was sexually abused when she was five or so by Gerald Duckworth, the older of her two half brothers, who was then in his late teens. Later, as a teenager, she was repeatedly sexually misused by her other half brother, George. Both her beloved mother and her adored half sister died before Virginia grew up. To get through all this, Virginia employed mental slippages, though she never slipped quite as far as Patricia Bartlett did. Instead, she felt removed and cut-off. "Every day," she wrote in "A Sketch of the Past," "includes much more non-being than being." Outside observers reported Mrs. Woolf as cold, distant, and inaccessible. But the interesting thing about her, I thought over my last few bites of sandwich, was how her fictional characters manage to achieve dissociation. Fiction, of course, reflects what the writer knows.

A young man in the Woolf short story "Solid Objects" repeatedly focuses his eyes on a starshaped fragment of china and eventually manages to remove himself from all human intercourse. He is a self-hypnotizing sort. Mrs. Dalloway, in the novel of that name, silently recites blank verse from Shakespeare's *Cymbeline,* eventually achieving a kind of mindless automatism as she goes about her day's duties. Perhaps she doesn't later remember her day too well. In *To The Lighthouse,* Mrs. Ramsay takes note of every third beam of the St. Ives lighthouse—the very lighthouse Woolf herself watched in the childhood summers when she was first abused. By doing her eye exercises, similar to following a pendulum, Mrs. Ramsay is able to achieve an inner peace. An expert at dissociating, she also lulls herself into oblivion by repeating, "Children don't forget, children don't forget." How ironic that this spell to insure forgetfulness consists of words that mean exactly its opposite. Indeed, children do forget.

Patricia Bartlett was not as habitually dreamy as Virginia Woolf. Like her strange, remote protagonists, Woolf lived most of her days perceiving a myriad of details but entirely walled off from any attendant feelings. She dissociated emotion from memory. Her biographer Louise DeSalvo thinks Mrs. Woolf may have lost the memory of her early abuse by Gerald Duckworth until a few years before her death, when she alludes to it in her diary and talks of it in "A Sketch of the

Past." Twenty years earlier, she had told a literary club about her unwanted teenage experiences with George.

Patricia Bartlett seemed a more everyday and normal person than Virginia Woolf, except when, under unusual stress, she experienced her great spurts of dissociation. But the two women had much in common when one looked at their defenses against awareness and their techniques for achieving self-removal. The extreme fright that spurred Virginia to her long slow trip into spaciness impelled Patricia to rocket from Lucas Valley to Mill Valley in a fog. "Children don't forget, children don't forget" does not differ much from "Stick with him, stick with him, we'll be O.K." Sitting mindlessly at a desk overlooking the River Ouse does not differ greatly from sitting mindlessly in the kitchen of a California condo.


Patricia Bartlett and her aunt returned from lunch looking animated and bubbly. "We haven't had such a good time in years," Aunt Gertrude told me as she picked up a magazine and settled into a waiting-room chair. Patricia noted, after we'd gone into my office, "I'm not going to make that mistake again. Family is to keep, not to discard like shorthand notes."

"What caused the recent distance from your aunt?" I asked.

"Cam didn't like Aunt Gert. He told me to stay away."

"What made you go along with that?"

"I don't know. Family—it's never been comfortable for me. The idea of it, I mean. My dad left home one day and he never said why. I used to think as a little kid it was because I did something wrong. Maybe I wasn't perfect enough, I thought. Then my mom's death happened. Nothing could have been more terrible for me. I should have died with her. Maybe I did die inside. Who knows?"

"Tell me what you remember. Where do your memories begin?" I asked, looking in a general way for anything about Patricia Bartlett's earliest memories that might help with Jane Thacher's "impossible" amnesia defense.

"I don't remember much until I was twelve or thirteen at a girls' school in Palo Alto. I liked it there. I 'woke up' somehow during my teenage years. Made friends. Had fun. Went to dances. Clubs. Made out with some boys. Cheated a little on my Aunt Gert. She tried to be strict, but I was able to get around her."

"How about before that? Do you remember things from before?"

"You mean earlier? I don't like to . . . ," her voice trailed off.

"Go back a little, if you can. Give me some earlier memories, if it's possible."

"There's not very much there. My dad. That's almost a blank, except I think—I'm not sure—I can still remember the rub of his whiskers. I've always liked men in the morning—maybe that's why. My mom. There's very little of her left in my memory. She was nice. Loving. She spent a lot of time in bed, I'm pretty sure of that. Used to wear a pink flannel gown and a matching robe a lot."

Patricia seemed to drift off. Her gaze focused inward; she was no longer looking at me.

"Go on," I said, and her eyes flickered as if I had startled her. She had "left" my office for an instant. It was my first glimpse of Patricia in the act of dissociating.

"Mmm. My mom, right? Let's see. She was nice, but I think she had a drinking problem. A quiet drunk. She'd sometimes be in bed when I came home from school. She had some money from my grandparents, I think. But she spent it—quite unlike Aunt Gert, who invested most of hers. I didn't inherit anything when my mom died. Not that I really cared. Aunt Gert made sure I could always earn my own way. And she did her best with me, I guess."

By talking again about her aunt and dropping the emotional subject of her mother's death, Patricia was using a defense called displacement. (Freud called it *Verschiebung*—a "sliding out of place"). This defense helps make parts of a memory disappear by diverting attention to something less intensely felt. I encouraged Patricia to go back again to the time before she came to live with Aunt Gert.

"My childhood? Well, I was kind of a frightened child, I remember," she said. "I was always scared of the water. I couldn't even take a bath. Still can't. Just showers. The time Cam and I went to Europe, I asked the hotelkeepers if there was a shower there—otherwise I couldn't stay. Let's see. I'm scared of fire—like of houses burning up and stuff like that. I made my boss fit our office suite with extra smoke detectors. You know, the movie *Towering Inferno* was made in our office building. That film absolutely terrified me. Cam brought home the tape. He said he loved the way I trembled while we watched."

"Your mother died in a fire, didn't she?"

"Yes. I was taking a bath. The firemen came in and found me taking a bath, with my mom dead on the kitchen floor."

"I need to know about that, Patricia. Do you remember anything?"

"No. No memories. I think I went blank. I can't remember the firemen. Or them carrying my mother out. Or the smell. Though I must say there are certain kinds of burning smells—especially if they're grilling meat—that make me go weird.

"It must have been after school when Mom died—about four or five o'clock. I was in the third grade. The firemen got me out of the bathtub, but I don't remember that. And then—wait, I do remember this one thing now—while somebody was drying me off, I saw them throw these black rags, with some pink flannel showing in a couple of places, into the tub where I was soaking minutes before. That must have been Mom's robe. Yes, I saw that. But I haven't thought of it until now."

"You're concerned about cooking smells, you say. Could your mother have been fixing dinner when the accident took place?"

"Hmm. Let me think for a second. My mom usually waited for me after school. And then she usually talked with me a while. And I would set up to do a little reading or spelling at the kitchen table. She was good to me, my mom, even though she was such a sad person. Anyway, then she would make dinner—usually something easy, like a couple of chops, some fish, or a piece of grilled chicken, a salad or a cooked vegetable, and some rice or a baked potato."

These memories are specific because they represent an amalgam of household routines during which the child, Patricia, had been alert.

Patricia continued, "I wanted to help my mom. She was usually stumbling a little by the time our dinner was ready. But I was young, and I couldn't really do much for the two of us. So I'd sit there and watch her."

"If you were usually sitting there doing your homework, reading, and chatting, then why do you think you took such an early bath that one particular day? It was right after school. Your mom must have been cooking—she was burned in a kitchen fire. Were you being punished—being sent early to bed? Were you dirty from some game after school? Help me figure out why you were bathing so early."

"No, it doesn't sound right about being punished. Or dirty. I wasn't much of a sports enthusiast. I can't see the picture in my mind. It's just not there. Anyway, my mom didn't punish me much. I was always trying to be good. 'Perfect Patsy,' that was me."

Patricia's story was curious and a little inconsistent. On most late afternoons, she sat and chatted with her mother in the kitchen, while her mother puttered over dinner. Yet on this one particular evening, at around four or five o'clock, this little girl had broken the pattern—had taken a bath. Strange. We'd get back to it. I decided to change the subject.

"The stories of your argument with Cameron and of your exams at secretarial school sound as if you might have made mental escapes at other times. Do you know of any other times?"

"Once on a plane from California to Boston—I must have been eighteen or so—there was a lot of turbulence, and I could see lightning. It was nighttime. I was afraid we'd get struck. I thought we'd catch fire. I hate fires! I sort of blanked out. My memory of this is faint, but I think I tried to go up front to talk with the pilots. Our seat-belt signs were on, and the flight attendants were belted in. I headed for the front part of the plane, but the attendants in first class—they faced backward in their jump seats—saw me coming. One of them grabbed me. And I dimly recall telling her that I was a pilot with two, maybe three thousand air hours, and that I wanted to help the pilots get through the storm. You know, I can't really fly a plane at all. She looked at me like I was crazy and said if I didn't get right back to my seat immediately, I'd be arrested when we landed in Boston. I went right back. And we made it. But you know, I forgot the whole thing until we had a little turbulence on a plane that Cam and I were taking to Paris last year. Then I sort of saw myself at age eighteen lurching along toward the front of that plane to Boston—being so scared of burning up from a lightning strike that I needed to talk with the pilots."

"Other times?"

Patricia's color was draining again. She did not answer. She said, "Wait a minute. Wait."

She reached for her throat. She gasped. I sat still. Even a look might divert her from her thoughts.

"What is it? Are you remembering something?" I finally said. "Feeling something? Tell me." I held still.

"It's Mom," she said, barely whispering. "I think there was something when she died like the time on the airplane I was just telling you about. I'm feeling it. God! It was bad when she died. The fire. I think I saw her. The burning. Yes. Burned up. That's what it was. I was there. In the kitchen."

And there it was. A little girl on an ordinary afternoon in the kitchen after school with her nice but inebriated mom, when the sleeve of her mother's bathrobe suddenly caught fire at the stove. Within a couple of seconds, the robe, matching nightgown, and mother were ablaze. Patricia watched horrified from her seat at the table, while the person she loved most in the world burned to death. The child then wandered into the bathroom. She drew the bathwater, put her clothes into the hamper, settled into the tub, and drifted into a weird shut-off never-never land that lasted—Patricia could not say how long—until somebody in the apartment building smelled smoke, called for help, and the firemen broke in.

Patricia did not remember the real story of her mother's death from the time it happened until the moment she stopped short in my office and whispered, "Wait." The act of telling me about her lifelong fear of bathwater and fires, and about her memories of incidents associated with those fears, forced the ugly memories forward into consciousness. (The name she had assumed as a *Globe* reporter, "Sally Burns," is interesting in this connection.) The memory Patricia retrieved about ten minutes before the ultimate remembrance of her mother's death—the recollection of seeing burned flannel soaking in the bathtub—also awakened her old hidden perceptions of singed cloth, hair, and flesh. Repressed memories surmounted Patricia's defensive barriers and spilled into consciousness. She saw the terrible sights she had put out of her conscious mind two decades before.

Patricia Bartlett probably did not dissociate before or during the time her mother burned to death. It was so fast and so surprising that she may have completely taken in what happened and then repressed it. But she dissociated afterward, in the tub. In the same fashion, she may not have dissociated as she walked in on Cameron and Midge. There's a good chance she took in the scene and then repressed it. She dissociated afterward, in her condominium kitchen and in her Toyota. That is why so much of Patricia's memory of the terrible events themselves remained available to her for retrieval, while the aftermath of each event became virtually lost to memory.

At age nine, the green-eyed girl watched one of the most horrible sights there is to see—a person being burned alive. Worse, it was her own mother—her only remaining close family member, a flawed but loving parent who died in the most dehumanizing kind of way. Patricia responded to this horror by separating herself from reality—by wandering away, both physically and mentally. As nine-year-old Patricia settled into the family bathtub, probably the last bath she took for twenty years, she felt, at least for a short time, entirely invisible.

Aunt Gert had arrived to help within an hour. Here began the second half of Patricia Bartlett's childhood. Gertrude did not speak to Patricia of the painful episode—then, or in the years to come. Perhaps, she hoped, the child had seen nothing, had smelled nothing, had ventured nowhere from her bath. Why upset the child unnecessarily? As Patricia Bartlett grew up, all that was unusual about her, as far as Aunt Gert was concerned, was the single event at secretarial school, when she seemed about to run away and assume another identity—and at that, only under extreme pressure. Yes, Gertrude Demerest told me a few days later, she had noticed that Patricia occasionally drifted into the land of dreams, glassy-eyed and pale. But no, Gertrude had not considered psychotherapy for the child. "It never seemed bad enough," she said.


Jane Thacher did put on her "impossible defense" in court. She pleaded amnesia for her client before a judge, a few curious spectators, a couple of fellow attorneys from the Public Defender's Office, and a pair of reporters, one from the *Recorder* and one from a small Marin County newspaper. I sat on a bench outside the courtroom until they called me in. By the time I arrived, Jane had already extracted the admission from Patrolman Lewisell that he had expected to find Patricia Bartlett drunk and therefore may have mistakenly smelled liquor on her. Gertrude Demerest had testified about the blackout at Patricia's secretarial school in Boston; Sarah Schubert had testified to her friendship with Patricia and Patricia's abstention from alcohol whenever they went out together; and Patricia had testified to the dissociative episodes—the one at age nine in the bathtub, the one on the plane, the one in Boston, and the one at the Lucas Valley condominium. Patricia's first experience with dissociation was by far the worst; the others followed only upon similar threats—of abandonment, loss, or death.

My testimony took no more than ten minutes. Patricia Bartlett had suffered from psychogenic amnesia, I said. Under the pressure of a shock at her apartment and an ugly breakup with the man she loved, she had automatically and unconsciously shifted to a different state of consciousness. In this state, she formed little memory and retained only bits. She could not control her actions. She could not judge her behaviors by standards of right and wrong. She could not understand the nature and quality of her acts. Jack Lewisell and Marty Neal had found her at the Mill Valley exit in this dissociated state—the early stages of an episode in which Patricia probably would have assumed another identity and some purpose to her travels. The highway patrolmen mistook her confusion for drunkenness. It was an understandable mistake. Patricia needed psychiatric help, I said. But she did not need incarceration.

Jane Thacher won her impossible amnesia defense. The judge pronounced Patricia Bartlett "not guilty." Dr. Bernard Diamond lived to hear about the big "amnesia win," as we called it; and in the couple of years before he died I never once heard him disparage the amnesia defense. Patricia Bartlett walked out of the courtroom that day; the judge did not remand her to a state hospital. Because of the temporary nature of her mental illness, she could go home.

Patricia is free. But whether or not she will ever be free of her slippages in and out of her own persona—that, perhaps, I will never know. Patricia moved to Boston shortly after her case was decided. Cameron had dropped her. I doubt he did it for Midge, but who can say? Aunt Gert moved to Boston, too; Patricia was her only living relative, and Gert wanted to live close to her.

Psychiatrists ordinarily do not get to hear the ends of their patients' stories. I hope Patricia sought some treatment for her tendencies to dissociate. The treatment of childhood trauma may feel painful to the patient, but it is well worth it in the long run, considering the problems that early trauma creates.

There are very good psychiatrists in Boston. An excellent group of trauma researchers, too. I hope Patricia finds them. And if she doesn't, I'm betting that Aunt Gert will.

# 4

# The Silver at the
# Surface of the Water

"Do you want to hear an incredible story?" The black-haired
woman at our table is not one to be ignored. Eliana Jacob is a neuro-
scientist, whose brain-chemistry experiments command national
attention. Four of us sit around eating Italian food family style in a
café on New York's Upper West Side. We are winding down from a
postgraduate conference we've given that day at Columbia. Eliana's
story, she says, is about a colleague who worked on his Ph.D. at
Columbia in the lab next to hers, and has remained a good friend.
He's a cell biologist, she tells us. A nice guy.

I dip into the community ravioli plate and take a stab at a couple
of rigatoni. Ready for Eliana's tale, I offer her my full attention.

"This fellow, he's brilliant," she says. "Well, his mother tried to
drown him. She tried it three or four times while he was growing up.
Can you believe that? She must have been nuts! So anyway, the guy
didn't remember a thing about it for years. I don't know how he managed to shut it off, but he managed it. He could remember nothing.
Nothing! Then one day his whole memory came back. And he fainted
from the sheer power of it."

"Did you find him in a big heap in your lab?" The lone male at our
table receives Eliana's tale with considerable skepticism.

"Oh, you know me, Tom," she says. "I don't usually put much
stock in anecdotal data. But this fellow is a friend. I trust him. And
he was in his car when he fainted, as a matter of fact. He was lucky he
didn't get himself killed."

Tim Tully, Gary tells me, teaches tricks to fruit flies. He calls his subjects "Pavlov's flies," and conditions them by means of electric shock to avoid a certain odor. He exposes them in sequence to two alcohol smells, both of which are slightly unpleasant as far as fruit flies are concerned. While one smell permeates the training cage, the flies receive twelve one-second shocks to their feet. The other smell is associated with no shocks. Tully then puts the flies into a tiny "elevator," which takes them to a T-shaped cage that offers them a choice between the two odors. With no training, an ordinary fruit fly has a fifty-fifty chance of choosing either odor—of walking down either corridor of the T-bar. Ninety-five times out of a hundred, however, the trained fruit fly will choose the direction associated with the safe odor. *Dunce* and *rutabaga,* however, flunk this test. Missing the enzyme to generate cyclic AMP inside its nerve cells, *rutabaga* cannot learn or remember. *Dunce,* on the other hand, has too *much* cyclic AMP in its nervous system, and cannot generate the sudden bursts needed to move neurotransmitters across the synapses. *Dunce,* too, is stuck with a bad memory.

Repressed memory, however, is not "bad" memory. Gary Baker's old experiences were unavailable for retrieval because they had been repressed. When Gary started taking diving lessons, his brain cells signalled some of these old memories back to him. They were state-dependent memories—things he had learned when he was underwater. The thirty-year-old Gary, however, had no idea where the ideas were coming from. "What came back was not a friendly memory," he tells me. "When you're underwater and you look up, there's a silver surface to the water. That's what I remembered."

The first time he dove, Gary knew that he had seen this silvery surface before, at another time, in another place. He recaptured the memory with a terrible sense of dread. He also associated the silvery vision with a dream that had bothered him for many of his younger years. "I didn't know where or when I first saw it," he says, "but the silver surface was always there somewhere in my mind."

Gary had two hundred, maybe three hundred water dreams in his childhood. They were all the same. "I saw the silver at the surface," he says, not bothering to add any new content to something so ancient and so simple. "Do you know how the top of the water looks from the bottom? That's what I watched in hundreds of my childhood dreams."

"Well, that shows you the power of a memory," the youngest of us chimes in. "One time in 1974, I was—"

Eliana temporarily prevents our young tablemate from running off with the conversation. "Just one more thing," she says. "Do you know what my friend's hobby is? What he does almost every single week-end? Well, he's one of the greatest river divers in the world. Now, what do you think of that?"

We are all speechless for several seconds; a fork or two is suspended in midair. But then the young psychiatrist recovers and launches into her own memory story, which is not as good as Eliana's and much, much longer. I make a promise in my head to remember this moment. I will phone Eliana Jacob soon.


Dr. Jacob is cooler and more careful on her laboratory phone than she was by candlelight over a couple of bottles of Chianti. She wonders about the wisdom of having told us about Gary—his name is Gary, she says. Maybe Gary wouldn't have liked it.

I ask her whether she could tell Gary about me—tell him I'd like to interview him for a book on memory.

She says he's in treatment now, and his psychiatrist might not approve.

"Can't he decide for himself?"

After a pause, Eliana says, "Yes, that's O.K." It will be awkward for her to ask Gary, because it will mean admitting that she told us about him at dinner, but she will do it. And she will give him my number. Suddenly Eliana softens. "Good luck," she says. "I hope he talks to you."


"All my life," Gary Baker tells me, "I've been fascinated by water." He sees me in his lab on a Saturday. He is missing his diving in order to be interviewed. He thinks the book I'm writing could help people. He'd like to be in it. Gary works in a sprawling biochemical-research laboratory in upstate New York during the week. On weekends, or whenever he can, he drives an hour or so farther north to test the four-to six-knot currents inside the cool upstate rivers.

"I always watched the 'Sea Hunt' kind of show as a kid," he says, "the Jacques Cousteau stuff, the minisub. That's always been a fascination for me. At the same time, I was terrified of water. Absolutely terrified. When I was in high school, I would run seven miles a night. Yet I couldn't swim fifty feet without feeling totally exhausted. In hindsight, I realize that my exhaustion came from being so frightened."

Gary Baker is tall—well over six feet—and powerful. His hair is the pale blond of the dedicated water seeker. His eyes are the blue of the depths. He must be forty-five, but he looks much, much younger.

"Did you have trouble meeting the high-school swimming requirement, or anything like that?" I ask, wondering how his fascination with water eventually replaced his boyhood terror of being drowned.

"No trouble," he says, a smile creasing his face. "I even earned swimming and lifesaving badges to qualify as an Eagle Scout. But I went out for those badges only because my parents had paid money for me to take the course. And somehow—I don't know how—I survived. But I was still scared to death of the water. And that's why, at age thirty, I took up scuba."

While he was working on his advanced degree in cellular biology at Columbia, Gary became friendly with David Mortimer, a technician in his lab. Mortimer had recently earned his scuba-instructor papers, and he found himself missing what every new instructor is missing—students. So Dave offered his young lab colleague free lessons. "It probably cost me fifty thousand dollars in equipment and twenty thousand dollars in dive books and God knows how much else from that one free course," Gary says. "But hell, I had told Dave that I was afraid of the water. And he said, 'I know. But think of it this way—diving will help you get over your fear.' And I thought about it. Dave was my friend. There was also a little bit of peer pressure there at Columbia. Other people in our lab were going to take Dave's diving course. So I said, 'O.K., we'll do it.' And Dave was a very good instructor. I think he kind of fudged the two-hundred-yard swimming requirement for me. And so I learned to dive."

Gary shows me around his lab. He is working on fruit flies— Drosophila melanogaster—studying among other things the intracellular chemical compounds involved in associative learning, in a part of the Drosophila brain called the "mushroom bodies." He shows me the flies. There must be thousands of them in the lab, dozens of separate kinds—mutations. Each variety is sorted into half-pint bottles that look like the half-pint urine containers you see in hospitals. At the

bottom of each bottle sits a jellolike substance made of sugar, yeast, and cornmeal, which hardens into a permanent floor for the bottle and a permanent source of food for the flies. The stuff probably ferments, something Drosophila melanogaster loves. A hundred to a thousand of them live in one bottle. Since the days of the zoologist Thomas Hunt Morgan, who taught at Columbia in the early decades of this century, Drosophila has been the classic lab animal in evolutionary and genetic studies. Fruit flies breed quickly and deliver all sorts of mutants. If one wishes to breed them for a certain trait, Gary says, one feeds them ethylmethane sulfonate, a substance that encourages mutations. Thousands of mutant strains are then checked for the trait to be studied. When the single trait, unassociated with other abnormalities, appears in two flies of the opposite sex, they are mated in order to perpetuate the desired gene.

Gary tells me about the work being done at Cold Spring Harbor, on Long Island, by three distinguished Drosophilists working in the field of memory—Tim Tully, Ron Davis, and Yi Zhong. The two strains that occupy most of the team's time are dunce, bred by the renowned geneticist Seymour Benzer, of Caltech, and rutabaga, bred at Princeton in the mid-seventies by William G. Quinn, one of Benzer's close colleagues, and his technician, Patricia Sziber. Both of these fruit-fly strains are slow learners. They cannot memorize a thing. Dunce is characterized by low concentrations of phosphodiesterase, an enzyme that breaks down an organic molecule called cyclic AMP. And rutabaga is deficient in adenylyl cyclase, an enzyme that converts ATP (adenosine triphosphate, a modified sugar that serves as an energy source in the cells) to cyclic AMP. Too much or too little cyclic AMP in the neurons makes fruit flies forgetful. Cyclic AMP, Gary says, is also presumed crucial to the short-term memory of human beings.

Gary and his colleagues study the potent chemical messenger known as neurotransmitters, which move across the connecting space between neurons in connections called synapses. While neurotransmitters are known as first messengers, substances inside the cells promote activity are known as second messengers. Cyclic AMP is such second messenger: it prolongs the neurons' electrical polarization, allowing more activity than usual to occur across the synapse. Prolonged polarization along certain neuronal pathways is, in short-term memory.

At the beginning of his diving career, Gary also surprised himself with a behavior. He wondered whether or not it reflected some kind of memory. "One of the things you have to do in scuba class is hold your breath for a minute," Gary says. "When I was timed, I did it for two and a half minutes. The very first time! I was amazed. And so was my instructor." Not until that moment in scuba class did Gary Baker realize that he had an unusual ability to manage underwater for long periods of time. He could hold his breath amazingly well.

In human beings, short-term memories (or what the clinician might call immediate memories) last for a matter of seconds. But if a memory is consolidated and passed into long-term memory, it can be brought back days or years later. Gary's familiarity with a watery environment reflected long long-term memory—memory that was nonverbal. No one had taught him scuba-diving before. In his first lesson, he behaved as if he had been diving for years.

Gary knew how it felt to try to learn something and keep it temporarily in short-term memory. He had crammed for many an exam. He knew how to repeat a telephone number in his mind enough times to remember it past a busy signal, or how to retain a name for the period of a fleeting conversation. None of these working sensations came to Gary, however, when he held his breath under the water and watched the silvery surface above him. He did not have to perceive, register, and retrieve. He simply knew. His memories already were there—in long-term storage. Even though Gary knew the sensation of holding his breath underwater, he didn't know why he knew it. How could he know? All he remembered, at age thirty, was his dread of "the silver at the surface."

Learning is the modification of behavior by experience. And memory is the retention of that experience over time. Even the simple behavior of a simple animal activates many nerve cells and many connections to other cells. Modified and retained behavior is embedded in neural circuitry, no matter how simple the animal. Memory involves a lasting change in the relationship between cells.

Gary's memory of how it felt to hold his breath involved these same changes in cellular relationships. In order to understand learning and memory, scientists analyze what goes on inside the neurons of relatively simple animals—much simpler animals than human children. Scientists also watch the behaviors of simple animals as they unconsciously and implicitly remember. This is what the lab at

Columbia led by Eric Kandel does year after year with the marine snail *Aplysia Californica*.

Gary became familiar with Dr. Kandel's lab while he was at Columbia working on his Ph.D. Kandel's studies fall into two large groupings: his team trains the marine snail to behave in certain ways and then determines what substances are involved in perpetuating those behaviors; they also study *Aplysia*'s neurons in cell culture. What these studies show is how, on a simple cellular level, memory works.

The gill of *Aplysia* is covered by a sheet of skin called the mantle shelf, which ends in a fleshy spot named the siphon. If you touch the siphon, you get a brisk withdrawal of both the siphon and gill. It is like our own withdrawal of a finger from contact with a hot kettle. The snail's response can be exaggerated by a simple form of associative learning known as sensitization. If you give a mild electric shock to its tail, the snail will greatly exaggerate its gill response the next time you touch its siphon. The snail's memory of its learned response lasts for minutes—short-term memory. If you repeat the tail shock several times, the snail's enhanced gill response lasts for days—long-term memory.

When the snail's siphon is first touched, a change occurs in the electrical potential of the cellular membranes of its sensory neurons. Calcium and sodium move into the cells. Potassium moves out. The calcium is the critical substance as far as short-term memory is concerned. With a shock to *Aplysia*'s tail, the calcium activates adenylyl cyclase, which prompts ATP to manufacture cyclic AMP, the "second messenger" being studied at Cold Spring Harbor and other labs. In a sensitized *Aplysia,* while cyclic AMP is being made from the ATP in the sensory neurons, the neurotransmitter serotonin is released from a second kind of neuron, helping to produce even more cyclic AMP inside the sensory neurons. This double nudge to the cyclic-AMP system produces a great deal more of this substance than usual. *Aplysia*'s huge gill response reflects this sensitization. The cells, in other words, have remembered.

In order to understand the cellular mechanisms behind the long-term memory of the snail, Kandel's group puts three kinds of neurons—sensory neurons, motor neurons, and neurotransmitter-producing neurons—into a kind of a soup called a cell culture. When the neurotransmitter-producing neurons release serotonin into the culture medium, the cyclic AMP inside the sensory cells causes an enzyme to phosphorylate (add phosphates to) the sensory cells' proteins. As long as these proteins remain phosphorylated, they prevent an influx of potassium, which would repolarize the cell membrane. Calcium will thus continue to flow across the synapse, and calcium triggers even more phosphorylation of proteins. The snail's motor neurons also keep the process active by manufacturing a "retrograde messenger"—nitrous oxide, Kandel's team thinks—which stimulates the sensory neurons to continue releasing calcium and other activating substances across the synapse. Because of this feedback loop and other self-perpetuating activities, the cell no longer requires bursts of cyclic AMP to keep its memory going. Same cell, two different kinds of memory. A tiny but powerful package.

Genes are also an essential part of the neurons' ongoing ability to "remember." Kandel's group has created an artificial neuronal gene that matches the gene responsible for producing the proteins that are phosphorylated. A color coating is applied to it which causes the gene to turn blue when it is turned "on." Such genes are apparently activated by the presence of cyclic AMP. When serotonin, that great stimulator of cyclic AMP, is added to neuronal-cell cultures containing the artificial genes, the cultures turn a deep blue. This boost in genetic activity in turn boosts the supply of phosphorylated protein in the sensory neurons. Kandel and his team believe that the retrieval of long-term memories is marked by this kind of genetic activity. And this must reflect what happens in our brains when we remember something from long ago—a rapid genetic activation.

Just as Gary Baker fell in love with diving, he fell in love with the way cells remember. He decided that this was his kind of biology. He took a postdoctoral position in another memory lab, in Göteborg, Sweden, and after a couple of years settled in upstate New York.

Gary loves intracellular chemicals because they are powerful yet they work at a level almost beyond our ken. As a boy, Gary was always interested in the power of exotic beings. All through his teenage years, he was a "Trekkie." He was a loner and deeply afraid of his father, who became more and more violent the older Gary grew. Gary's father beat the teenage boy so hard with his fists that the only way to stop him, Gary found, was "to roll up like a cockroach." As an adolescent, desperately needing to escape his dad, Gary sat for hours on the flat roof of his house in western Nebraska, waiting for space aliens of the "Star Trek" variety to beam him up.

When Gary was just into his teens, his father bought him a microscope, and the boy spent hours trying to increase the magnification with drops of oil to the lens. He wanted to penetrate each small thing he saw. A high-school biology teacher who lived two blocks away took an interest in him, and they began working together, with a much bigger and more powerful microscope than the Bakers could have afforded. The friendship between teacher and boy became the most positive influence in young Gary's life.

The boy looked for his exotic powers in odd places—inside mini-submarines, space vehicles, and the one-celled creatures that lived in the pond behind his house. He read science fiction till his eyes reddened. Though his younger siblings—Terri, Harry, Barry, and Mary (yes, their children's names all seemed to rhyme to Mr. and Mrs. Baker)—were available to play with, Gary found his fun alone. He trusted his own company most. And he could feel free to dream of powers, controlled and confined to tiny spaces.

Gary's family was to all appearances what he calls "a June Cleaver bunch." "The seven of us always presented the image of God, Mom, and apple pie," he tells me. "I remember my mom trying to create a picture of the perfect home life. Buying us a lot of toys. Whenever there was something at school that was needed, we always had it— you know, memberships in student organizations, gifts for the teacher or the other kids at Christmas and birthdays, and things like that."

Gary's parents moved from town to town in western Nebraska while their five children were growing up. They lived a middle-class life at the outskirts of these communities, where they could have one or two acres all to themselves. His father sold farm equipment in other men's stores. His mother ran day-care programs at their house. The land was dry, and irrigation was the main way to get things to grow. A small irrigation ditch formed a natural boundary to the first property where Gary lived.

Gary recalls his teenage space fantasies with some sadness. "I felt I didn't belong on this planet," he says. "In fact, I thought of myself as some sort of mutation. Like Spock, I guess." I glance around the lab, at the bottles full of altered fruit flies. Does Gary feel "at home" among them?

It took Gary about three years from the time he started scuba diving to recognize a painful fact from his past. The fact came with only one detail and no specific episodes. "Over the course of, I'd say, three years of diving in New York," he tells me, "I developed an awareness: 'Oh, wow! My mother threw me in that irrigation ditch outside our house! And that must have been where my fears of the water came from!'"

Gary's first realization about his lost past was strange. It was a thought, not really a memory. Our thoughts come from our word and association centers, but our memories come from every part of the cerebral cortex. They come not only from the frontal lobes, where we feel old motor movements and rethink old thoughts, but also from the temporal lobes, where we register the sounds, balance sensations, and emotions accompanying the memory; from our parietal lobes, where we apprehend physical sensations and spatial arrangements; and from our occipital lobes, for accompanying visual information, metaphors, and color. Many parts of the cortex fire simultaneously, as our memories come to us—more parts than are necessary simply for thinking.

Gary was thirty-three years old when his "Oh, wow!" idea popped up. Three years later, his mother developed terminal diabetic complications. Gary went back to Nebraska to visit her during her final ordeal. On her deathbed, she confessed nothing about throwing Gary into the water. And Gary did not dare question her about it. He did not know whether to trust his own thoughts. The idea had been a shocking revelation to him, yet it was accompanied by only one detail: he seemed to know which particular irrigation ditch it was. He had no accompanying mental pictures, however, and no physical sensations. Gary wasn't even sure the whole thing was true.

"It was just a cognitive awareness—a cold idea," Gary says. "There was no validation of it. I just had some sort of sense—'Mom threw me in the irrigation ditch.' That's all." And so Gary Baker's mother died without Gary's knowing with any certainty what, if anything, had happened between them. He couldn't ask.

The man who loved small powerful things—minisubs, microscopes, and cells—married a small powerful person named Jill while he was still in graduate school. She was under five feet tall, taught high school in Manhattan, and was very smart and stimulating. But Gary Baker was unable to keep her. Five years into their friendly and uneventful marriage—they had both agreed not to have children—Jill told her husband that she was leaving. She liked him, she said, but their life wasn't what Jill had expected. There were no "other men" in Jill's life, and no "other women" in Gary's. Things were just too unexciting. Jill left without Gary's knowing exactly what had happened—or failed to happen—between them.

By the time Gary Baker left Columbia for Sweden and his postdoctoral studies, his adult life had hit an all-time low. He still hurt from his breakup with Jill. Swedish women, as appealing as they might be by reputation, did little to brighten his spirits. His laboratory work had become far less imaginative than it should have been. His habits were rigid: he'd wake up at the same time of day, eat at the same time of day, and fall asleep at the same time each night. He had very little contact with his brothers and sisters—although once in a while he would talk on the phone to his youngest brother, Barry, who lived in Arizona. On weekends, Gary dove into a few submerged shipwrecks off the Swedish coast, but for the most part he wasn't having much fun.

Fortunately, he spent only two years in Scandinavia. He was offered a job in upstate New York at an excellent lab with a friendly group, not too far away from the waters of his dreams. Gary loves swift-flowing rivers. They call to him far more seductively than do shipwrecks at the ocean's edge. The cell biologist found new hope when the letter confirming his appointment arrived. He would be going back "home."

New York was definitely home now, not Nebraska. Gary's mother was dead, and he was virtually estranged from three of his siblings, with whom he had never developed much in common. He was unremittingly angry at his father, who had beaten him so badly as a teenager that he felt amazed to have made it into adulthood at all. Barry was his only remaining friend in the family.

Gary found a house near his new laboratory and signed up for a Dale Carnegie course, so that he could make more friends and play better politics at work. Things would be different, he promised himself. He met Anne, a woman he liked more than anyone since Jill. They went out three times before Gary discovered, once again, that the behavior of women could not be predicted—at least, not by him. Anne told Gary that she did not want to see him anymore because he was far too intense. Gary was hurt and puzzled. Too intense? She was undoubtedly right—he did seem to be driven by some mystifying inner engine. What in the hell was wrong with him?

A week after Anne rejected him, Gary Baker erupted. It was a silent eruption, but powerful all the same. Gary was forty-three years old when it happened and two years into his staff position at the laboratory.

"It was a hot, humid day," the blond scientist tells me, his voice slightly rough. "I had driven almost all the way to a dive site about two hours and a hundred miles from home. By the time I turned off the highway toward the river, I was really tired. It was so damn humid.

"And, ah—and I got halfway up the exit-ramp, and suddenly I had three memories. One after the other after the other. They were like three slides—black-and-white slides—shown in rapid succession. First, me at eleven. Next, me at seven. And last, me well before kindergarten. In each, I was lying naked on the bathroom floor. My mother had tied me up, and she was inserting things into my rectum. In the first picture, she was putting in a red baseball bat, about this long"—Gary holds his hands about a foot apart. "In the others, she was inserting something else—I'm not sure what. The pictures were of three different bathrooms. Three different houses. That meant three different ages for me. And, um"—Gary's voice gets even rougher—"the suddenness of the memory, the shock— Well, I just blacked out in the car."

Gary must have been unconscious only a few seconds. He came to as he slammed into the rear of a car that had stopped at the top of the ramp. The collision did twelve hundred dollars' worth of damage to Gary's car, but none to the car ahead of him. "I didn't even try to turn in an insurance claim," Gary says. "Because I didn't want to put down that I had hit a car after I blacked out."

Here were repressed childhood memories that returned with such force that they caused a well-built, husky athlete to faint dead away. The memories had probably been repressed, not dissociated; dissociated memories rarely come back clear and complete. For more than three decades, they had been totally blocked from retrieval. And these memories were not of drowning, as Eliana Jacob had said, but of incestuous rape. Eliana Jacob had not heard the whole story. Or if she had, she had chosen not to share it over ravioli.

On the day that Gary's memories came back, the air was so humid that it may have cued a memory of humidity in bathrooms past, especially if Gary's mother had raped him in connection with his bathing. It is hard to identify any other immediate cue to his memory retrieval; Gary cannot think of any himself. Perhaps there was no cue. The ground on which the returning memory fell was a tiring drive, after a week's worth of stress and soul-searching. Gary had started questioning himself from the moment Anne rejected him. "Am I a primitive character?" he had wondered. "Is there something 'off' about me?"

Gary pushed his car onto the shoulder of the exit-ramp, and the car he hit went its way. Then Gary waited. Eventually his diving friend drove off the same exit, and Gary flagged him down. "My diving buddy helped me get my car started," he says. "But I couldn't go diving that day. No way. In fact, over the next week I couldn't sleep. I was feeling incredibly anxious. Worst of all, I knew there was much, much more in my mind. More terrible stuff. I cancelled some of my scuba teaching appointments, because I didn't feel comfortable in the water. And I asked a psychiatrist friend about my memories. I asked him, 'How do you know, if you remember something, whether it's real and not some psychotic illusion?' Those pictures I saw—that's *not* how I chose to remember my mother."

The psychiatrist gave his friend five sleeping pills, so that Gary could get a few nights' rest. And he gave him the name of a female colleague in the area who works with victims of childhood trauma. Gary asked for an emergency appointment—despite the pills, he was still not sleeping—and she gave him one. Thus Gary came to embark on a course of weekly psychotherapy.

By the time of our meeting, he has been on this therapeutic regime for two years. Gary tells me that he has grown more in those two years than at any other time of his life, childhood included. "If I could do it all again," he says, "maybe I'd be a psychiatrist and study memory on the macro level."

On the micro level, memory actually causes growth in the nervous system. Perhaps someday we will be able to prove that psychotherapy does the same. Recent research in cell biology demonstrates that when neuronal genes are turned on in the process of handling long-term memory, the brain actually grows. Things happen. In animals as small as *Aplysia,* long-term memory has been found to encourage the growth of new neural connections. An increase has been found both by the Columbia group and a group at the University of Texas Health Science Center in the number of presynaptic terminals in those sensory neurons of *Aplysia* involved in long-term memory.

A traumatic memory established in childhood remains an important influence into adulthood. It is possible to prove how lasting and influential childhood memories can be, in lower forms of life, at least. Using his shock-aversion technique on fruit-fly larvae, Tim Tully of Cold Spring Harbor has shown that childhood memories last through something as strikingly disruptive as metamorphosis. Once put through eight shock cycles, the larvae will retain their memories over the five days that it takes them to metamorphose into adults. These experiments carry important implications for human children. And they fit in with a clinical research study I published in 1988, concerning twenty youngsters who had been traumatized in various ways under the age of five. There was documentation of the traumas of each child—police reports, confessions, eyewitness testimony, and so forth. No matter how young or how nonverbal these children were at the time of their traumas, their nonverbal behaviors—how they played, what they feared, how they acted—indicated that their memories had been stored and remained strongly operational. These behaviors reflected the traumas, though many of the children could not remember their terrible experiences in words. Like Gary's "silvery surface" and his uncounted childhood nightmares of deep metallic-hued waters, the nonverbal behaviors of nineteen of the twenty children demonstrated that they had perceived, registered, and stored their terrors. The twentieth child had not actually seen the traumatic event, although she thought she had seen it. She had only heard family lore about it. She had a false memory, and not one behavioral symptom accompanied it.

Once Gary Baker's mental pictures returned he felt continually uncomfortable. "I had the sense that I had a lot inside, and that the dam was about to break," he tells me. "I've always been very rigidly controlled, and in hindsight I think it's because I clamped down on my memories at such an early age. But after I started therapy—that was two weeks after I fainted at the highway exit—things started to happen extremely fast."

Within the first few of weeks of their return, Gary's three black-

and-white mental snapshots started running like videotapes. They took on color and then sound. He could see his position on the various bathroom floors in relation to the various sinks and tubs. "The last thing that came into my memories was the terror," he says. And then he remembered another scene, from age four or five. "It was the house we left by the time I was six. My mother masturbated in front of me with a white dildo. I remember running out of the room screaming in terror because I thought the moans and the red color [of her genitals] meant she had hurt herself."

When he started his psychotherapy, Gary felt that his memories were all blocked up. He believed he was holding onto a series of personally meaningful recollections that were still heavily repressed. He strained for them. "I felt," he says, "as though I had come to a cold black wall."

Memories usually do not emerge when a person tries too hard. Gary's psychiatrist told him to let up a bit. He had just begun his therapy, she said. The rest of the memories would come when he was ready. But Gary repeatedly bucked against his "cold black wall." It felt almost palpable to him.

"I wrote a letter to my dad," Gary says. "It was my idea. My doctor never suggested it. My letter said, 'Dad, I'm starting therapy right now. I'm in a lot of pain. I don't feel good. I'm having memories of what Mom did to me. I don't believe you knew what was happening, but if you recall anything, I would appreciate any help you could offer.'

"Now my dad, who formed his opinions back in the forties and fifties, thinks that all psychiatrists are evil and the only people who go to them are criminally insane. He came to see me right away."

As a scientist, Gary wanted some sort of external confirmation for his memories of his mother's sexual attacks. But none of his siblings professed to know a thing about it. Nor did Mr. Baker. When Gary first saw the huge man in his living room, he mistakenly perceived him as wearing a Nazi uniform. "The whole visit felt like the Nuremberg war trials," Gary says. His questions to his father over the two-day visit elicited no confirmations for Gary's memories. Moreover, Mr. Baker adamantly denied that he had ever initiated any physical attacks on Gary, and he adamantly denied that Gary's mother had ever had an emotional problem of any kind. Gary's brother Harry, who had come along on the trip, took an immediately hostile approach. His first words to Gary were "What's wrong with you?" Both father and brother said that Gary had watched far too much "Star Trek" as a teenager. They told him that he was now under the influence of "too many psychiatrists from New York City."

"I was at work when they left to fly back to Nebraska," Gary says. "My dad broke some stuff in my house before he left—he must have really been mad—and I wouldn't take the money he offered me later for it. I thought the money was a kind of payoff. He broke the glass on a topographical map of the world oceans on my wall; he must have knocked it to the ground. And he destroyed something on my desk; I can't remember what it was. But when I got home I totally cleaned out the parts of my house where they stayed. I mean I scrubbed the walls of my guest room and kitchen, and I scrubbed all the bedding a couple of times. And as I was doing the scrubbing I was saying to myself, 'Now I know what a rape victim feels like. Now I know why she wants to get clean.'"

It is about five o'clock in the afternoon, and the light hits the glassware around the lab the way it hits the pearls on the earlobes of a Vermeer model. "One night after their visit," Gary continues, "I was in Ohio doing a scuba dive in an old salt mine. It was a unique research institute, now defunct, where physicists had been looking for evidence of proton decay in a huge tank filled with ultrapure water. I was two thousand feet underground in this tank when I suddenly heard a train whistle. Well, there were *nooo* trains anywhere around— *nooo* way! And right afterward I remembered my mother taking a transformer from my electric train and using the wires to shock my hand."

"Do you know which hand it was?" I ask, wondering if Gary senses the pain as we speak

"My right hand—the first and second fingers. I was a first grader." He pauses a moment, and gingerly flexes the hand. "It's fascinating to me about my mom. I mean, why did she do these things to children? She never went to a mental hospital. She never had a diagnosis. She ran a day-care center, and I think she badly hurt the kids there, too. In fact, I know it.

"But getting back to the transformer. After I remembered that, I phoned Barry and he remembered the same thing happening to him. He had always remembered it. But Barry remembers the instrument as a gray box with a red handle. He's five years younger than me, and

I don't think he thought of it as a toy-train transformer. And that was my first validation of my memory as real and not some kind of psychotic delusion. For the first time, I was sure I was right. I truly remembered my real life. Barry confirmed my memories—at least, the one that came back to me right after I heard the train whistle in my head."

Gary retrieved a second train-related memory immediately following the first, while he was still at his dive site under the State of Ohio. He remembered being five years old and being forced to lie down on the railroad tracks a half mile from his house. First his mother made him sit a few feet off the tracks as a train went by. Then she forced him to lie on the tracks, telling him that the train would run him over. When the train got close ("you know how sound transmits through a steel rail," Gary says), she let the little boy get up, "with the threat that the next time the train would really run over me."

Why would a person do such a thing to her child? I wonder as I listen to Gary's tales and watch his laboratory flies walk all over their food. He was her favorite child, Gary tells me. The oldest. She wanted him to be wonderful. But there must have been a terrible hate there, too—not just love and sexual fascination. She must have feared her firstborn son and exaggerated his powers. Did she hate Gary for being a boy? Were only boys in danger of her attacks? Gary says that his mother always had a favorite boy in her day-care programs—a young lad who would have the privilege of taking his afternoon nap with Mrs. Baker. "I'm sure the sexual abuses happened to them, too," says Gary, deep regret penetrating his voice.

Years ago, the child psychiatrist Richard Galdston, at Harvard, and I, then at Case Western Reserve University Medical School, separately came up with the same finding from our clinical studies of child abuse. People who physically assault their children magnify their children's powers, capacities, or attributes. They see their children entirely unrealistically—as Galdston put it, with "psychotic transference." There is a good chance that somebody did terrible things to Mrs. Baker when she was a child. Terrible memories create terrible behaviors. This is no excuse, just a very sketchy, incomplete explanation. Mrs. Baker did not live to explain her actions to her sons. Nor does anyone alive today know why she did what she did.

Gary stops me from staring into a jar where at least a thousand fruit flies with odd-colored wings swarm. He tells me that the last memory he retrieved at the Ohio dive site explained the "cold dark wall" to him. He was back at his motel trying to sleep when the memory returned. When he was about four years old, Gary remembered, his mother emptied the refrigerator, put him inside, and slammed the door shut. Several months after Gary retrieved this memory, Barry told him that he had retrieved his own memory of having been locked in a freezer chest when they lived in a different Nebraska town. In that conversation, Barry remarked that as a child, he had always wondered whether the light inside the refrigerator goes out when you close the door. "It does," Gary says. "I know."

He sighs. "I guess it was one of my mom's neat little ways of dealing with children," he goes on. "Locking them inside a refrigerator. And the interesting thing is, once that memory came back I no longer had the feeling of being up against a cold dark wall. The cold dark wall *was* the refrigerator."

People who, like Gary, have "cold dark walls" around their memories, are of interest to Larry Squire, a psychologist at the San Diego Veterans Administration Medical Center. For several years now, Dr. Squire has been conducting studies on organically amnesic patients, using ingenious psychological tests and brain-imaging techniques. In 1989, he studied a group of individuals who had become amnesic on a known calendar day. He found that although these people had trouble answering questions about world events that had taken place ten or twenty years before their amnesias set in, they were quite normal in their responses to questions about things that had occurred thirty or forty years before the amnesias. This suggests that very long-term memories eventually reassemble themselves. "The new perishes before the old," the French psychologist Theodore Ribot wrote in 1881 of memory. Dr. Squire had found at least one way to prove Ribot right.

Squire's team carried out a related experiment on a group of monkeys, who were taught to recognize twenty object pairs a day. After the monkeys had learned a total of a hundred pairs, the hippocampal regions of some of the animals were removed. The monkeys who had not been operated on remembered the most recently learned object pairs better than the pairs they had been taught earlier in the sequence. But the surgically altered monkeys remembered the early object pairs better than the later ones. This experiment suggests that the hippocampus is important to memory only for a limited period of time. Long-term memory located in the more recently evolved areas of the cerebral cortex eventually replaces hippocampal memory.

Dr. Squire's principal human subjects suffer from anterograde amnesia—that is, they cannot transfer explicit short-term memory into long-term memory. They do very well at long-term storage of implicit memories, however. For example, after several days of practicing they are able to mirror-draw as well as any normal individual who has had the same amount of practice. Although these patients deny that they have ever tried a mirror-drawing task before, because they cannot explicitly remember having done so, they perform at a practiced level. One of the originators of the idea that there are multiple forms of memory, Dr. Squire clearly shows here that human memory consists of separate systems, some including conscious knowledge and others having nothing at all to do with thought.

I look over at Gary's clock. It is nearly six o'clock on this summer evening, and a half-dozen kites dive and then rise high above the grassy field outside the lab. Gary tells me that two scuba students will be coming over to his house at eight. "Listen, let me stop off for a pizza I ordered and bring you home with me for about an hour," he says. "I think we'll be done by then."

"Sure," I say. I would very much like to see how this cell biologist and diver lives.

We arrive within twenty minutes—extra-large pizza and all—at a ranch-style house. Gary says, "I just moved in here with my girlfriend. We're trying to see if it will work out. Both of us are divers, so we have a lot in common." I meet Brooke, a tall, informally dressed brunette in her mid to late thirties. Like Jill, Brooke teaches school. But unlike Jill, she seems devoted to Gary. "How's it going?" she asks him, and glances at me with open curiosity and a little concern. Gary brushes off the question, saying he's fine. But I notice he gives her a tiny hug before he leads me to his study.

Gary steers me downstairs to a large basement room that looks more like a library than the usual basement rec room. He eats his half of the pizza at a big conference table at the center of this rather remarkable place and opens two Cokes, offering me one.

I glance around the room as Gary savors his pizza. Three of the walls are lined with charts of the freshwater and saltwater fishes of the world. In the space not taken up by the fish are framed prints of Chinese junks and photographs of waves, of waterspouts, and of water-filled caverns. An amazing photo shows Gary in full diving regalia plunging into a concrete-lined hole—"the research facility in Ohio," he reminds me. At right angles to the fourth wall are eight or ten wooden bookcases. "I have one of the great scuba libraries in the U.S.," Gary tells me. "I try to be a scholar even of scuba."

Gary has saved his most important memories for last. They came to his mind late in the process of his introduction to psychotherapy. He remembered them a month or so after he saw himself lying on the railroad tracks of his childhood. The group of memories Gary describes now, as we sit in this room dedicated to diving, explain the course of his life better than any of his other memories. Gary does not have serious sexual difficulties as a result of having been repeatedly raped by his mother while he lay naked on the bathroom floor. He does not have any problems with railroad trains. Or with refrigerators. But he has dedicated his life—at least his avocational life—to the water. And it is his water-related memories that he brings me now, at the end of our afternoon.

"So the big thing that came to me in the last year was about the water," Gary says, throwing his pizza-stained napkin and paper plate into a blue wastebasket embossed with a map of the continental shelves of eastern North America. "My mom did some things to me that made a hell of an impact on my life, you see. And I've been trying to work them out unconsciously since I became a diver."

"And before," I add in my own mind.

"When I was in the three- to four-year-old range, we had this little dog," he goes on. "I guess it was her dog—my mom's. But I never thought of it that way—'her dog.' One day, I went down to the irrigation ditch that bounded our property. I mean, it was no Grand Coulee Dam or TVA project, just an irrigation ditch no more than four feet deep. So I threw her dog in to see if he could swim. I was curious, you know. Damn, I was only three or four years old! I just wanted to see the dog paddle.

"So she comes running across the backyard, and she retrieves her dog. But then—and this is where my memory feels so horrible—she lifts me up over her head. And she screams at me as she holds me up high, 'I hate you! I hate you! I hate you!' And then she throws me into the water. I am shocked. I look up. The water is way over my head. And I see the silver at the surface."

Gary's voice catches. His eyes suddenly look paler than pale. He pulls out a handkerchief. I murmur my sympathy, but Gary says, "It's O.K. It'll go away. This memory—it's only been back in my consciousness for a year, so it's very close to my feelings. Some of the other memories that came back to me almost feel as if they're out-of-body—beyond my feelings. But this one, I just can't defend against it. I know because of this memory that my decision to learn how to dive was not really a decision to overcome my fear of the water. It was my need to overcome my certainty that I would drown."

I can see now why Gary was practiced at holding his breath in his first scuba class. And I can see why he specializes in braving waters with intense currents. "One-trial learning" can do that sort of thing. Eight electroshock cycles to a fruit-fly larva suffice to alter the behavior of the adult fly. One drowning attempt can change a child's life. I understand why Gary dreamed hundreds of dreams of the silvery surface. And I can also understand why he has become a world-class diver.

Gary goes on, still trying to talk past a catch in his voice. "I had the sense that I would never get back up to the surface. I saw it up there, all silvery. There was this cold sensation. And there was also a sense of movement. Like I was being swept away. But I'm sure the velocity of the water was nothing like the velocity of the rivers I play in now. I teach people how to handle intense currents. That's my forte. And they love it. But it is also the story of me as a little kid. Maybe still within me is the drive to overcome that fear of being swept away."

"How did you finally get out of the irrigation ditch?" I ask.

"She pulled me out," he says, and he dabs at his eyes with his handkerchief. "You know, I can't understand what stopped my mother from killing me. She had my head in a toilet bowl other times—I have memories of that now. She even had me immersed underwater in my bathinet. I can remember it as though I'm seeing it all through gauze. There were light gray walls all around me, a foul smell in the air—I've never encountered that odor since. And the sense of giving up on something—just the sense that the end is here. But my mother always pulled me out of the water. And I don't know why."

• • •

It is ironic that something so dangerous, so terrifying, and so forced upon a child can become the voluntary activity of the child's later life. But artists have repeated their childhood traumas time and time again in their art. When he was fourteen years old, René Magritte lost his mother to sudden, unexpected death. She committed suicide by jumping into the Sambre River, and her body was not recovered for days. Magritte repeated his memories in his artistic life—"played" with his mental images of his mother's body after she was fished out of the eel-infested industrial river and then laid out at home. The corpse most likely had a ruined face and bloated abdomen. Some say that Magritte's mother's nightgown was wrapped around her face when they found her. Magritte repeats these memories too many times to count, in his depictions of veiled or faceless people. He shows you cloth wrappings, apples, bowler hats, sky—anything but faces. He frequently paints watery backgrounds. He reproduces a sense of dread. He draws strange women, part human and part fish, with bloated bellies—as close to a woman fished out of the water as you can get.

Edvard Munch's mother died of tuberculosis when he was five, and his sister died of the same disease when he was fourteen. Those deaths are often repeated in Munch's paintings of women and babies (or fetuses) in coffins. He depicts deathbeds. He depicts terror. Even his living women look dead. But the worst images of all, the most frightening, are the images of Munch's terrified survivors. Himself.

When the celebrated Mexican painter Frida Kahlo was a teenager, she was impaled by a railing when the streetcar in which she rode was hit by a bus. The painful, deforming effects of the accident appear over and over in her terribly blemished, often broken-looking, unblinking self-portraits. As a six-year-old, she had been confined to bed for nine months with polio of the right leg. At that time, she "visited" an imagined little girl who lived at the center of the earth and could dance. She appears to have held on to this memory, too. At age forty, Kahlo painted *The Two Fridas,* one of her most celebrated works. In it, a healthy Frida gives a blood transfusion to an identical but weaker Frida.

Gary Baker was no artist. But he constantly reënacted something that had been lost for years to his conscious memory. He reënacted it within the swift-running currents of his beloved New York State rivers. He termed this activity "play," something I think that Magritte, Munch, and Kahlo would have called their work, too. As a kid, Gary could hold a note on his saxophone longer than anybody else at school. He practiced breathing without even realizing it. It was a kind of lifesaving habit of his. In high school he was a Trekkie, living an imaginary life in a space world as devoid of air as was the water that had so terrified him. In college he wrote down his chess moves ahead of time, so that his opponent would know after their game that Gary had had him under his control from the very start. Gary strove for control because he once had none. His mother's games of death had given him plenty of ways to "play" with his own anticipated demise.

Eventually, Gary's diving became the main behavioral expression of his active though still repressed memories. In diving, he was unwittingly facing his terror of toilet bowls, of a bathinet, of currents that threatened to sweep him away beyond any help. He strove to master what ordinarily cannot be fully mastered in a lifetime.

Gary's traumatic experience in the irrigation ditch does not stand alone among his traumas. There were many other times when his mother threatened his life, his love for her, and his boyhood sexuality. But the ditch sets the tone and pattern for much of the rest of his life. He would study one-celled organisms, the inhabitants of watery ditches around the world. He would eventually probe the cells of the human brain. He would challenge rivers with currents that run along at a reckless clip. He would teach others to do the same. He would master the silvery surface at the top of the water.

Gary's moment in the ditch represents a moment of inextinguishable learning. This mental representation must have moved with ease from short-term into long-term memory. If very old memories reassemble, as Larry Squire's work tells us, these memories must have been repackaged in Gary's cortex without losing any of their enormous impact. Entirely hidden from Gary's consciousness, they exerted influence over much of what he did, and after forty years in hiding they reëmerged, in all their powerful detail.

I see Gary Baker's name these days in the scientific literature on brain and memory. His group at the lab is doing interesting work. We speak once in a while by phone, and Gary tells me that he is freer, more creative, and far happier than he has ever been. His psychiatrist has set a termination date for his therapy, but Gary has mixed feelings about that. "The more therapy I do," he says, "the more productive I get and the less 'Mr. Spock-like' I feel." He and Brooke are marrying soon. But diving is still at the center of Gary's life. He must continue to play in the depths, where he can look up toward the silver at the surface of the water.

# 5

# The Two Miss Americas of 1958 and Her Sister

In the 1951 newspaper photograph, a man sits on the arm of a couch, his knees spread, his hands relaxed. Even though the jacket of his pale spring suit is casually unbuttoned, his handkerchief peaks sharply at the pocket. The gray in his hair frames his patrician face, which angles toward the other occupants of the couch, his four daughters. He relates to them in a friendly fashion. He says something of interest. Parted lips reveal straight white teeth. His body is lean and athletic. He looks easygoing, the very picture of middle-aged health and success.

Girls' legs in very high heels fill the bottom half of the picture. Lean and well shaped, the legs suggest horseback riding, golf, swimming, and skiing. Three of the girls are blond; one sister has dark hair. Their pin-curled shoulder-length hairdos shine from attention and good health.

The father's right hand barely touches one daughter's back. She looks up at him. This is Gwen, the oldest. Her hair is so light that it rivals Jean Harlow's in the old movies. The dark-haired girl is Val, the second oldest. One girl dresses in black, while the others wear the pale shades of late spring. This is Nancy, who looks sophisticated but whose feet, in their high heels, land awkwardly on the floor.

The youngest girl sits in profile and clutches her gloves with tightened fingers. Her curls are not fully combed out. She is the tallest and the thinnest. She is Marilyn Van Derbur at thirteen. In this photo,

Marilyn and her sisters are attending a ceremony at the University of Denver to honor their father. The handsome man at his ease is Francis S. Van Derbur, who has been named the Outstanding University of Denver Alumnus for 1951.

Francis S. Van Derbur and his wife, Gwendolyn Olinger Van Derbur, were two of the best of the best people in Colorado. Bill McNichols, a former mayor of Denver, called Francis S. Van Derbur "a figure in the state's history." Mr. Van Derbur was an ambitious boy who made good. He went through college on scholarships. He worked every spare minute. He played piano by ear and recited poetry by heart. While finishing his studies at the University of Denver, he met a charming, rich, and socially connected coed nicknamed "Boots." Once introduced, they never parted. Boots Olinger was absolutely swept away by "Van's" looks. "He was an Adonis," she later said of Francis S. Van Derbur. "I took one look at him and fell in love."

The couple married on June 13, 1930, after Francis had worked a full year for Gwendolyn's father. Francis then began the long task of building up the Olinger family's mortuary firm. By 1959, when he became the company president, it was a multifaceted giant. Of their fifty-five years together, Boots Van Derbur told *People* magazine, "It was a perfect life. . . . My heart beat fast every time I saw him—from [the] first moment until the day he died." Boots, well into her eighties now, tries to remember "the good things" Francis did. She remains active and committed to charities and to her family. Family has always been the center of Gwendolyn Van Derbur's life.

Francis S. Van Derbur was an outstanding philanthropist, board member, socialite, businessman, and pillar of the Denver community. When he died in 1984, at age seventy-six, of a heart attack, the Denver papers put the announcement on their front pages. He is interred in a mausoleum at the top of Mt. Lindo, near a huge neon cross he built years ago so that his mother could spot his father's grave from her house. The lighted cross, an official Jefferson County landmark, serves as a reference point for airline passengers flying into Denver. Mr. Van Derbur also left less visible but more important marks on Colorado institutions. Among his favorites were the Cleo Wallace Village for Handicapped Children, his alma mater the University of Denver, Colorado Women's College, the University of Colorado, the

Denver Center for the Performing Arts, the Civic Theater, the national Intrafraternity Council, and the Boy Scouts.

The four Van Derbur girls arrived in quick order, beginning in 1931. The family lived first in an old three-story white frame house in East Denver. In 1948, they moved to an even more commodious house a little closer to town. The girls skied in winter and sported over the Colorado countryside the rest of the year. There were schools, music lessons, games. Everybody strove to be the best. Marilyn, a skinny, bony kid, was horse-crazy. Her sister Gwen remembers that there were switches of horsetail hair, statues of horses, and horse paraphernalia all over Marilyn's room.

It was a must in this excellent family that each child volunteer. Marilyn spent hours at the Wallace Village helping in programs for emotionally disabled children. Gwen developed a lasting love for all sorts of causes. To get their allowances, the Van Derbur girls had to sign "initiative slips" detailing their good deeds.

Rather than collecting pictures of movie stars, young Marilyn kept a scrapbook all about Gwen, who was six years her senior. In 1949 Gwen was named Homecoming Queen of the University of Colorado. She was the Queen of the first Wintersköl at Aspen, and her face appeared on the July 1952 cover of *Photoplay.* Nothing impressed young Marilyn more than Gwen. Marilyn's scrapbook was filled with newspaper and magazine clippings and photographs, and it was somewhat puzzling to Gwen, who did not bother to save such things.

In 1957 Marilyn, then nineteen and a sophomore at the University of Colorado, entered the Miss Colorado beauty contest and won. As her junior year of college began, she competed in Atlantic City for the title of Miss America of 1958, playing two pieces that her father had selected for her—"Tea for Two" and "Tenderly"—on the Hammond organ. ("He's never wrong," Marilyn remarked later to the press, in reference to these choices.) She was clearly one of the crowd favorites in the evening-gown and bathing-suit contests, but she had to fight off a strong challenge by Jody Elizabeth Shattuck, an extraordinarily attractive Miss Georgia, in order to win the crown. When Marilyn was selected Miss America, she was surprised. "Even my sisters wouldn't bet on me," she said. Following her year as Miss America, she completed her junior and senior years at the university, functioning at the same time as the television spokeswoman for AT&T. Academic achievement stayed important to Marilyn despite her celebrity status, and she graduated Phi Beta Kappa.

Four smart pretty girls, each of them busy with charity work and "initiative slips." The Van Derburs appeared to have realized the American Dream.

On the night of May 8, 1991, in Denver, a group of incest survivors, their families, their therapists, and one reporter gathered in a small auditorium on the University of Colorado Health Sciences campus to hear plans for a new program at the Kempe National Center, a well-known university-affiliated institution dedicated to the prevention and treatment of child abuse and neglect. It is named after the Denver pediatrician C. Henry Kempe, who in the summer of 1962, along with a psychiatrist, a radiologist, and two other physicians, published "The Battered-Child Syndrome" in the *Journal of the American Medical Association*—an article that has become the classic medical paper on diagnosing physical child abuse. A surprise speaker came to the podium the night of the Kempe benefit. Wearing a smart white suit, she spoke in a practiced and compelling style. She had come with an offer, she said. She, her mother, and her sisters would establish a Kempe Center program for adult survivors of childhood incest, with a start-up donation of about a quarter of a million dollars. But what truly jolted the small audience was the speaker's revelation about her own life. "Tonight I stand before you an incest survivor," she said. The speaker was Marilyn Van Derbur Atler, Miss America of 1958.

Marilyn told her audience that Francis S. Van Derbur had "violated" her from the time she was five years old until she left for college. He had expected the true nature of their relationship to stay secret. "This was his greatest weapon," she said. "He knew I would never tell." Marilyn then delivered an apostrophe. "I say to my father tonight, 'You were wrong!'"

A shocking revelation even in an era when such confessions were becoming almost commonplace, Marilyn's story carried the immediate fascination of an incest situation at the highest levels of society, and it commanded media attention nationwide. The part of the story that held the most interest for me was Marilyn's statement that she had remembered nothing about her sexual ordeals until she was twenty-four years old. She had lost all memory of what was happening *as* it was happening. From the first episode to the last, Marilyn

did not consciously think anything was amiss. While she was dating
Larry Atler, the boy who would later become her husband, she did
not know that many times after they had kissed goodnight her father
forced her into unwanted acts of sex. While she reigned as Miss
America, she was entirely unaware of her incestuous past.

The technique that Marilyn Van Derbur used in order to put her
incest out of mind is relatively uncommon. Marilyn explained to her
audience at the university that as a child she had "split" into a happy
"day child" and a terrified "night child." She had evidently used
the defense that Freud discovered late in his career and named *Ich-
Spaltung* (literally, "I-splitting"). Her "day child" never knew what her
"night child" experienced. All memories of abuse were sequestered in
the night child's mind. Splitting is a defense mechanism that allows
you to see yourself or others as "all good" or "all bad." The person who
splits cannot integrate positive and negative qualities of self or others
into full and cohesive images. Occasionally the memories of one of
these "selves" are lost. Apparently this had happened inside the mind
of Miss America.

Marilyn told her audience that she considered her ambition, ath-
leticism, and academic successes characteristic of the day child. She
applied "night child" to that side of herself harboring unspeakable
shame, dirty secrets, and terror. The night child could hardly sleep.
The night child could not speak. But Marilyn's day child was completely unaware of all this. Neither side knew about the other. The
incest memories were stored in only one half of Marilyn's consciousness. "During the days," Marilyn told her audience, "no embarrassed
or angry glances ever passed between my father and me, because I, the
'day child,' had no conscious knowledge of the traumas and the terrors of the 'night child.' . . . I believed I was the happiest person who
ever lived. I truly believed that."

Marilyn was twenty-four years old before her memories returned.
The occasion was a lunch in Beverly Hills with an old friend, the
Reverend D. D. Harvey, who had at one time run the youth group
Marilyn attended at the Montview Boulevard Presbyterian Church, in
Denver. Marilyn was in Los Angeles to make TV commercials for
"The Bell Telephone Hour," and the Reverend Mr. Harvey, who had
moved to Los Angeles and was now a counselor for Synanon, invited
her to lunch. Since becoming a spokeswoman for AT&T, Marilyn had
come to Los Angeles a number of times to make commercials, but she

had avoided D. D. Harvey. This time he insisted. He wanted to ask her something. Many adult victims of child abuse took part in Synanon's drug-rehabilitation program, and Harvey worked with a number of them. He had suspected for years that something was wrong with Marilyn, and now he thought he knew what it was. At lunch he brought up the subject of incest. Marilyn fell into instant sobs. Just the mention of the word triggered a huge outpouring of forgotten emotion. Choked out through the tears, Marilyn's first words to the minister were "Don't tell anybody."

"Who is it that you do not want to tell?"

"Larry."

"Then he is the only one we *have* to tell," Harvey responded.

Larry Atler was by now an attorney in Denver. His relationship with Marilyn had been an on-again/off-again thing. In fact, the year she finished college Marilyn had married a former University of Colorado football player. The marriage lasted all of three months, and then Marilyn went back to Larry, as she had so often done before. When the Reverend Mr. Harvey telephoned Larry, he agreed to fly to Los Angeles immediately. Marilyn found it almost impossible to discuss with him in concrete detail what had happened between her father and her. But Larry understood quickly and offered her all the comfort she could have desired. They married two years later.

Marilyn Van Derbur's split into "day child" and "night child" is a defense occasionally employed by young children enduring very long or repeated traumas. Like all psychological defenses, splitting can be used for purposes other than warding off traumas, but it is ordinarily set up by child abuse or other extremes of family dysfunction. When children are past the toddler stage, they become able to attribute "good" and "bad" qualities to other people and to themselves. If they experience a severe trauma at the age of two or three, they may have to wait until the age of four or five to develop this capacity more fully and then to split.

Young "splitters of the object"—those who divide their views of others—show extreme rage alternating with good humor. Such a child may hit the teacher while being scolded. "She's a witch," the child thinks. But later the child may be particularly gracious to the same teacher as she gives out cookies. "She's an angel," the child thinks. This behavior often stems from an attempt to handle the overly exciting yet horrible feelings engendered by an abusive parent or caretaker while retaining the memories of gentleness and kindness displayed by the same abuser. The child has trouble justifying two diametrically opposed feelings. The feelings are therefore sequestered, one from the other, and the child is aware of only one set of feelings at a given time.

Splitting of the object is seen particularly in those people burdened with what psychiatrists diagnose as "borderline personality." The term refers to people who behave erratically, angrily, and moodily and who harbor radically shifting views about key individuals in their lives. The "borderline" diagnosis has recently been correlated with child abuse—although many individuals prey to early abuse fall far short of borderline characteristics. A number of victims of child abuse use the defense of splitting, however; as a result, they often end up with holes in their memories.

But splitting of the object was not the kind of splitting Marilyn Van Derbur Atler described to her Kempe benefit audience on the night of May 8, 1991. She said that she had split herself. The Cambridge, Massachusetts, psychiatrist J. Christopher Perry, a leading defense theorist, has written that when people split their own persona they demonstrate "contradictory views, expectations [of themselves], and feelings . . . that cannot be reconciled into one coherent whole." A day child plus a night child, in other words, does not equal a whole child. Children define their split selves as "sick" and "healthy"; "old" and "young"; "smart" and "stupid"; "helpless" and "powerful"; really any set of opposites. Most commonly, children split "bad" from "good."

The child who employs "splitting of the self" considers the unwanted side a kind of gangrenous appendage, and tries to cut it off. This mental amputation costs the child fullness of character, mental energy, and considerable memory; the sick, or bad, or night side remains intact though hidden—as though the child had to drag around a rotten, half-severed limb. Children who split lose awareness of the link between their "selves." For instance, they will attribute certain characteristics to a doll or an imaginary playmate, but they do not recognize these characteristics as their own.

Some children who split themselves can go further than Marilyn Van Derbur ever did. They may break off more characteristics—hopeless ones, dependent ones, and angry ones, for instance. They may dissociate along with their splitting, temporarily stepping away from thinking, from bodily processes, from the world altogether, while in the guise of one persona or the other. If the splitting and dissociation is frequent, the child will be unable to account for time. He or she will repeatedly exhibit gaps in both short-term and long-term memory. There will also be, perhaps, gaps in learning—in such areas as arithmetic or history, for example. The combination of dissociation with splitting is one of the few defensive clusters that can affect priming, conditioning, and knowledge-and-skills memory as well as episodic memory—the memory of events. The person may develop the condition known as multiple-personality disorder, or MPD. At the center of this very grave condition lie problems with memory.

Childhood splitting frequently combines with the defense of displacement. The child who employs displacement redirects his powerful feelings or impulses toward an object less emotionally charged. This leads during development to the imaginary playmate, a perfectly normal phenomenon in the lives of five-year-olds.

Here is an extreme example of displacement by a traumatized child: Markie Stanton (as I shall call him) was seven years old when his father was severely injured in a car crash. Markie's father lingered, brain dead, in the hospital for two months before his death. For the next two years, Markie invariably slept with a plush elephant he called "Li'l Boy." If the real boy Markie went anywhere, "Li'l Boy" had to come along too.

I met Markie when he was nine. At first I thought that "Li'l Boy" was a typical transitional object, like a blanket or a teddy bear. I soon learned, however, that the bereaved boy had valiantly attended his father's gruesome bedside at the hospital, gone through the funeral, and helped his mother afterward in as grown-up a way as he could. At age nine, Markie was acting far too adult. At seven, he had split, dividing "young" from "old" and turning over all his childishness to the stuffed animal he called "Li'l Boy."

Markie suffered because of his split. His peers did not especially like him. His schoolwork was not as brilliant as it might have been, because he feared he might make a mistake. Not only did his splitting defense fail to grant him relief from his unhappy memories but it deprived him of friendship and self-esteem.

Like Markie Stanton, Marilyn Van Derbur Atler suffered a number of problems related to her split. The day child would never take a nap, she said in her Kempe benefit speech. The idea of general anesthesia was unbearable to her. She dreaded sleep. And in fact the night child awoke almost every night at 2:00 A.M., sensing a male intruder in her room. "Sleep," she told her audience, "is when a man can do anything he wants with you and you have no power."

Marilyn and Larry's only child, Jennifer, was born when Marilyn was thirty-four. It was a difficult breech delivery, but Marilyn allowed no anesthesia. When Jennifer turned five, Marilyn experienced a surge of mental symptoms in physical disguise. She lived through a long bout of paralysis, lying immobile for several weeks while her mind worked overtime. She gradually realized that these problems were related to Jennifer's age. Her daughter was now as old as she had been when her father first abused her. Jennifer's age had acted as a memory cue. Marilyn's memories of sexual abuse were largely sensory memories—bodily sensations that reflected her physical feelings at the time the abuses were taking place—and they were the only memories Marilyn reported in her public revelation of May 8.

When Jennifer entered puberty, Marilyn began to suffer excruciating pains in her back, chest, and legs, and on her skin. Again, Jennifer's age had cued her to the agonies she had experienced at the same age. She often sobbed uncontrollably. By now she had remembered the incest for more than twenty years, but the pain had grown right along with the child Jennifer. Marilyn's speaking career virtually stopped. She sought a number of types of psychotherapy, including groups and individual treatment. She was hospitalized more than once. She could see no way out.

Marilyn was forty-six years old when Francis S. Van Derbur died. The person who had caused her problems permanently disappeared, but the problems stayed with her, and in fact became worse. "In deep despair, I was often dysfunctional for long periods of time," she told her Kempe benefit listeners, "I looked upon death as peace—as a release from a mind and body that could no longer contain the agony." Near the end of her prepared text, Marilyn expressed her wrenching ambivalence about Francis S. Van Derbur. "I loved my father," she said.


I have watched the Miss America Pageant enough times to know the routine—evening gowns, bathing suits, a prize for the most congenial contestant, the talent show, talking with the finalists, and then the swift elimination down to the one beautiful girl, the one who cries and walks the ramp with a crown, wrap, and roses. But in the fall of 1957, when they selected the 1958 Miss America, I was not watching. I was in medical school.

In 1991, when Marilyn made her public announcement, I decided to watch—to collect some clippings and record what I couldn't catch of Marilyn directly. I had found her "splitting" fascinating. Splitting is an unusual enough defense in adults to claim my attention, especially when the splitter is a highly successful individual without obvious MPD or borderline personality. Then, too, I found myself equally fascinated with Marilyn's three sisters. Had they split, too? It seemed highly unlikely that the other Van Derbur girls had been spared their father's warped attentions. What kind of defense had they used? I found myself as much interested in Marilyn's sisters' memories as in Marilyn's. If the chance presented itself, I would try to interview one of Marilyn's sisters.

The June 10, 1991, issue of *People* featured a small section on Boots Van Derbur in an article about Marilyn's revelation. Boots said that in retrospect she could remember moments when her husband had left their bedroom to make sure the girls were falling asleep. Boots recalled that after he had ostensibly rubbed their backs or sat with them talking, he would return to his bed saying, "The girls will sure sleep good now." It never occurred to Mrs. Van Derbur to question her husband. "In those days," she said, "we didn't even think about those things."

Those things. Boots inadvertently reveals a problem here. She could not say the pertinent word. Boots was still in the grip of denial (*Verleugnung*), a mental defense that cancels or negates external reality. The person cannot later remember an unpleasant event because she has attached no emotional significance to it. What is perceived as insignificant may not even get into what we know as episodic memory.

When Van "rubbed" the girls to get them to sleep, Boots did not wonder. When he came back to his bed (they did not share one), Boots did not ask. Later in their lives, Boots and Van slept in separate rooms. But at the time "things" started happening, Boots did not let the odd behavior going on in her own bedroom enter her mind as meaningful. Denial stops memory before it gets much of a start. Mrs. Van Derbur sniffed danger but then extinguished any related imaginings. Very little registered. By denying, Boots saved her marriage. But by denying she also imperiled her daughters.

The city of Denver, in a kind of communal denial, did not unanimously respond to Marilyn's startling Kempe benefit speech with empathy or belief. Denver radio talk-show callers asked such things as "Why should we believe her?" Or "Why did she wait to tell her story until Francis Van Derbur died?" Or "Is she just trying to be famous again?" Marilyn had described several symptoms that bore out her memories. But Denver did not unanimously accept these symptoms as evidence that her memories were true.

Convincing confirmation arrived, however, three days after Marilyn's speech. On May 11, Fawn Germer, of the *Rocky Mountain News,* reported a phone interview with Gwen Mitchell, Marilyn's oldest sister, who had moved to California. Gwen said that she, too, had been sexually abused by Francis S. Van Derbur. But unlike Marilyn, Gwen had always remembered.

This strong external confirmation broke through the city's denial. Denver stored a long-term memory of significance. Gwen Mitchell was an attorney working in estate planning in the affluent Bay Area town of Hillsborough, Bing Crosby's hometown. Gwen had been married twice—for seventeen years in Kansas City to the father of her two children, and then for nineteen years in California to her current husband. She had experienced anxiety attacks toward the end of her first marriage. But Gwen offered more than her symptoms as evidence of incest. She actually remembered the incest, which had begun when she was seven and continued until she was eighteen. She had always remembered. She did not tell anyone about it until she was thirty years old and Marilyn, then twenty-four, approached her about her amazing return of awareness. Until that moment, Gwen had assumed that she was the only abused child in the family. Gwen told Fawn Germer that with this realization she had developed guilt about her silence and had vowed to back her younger sisters whenever they needed it.

Incest and other forms of unwanted sex are the most tightly held secrets a child can have. For some reason, youngsters know, without being told, that they must keep quiet about this kind of thing. Gwen Van Derbur had apparently imposed this prohibition on herself without any overt threats or mandates from her father. She kept quiet until her sister came to see her.

Gwen had had to back Marilyn on one other occasion. In 1985, a year after their father died, Marilyn tried to inform her mother about the incest. "It's in your fantasy," Boots Van Derbur had responded. Boots' dismissal was intolerable to Marilyn, and Marilyn reported it to Gwen, who phoned Boots and then went to visit her in Denver, revealing to her mother at this point that Francis Van Derbur had abused her, too. Mrs. Van Derbur had no choice but to believe. Her denial broke.

Before Gwen Mitchell went into estate planning full time, she handled a few child-custody cases in the San Francisco courts, and, as it happened, we had once worked on the same case. When I phoned her, Gwen said she was very willing to be interviewed. And thus my plans unfolded. I would compare what could be gleaned from Marilyn's television appearances and public statements with my own interview of Gwen. I would concentrate on the question of why Marilyn's memory had been lost while Gwen's memory remained. I would try to understand why and how two people from the same family would defend themselves so differently from virtually the same kind of trauma. And I would try to learn how much each woman remembered now.

Childhood incest is one of the most difficult traumas for adults to remember. Incest feels particularly shameful. It engenders tremendous loyalty conflicts. And it can be anticipated. The young victim *knows* another incestuous episode is going to happen. The perpetrator, after all, has continual access to the child. So the child anticipates. A little girl may self-hypnotize—for example, she may count dots on the ceiling or repeatedly say her prayers. She may also use visualization of other scenes in order to dissociate. Or she may split. The child readies herself. She cannot stand the idea that somebody she loves is coming once again to overexcite and scare her. And she cannot stand her own response.

In the years that followed Marilyn's realization that her dad had abused her, she did recapture a few episodic memories of the abuse. "There were days," she told Maria Shriver on NBC's "First Person," "when all of a sudden a memory would come back of what my father had done to me. And it was so horrific to me and so unacceptable to me that I would—I would say in therapy, 'I have no place to put that in my head! I have no place to put that in my head!'" Even after Marilyn became aware of some of her early memories, she could not tolerate her own awareness. Her immediate impulses continued to run toward defense.

It quickly became apparent to me that the Marilyn I was meeting in the press and on TV was not the entire woman. This was "day child" all the way. Because Marilyn's day child incorporated only parts of her personality and memories, the whole Marilyn Van Derbur Atler, I began to realize, might be hard to know. I had done this kind of indirect analysis before, writing in 1989 about Stephen King and basing the analysis on his books and films and the statements he made in interviews. But King was very different from Marilyn—he answered any question his interviewers asked him, even if the answer was personally revealing. Marilyn appeared to guard herself closely. She often used the exact same words in various widely spaced appearances, as if she had prepared her remarks in advance and then memorized them. She did not answer everything asked. Many times she graciously changed the subject.

There is no doubt about it—the "day child" was still extraordinarily beautiful. In her early fifties, Marilyn was tall and thin, athletic and trim. Her graying hair, lighter in front and darker toward the back, was sleeky brushed up and away from the handsome face. On TV, she seemed to be making intense eye contact with her interviewers. A dimple perpetually played in her left cheek, adding oomph to her frequent smiles and exclamation points to her heavily underlined words. She wore striking clothes—a white suit with a black collar and brown lapels for her appearance with Sally Jessy Raphaël, for instance, or, for *Newsweek,* a blue-and-white striped blouse that perfectly matched her eyes, so reminiscent of her father's.

The day child's *Social Register* upbringing showed on TV. She behaved with grace and charm to all. When Jennifer, Larry, and Lynda Mead Shay, a former Miss America with whom Marilyn had become friends, joined Marilyn on the Sally Jessy Raphaël show, Marilyn made a point of holding hands with each of them as they took the seat next to her. She turned to the other guests easily, including them in what she said.

The day child's professional attention to speech—Marilyn had been a successful motivational speaker after her five-year AT&T television contract ran out—also showed. She spoke as if some of her words were composed of capital letters. (In a printed copy of Marilyn's Kempe benefit speech, certain phrases are actually spelled out this way.) Marilyn also repeated her language for emphasis: "never, never," or "*if* and *only if*," or "I didn't *know*. I *didn't* know." On the Sally Jessy Raphaël show, she received a spontaneous ovation from the studio audience for her recitation of a self-help creed for incest survivors, which she delivered with great style, flawless timing, and heavy verbal underlining. One could conclude that the day child, to compensate for the muteness of the night child, was almost fanatically attentive to the ways and means of speech.

Francis S. Van Derbur did not give her any significant daytime attention, Marilyn told her public. As a result, the day child pushed herself harder and harder to win his approval. As Miss America, Marilyn sometimes made twenty appearances in one day. Today, as an advocate for adults who were sexually abused by their parents as children, she works at an extraordinary pace. All this work has apparently been, in part, an effort to impress Francis S. Van Derbur—even if only his ghost.

"I just wanted him to put his arm around me once," she told Maria Shriver. "There was a part of me that believed that 'Maybe tomorrow. Maybe if I cooked one more dish, maybe if I walked his dog just one more time, maybe today would be the day that he would love me.'" Nothing Marilyn did seemed to inspire ordinary fatherly love in Francis S. But she tried and tried. "I graduated Phi Beta Kappa, won Miss America, skied on the University of Colorado ski team. It's just exhausting," she said to Sally Jessy Raphaël.

Marilyn's day child indulged in a number of daredevil activities in her youth, such as breaking and training horses and ski racing. In an article in the September 1991 *McCall's,* she noted that this "fight-to-the-death kind of courage" was the day child's way to balance the night child's silent passivity. Whatever she did, however, Marilyn's day child appeared to do it for her father. She told the viewers of "Good Afternoon, Colorado" that each time she excelled at something she would say to herself, "Do you love me now, Daddy? I'm Miss America. Do you love me now, Daddy?"

In a June 1991 interview in the *Denver Post,* D. D. Harvey explained why he had long suspected that something was wrong with Marilyn. Beginning in her teens, she wouldn't let him get close, he said. "That constant smile, repeated references to her storybook life, idolization of her father, and insistence on distance from others" had alerted him. As an adult, Marilyn's friendship with the minister was "always on the run." On many occasions, she inexplicably "would pull away" and "sometimes avoid" him. In fact, whenever the young Marilyn was with Harvey, she kept a physical barrier—a chair, say, or a table—between them.

Because the night child had lost control of her life, Marilyn Van Derbur's day child took control—and hung onto it into adulthood. Marilyn seemed unable to abdicate, even for an instant. She prepared even when preparation did not seem necessary. In a "diary" chronicling the year that followed her Kempe benefit speech, published in two installments in the *Rocky Mountain News,* Marilyn writes of spending a whole day with a producer of "First Person" in order to get ready for her interview with Maria Shriver. She also writes about working with Roseanne Arnold for six weeks in the summer of 1991, in order to prepare for Roseanne's public announcement of her own childhood incest. It was up to Marilyn to manage the media for the indomitable Roseanne. "Maybe I'm the only one who believes we can pull this off," Marilyn writes in the *Rocky Mountain News.* But the day child did indeed "pull it off." She could conjure up inexhaustible energy for such things.

If a child has no options in dealing with a father who keeps her captive in her own house, she may well need to call the shots in whatever other situations she can. It was clear to me, for instance, that Sally Jessy Raphaël had to play by Marilyn's rules, not vice versa. The talk-show hostess gingerly stepped around the day child's sensibilities, accepting silence in answer to "What happened at night?" ("But I'm wondering if the night child hid under the bed? Or pretended it [the night child] wasn't there? Or stayed out [at night] so nobody could come into the room?") Her acceptance of Marilyn's silence was unusual for this particular talk-show hostess, who is a feisty person capable of persistent cross-examination. Perhaps Marilyn had set some rules in advance. The clincher came when, after Marilyn failed to respond, Sally asked her, "Have you answered these in your *own* mind? I won't ask you to answer them for *me.*" Marilyn did not answer this last question, either. There wasn't much doubt about who was running the show.

The day child's trust in the media of television and newspapers was coupled with a puzzling distrust of books. "As long as there is a camera available and a reporter with a pencil, I will keep [my] message alive," she told Fawn Germer of the *Rocky Mountain News.* "If I am told tomorrow that there are another eight interviews for me, I will do another eight." But Marilyn would authorize no books, nor would she write one herself. "I'm not about to go into my family with a microscope, and a publisher is not interested in a book unless you have the *National Enquirer* mentality," she said in the same interview. Marilyn appeared to prefer any medium in which she felt she could manage the process. The drafting and redrafting procedures in the book industry, with the attendant advertising and publicity, must have made the day child feel that she would be less personally in charge.

Marilyn's day child was her dominant, more fully realized half. Her split had not only caused her memories of incest to disappear until she was twenty-four but had also made it impossible for her to remember how she had managed to divide herself in the first place. She writes in *McCall's* that she doesn't know how she forgot. But her split must have sequestered a number of her episodic memories and made them well-nigh impossible to retrieve. Her memories of emotions and physical pain appeared to be more vivid than whatever smells, sounds, words, or quick mental snapshots she could recall. For example, Marilyn told Carol Kreck, of the *Denver Post,* that revisiting the house she had lived in until she was ten years old had not triggered any memory reclamation. The owner of the house let Marilyn come in after she paid him a hundred dollars in cash. The same heavy purple velvet draperies still hung at the windows. "I was terrorized as I walked from room to room," she said. "I had no memory of certain rooms. I had hoped for flashbacks, but none came—just feelings of terror and doom."

From what Marilyn told her ever-growing audiences, the "night child" was the half of herself that harbored all the traumatic memories. This night child lived in only one place, the bedroom. Perhaps if Marilyn had spent the night trying to sleep in that old room where she had spent her early years, she might have remembered something. But it was the day child who had come with her hundred dollars in cash to these rooms. And, as Marilyn said, the day child had little access to her nighttime persona.

"You have to make up a fantasy world you live in," Marilyn told *Newsweek,* speaking of the day child's attempts to compensate for the lack of coherent memories. "And you need it to survive." But Marilyn's day child lost something in the process of separating herself from her most horrible experiences. In the *Rocky Mountain News* "diary," Marilyn reports an encounter with a woman who had waited in line for a glimpse of her after one of her post-revelation public appearances: "Are you real?" the woman asked. "Are you really real?" Perhaps the questioner wondered about Marilyn's unshakable invulnerability, confidence, and control—her flawless presence. Here was a magazine cover come to life.

I watched for cracks in Marilyn's day-child façade on TV and in print. Perhaps through a crack I might view the beleaguered night child. But there were no real cracks, just a few thin spots, the most obvious being the strange dichotomy between her poise and self-assurance and the terrible sense of shame she described. She told a number of reporters that being Miss America had been especially difficult for her, because she always felt that her audiences were judging her. "Although I was painfully shy, my need to be the best . . . put me in the spotlight even though I was never, never comfortable there," she says in *McCall's*. Much of Marilyn's life was haunted by this dichotomy. She avoided getting close to people, yet she exhibited herself to them from a great distance. She states in *McCall's* that one of the best parts of being Miss America, as far as Marilyn's night child was concerned, was that everywhere Miss America went, a chaperone went, too.

When Marilyn married Larry, he instructed his warm and loving family never to touch her. He had known about the Van Derbur incest problem for two years, and he realized that the night child shrank from physical contact. Marilyn writes in her newspaper diary that it took several years for her to allow any demonstrative affection to flow from the Atlers toward herself. Much of her physical standoffishness must have been the night child's aversion to Mr. Van Derbur's dreaded nighttime touch. And Marilyn confirms this by alluding in her newspaper diary to having suffered (unspecified) sexual difficulties as an adult.

Shortly, after Marilyn began her reign as Miss America, she refused to allow publication of a commercial photograph for which she had posed, unconsciously sensing that this photo revealed the night child. The photo, which was reproduced in *People,* shows Marilyn in a white low-backed gown with a pointy bra. Dark moistened lips beckon beneath sleepy eyes. A couple of tendrils fall down and away from the upswept hairdo. This photo represents everything that the day child hated in her other half: invitation, awareness, messiness, and experience. The only aspect of the night child that does not show in Marilyn's hated photo is how shy, how very shy, she felt.

Marilyn's night child could not speak. Rather than describing her split as "day child/night child," Marilyn might have called the two parts of herself "speaking child/mute child." Marilyn, as a survivor of child abuse, wants now "to speak for children and for the mute adults who never were able to speak" ("Good Afternoon, Colorado"). The night child's speechless frustration was expressed in a quote from Oliver Wendell Holmes engraved, according to Gwen, for a number of years on Marilyn's personal stationery: "Alas for those who do not sing but die with all their music in them." In her early adulthood, Marilyn was the one dying with her personal feelings still unexpressed.

One wonders if many of the mute night child's memories were laid down as nondeclarative, or implicit, memories. Such memories could not have been retrieved in words. The stories Marilyn told the media strongly suggested that her father must have assaulted several different parts of her body. Her nighttime memories may well have been implicitly formed—planted time after time and then stored via entirely nonverbal pathways. For months during her daughter's adolescence, for instance, Marilyn's "skin screamed." This is a good way to describe how a child's skin feels after repeated and unwelcome touching. Of her feelings during Jennifer's adolescence Marilyn told Maria Shriver, "For me, the hardest part was my body feeling like it was going to blow up. I felt like a ghetto blaster with eighteen rock stations on all at the same time." When a father stimulates a little girl incestuously, she often feels shamed, humiliated, pained, angry, and excited all at once. What depicts such a cacophony of feelings more graphically than Marilyn's "ghetto blaster"?

In a therapy group she attended while Jennifer was growing up, Marilyn was asked to bring a doll to one of the sessions. She purchased a soft, almost bodiless doll and impulsively erased its mouth with white-out—not only, she said, because of the doll's inability to speak but also because of "what goes *in* the mouth." She writes in *McCall's* that during the same period she visited a practitioner of the deep-massage therapy known as rolfing. Marilyn felt "something" strange inside her left thigh, and asked her rolfer to get it out. When the rolfer inquired what the "thing" was, Marilyn used a word that both Shakespeare and Freud would have found of interest. "An asp," she said.

In the summer of 1984, when she and Larry took six teenagers including their daughter to Laguna Beach, Marilyn awoke in excruciating pain, feeling "as if I had an ax embedded in my anus." She hurt even when she was standing up. The problem, which was purely emotional, lasted for several days.

The night child was assaulted so intensely and so repeatedly that there was barely a part of her body that belonged solely to her. This brings the Marilyn-watcher to the sensations of crawly, overwhelming terror in the night child's implicit-memory bank. In her speech on behalf of the Kempe Center, Marilyn speaks of her fright as "what one would feel if locked into a small room with poisonous snakes." Her day child kept an explicit, declarative memory that strongly echoed the inchoate implicit fright of the other half. "Once I watched him [her father] pick up a small chow puppy that had disobeyed and throw it like a football over a back fence," she writes in *McCall's.* "The puppy was too terrified even to yelp." It is a testament to how well split Marilyn was that this violent incident did not evoke, at the time, any memory of her own violation.

Marilyn herself could not yelp. Nor could she disobey. She could remember the puppy incident, but she cannot remember much of what happened to *her* as a "young pup." Her defensive split destroyed many painful memories. And her consistently nonverbal behaviors and thoughts as a "night child" may have sent even more of her perceptions up entirely nonverbal pathways. Her language refers to her youthful ordeals again and again: "asps," "poisonous snakes," "pups," and "yelps" are things that populate the horror worlds of terrified children.

Marilyn does not know how she originally split. She speaks nowhere publicly about having an imaginary playmate or liking dolls enough to attribute her own characteristics to them. But most people who experience memory returns do not recapture the essence of how they originally made their memories go away. Their techniques escape retrieval, even after the memories themselves come back. What is left of Marilyn's splitting technique is often an intellectual description, based partly on what therapists have said to her about how a person might erase a memory. Marilyn frequently says that she "dissociated," alternating this word with the word "splitting," and even using the two words synonymously. The glossary of defenses published by the American Psychiatric Association considers these two defenses to be entirely separate and different. And certainly in childhood each defense is distinct. Marilyn did not have a dissociative disorder—she was not, for instance, a multiple personality. She apparently suffered no blank spells at school; she was an outstanding student and graduated at the top of her class at Denver's East High. No teacher seems to have caught her out of touch or mentally absent. She has not spoken of self-hypnosis or of going into trances. Whenever I saw her on TV, in fact, she was totally in touch, intensely engaged with her interviewer. If she dissociated, it happened well beyond the view of any television hostess or newspaper reporter.

A synchronized use of splitting and dissociation is the defining characteristic of multiple personality. In MPD, the host personality is vaguely aware that there are alien aspects to himself. He may feel under outside influences, often hearing the voices of these influences. He suffers amnesia for various periods of time, during which he acts in the name of split-off "alters." The host personality is frequently absolutely unaware of what the alters do. The person may, for instance, discover a dent in his car and not know how it happened. He may go off shopping and subsequently have no idea, when the bill comes, of what he bought or where it is. Other people will say he is excessively moody—or that his voice or dress or demeanor changes drastically from time to time. Sometimes he even gives names to the various sides of himself. He does not have a comfortable or well-formed sense of identity.

But Marilyn Van Derbur Atler displayed none of this extreme shifting of personality and memory. Nor did she reveal anything about such a history. There was a certain inevitable sameness to her. She told many of the same stories over and over, using the same language. She told her audiences that she had vacillated in her earlier years, in her relationship with Larry and her friendship with D. D. Harvey. But this unpredictability does not sound like the kind of radical alterations one sees in MPD. Even though she used the identical defenses, Marilyn, it seems, was spared the fate of "Sybil" and "Eve."

Marilyn probably dissociated when her father entered her room at night. And she depended on her simple splitting maneuvers to put her memories out of mind by the next morning. Like Marilyn, most traumatized youngsters who split tend to indulge in very simple maneuvers, and they do not ordinarily develop multiple personalities. One such child, a beautiful little Asian girl who had been abused for about a year by a neighbor, told me she wanted to be a blue-eyed blonde. She had at least considered splitting into what she saw as a pure creature as opposed to a dark, impure one. Another of my patients, five-year-old "Evie Jessop," had been sexually misused for several months when she was two by a man who hung around her day-care center. She was just getting started with her splitting when we met. Sometimes Evie accused her parents of being "not nice." Later she abruptly changed her mind, saying that they were "the nicest people in the world." Evie's parents wondered at her new behavior. The child had also started drawing picture after picture of hearts. For the six months before she came to see me, hearts of pastel colors were all, in fact, that young Evie would draw.

By the time I met the Jessops, the man from the day-care center was serving a sentence in San Quentin for sexually abusing another child. Though months earlier Evie had remembered her abuses—she had spoken to her parents of such things as "poop on the stairs," "yucky stuff in my mouth," and "chasing and hurting"—more recently she had behaved as if she had forgotten it all.

When I asked Evie why she preferred drawing pictures of hearts to pictures of people, animals, or houses, the little girl said, "Hearts are nice."

"What about the things that used to happen in the back of your day-care?" I asked her, at a different time.

"Not nice," she said.

Evie Jessop appeared to be making very sharp distinctions between "nice" and "not nice." She had recently stopped taking naps at preschool; "not nice," she said. She feared strangers—"not nice." She hated the four-year-old bully at her Montessori program—"not nice." It looked as if Evie Jessop's distinctions about the world fit into just two categories.

Evie's splitting had started shortly before I met her. The child did not have a long head start. She had not split herself, as far as we could tell—just others. Her parents and I would catch up before Evie got much further.

Evie drew myriads of pastel hearts in my waiting room before each of her appointments. When she brought them into my office, I scribbled squiggles inside some of them and added whorls around their boundaries. I put black crayon to the insides of a few. "Hearts are very interesting," I suggested. "Some are deep and dark. Some are messy." Evie inspected her altered pictures with great care. She took some home.

Our plan was to show Evie that things could be both "not nice" and "nice" at the same time. We demonstrated our point through her hearts. People could be both good and bad all at once, I wanted Evie to know. She had many interesting qualities and would grow up fine without chopping off all her "not nice" parts. It was O.K. to feel feelings, even the bad ones. By scribbling on her hearts and adding shades and nuances, I showed Evie Jessop that her parents and I liked her a lot, whether she was "nice" or "not." She was both of these and much more. In about a month, Evie stopped drawing hearts and began to draw people. She told her mom that she loved and hated her all at once. We knew Evie was well on her way to recovery. There would not be two Evie Jessops.

Splitting is not in any sense a disease. It is a mechanism. Someone who splits is not a "split personality"—the old misnomer for schizophrenics. Nor is he necessarily a multiple personality. Splitting seems to become possible when children project their own qualities onto imaginary companions or superheroes, as many normal children do. No memory loss is inherent in splitting. But *any* defense can be used to effect forgetting, splitting included.

Marilyn Van Derbur appeared to have lost many of her memories as a result of her split. She may have lost the memories because her mute night child did not rehearse them in words. She may have also dissociated by night ("My mind left my body," she told the *Denver Post*), and that, too, would have helped her to drift away from memory. In Evie Jessop's case, splitting, in and of itself, began to take away memory. Once we intervened, Evie no longer forgot. She began speaking again about what had happened to her at the day-care center. "The man put arrows on the floor," she told me. "He made us come to where he was. I was angry at Mommy and Daddy. They let him scare me." Was Evie better off forgetting? I think not. With her past partly out on the table, we could begin to deal with it. Evie spent four weeks painting a magnificent picture of a monkey named Abu (herself), lost and alone in the Cave of Wonders (the day-care center) getting in trouble out of Aladdin's (her parents') sight. Evie was now working on her problem in a productive fashion. "Aladdin couldn't help what happened to Abu," she told me. "He didn't know what was going on."

When Marilyn Van Derbur was young, she apparently did not have the benefit of psychotherapy. Her splitting made many of her nighttime experiences fall into the night child's black hole. And her dissociation must have put the experiences through a filter that let only her sensory memories and a few episodic memories register. The childhood memories that Marilyn offered her listeners and readers were disconnected and broken bits. Considering the defenses to which she admitted, this fragmentation was to be expected. What D. D. Harvey had elicited from Marilyn at age twenty-four was uncontrollable and massive emotion. But it was not coherent memory. Amputated experiences make for impoverished memories, at best.

Marilyn used one other defense that deserves note—projective identification. It, too, interferes with memory. As Jennifer Atler grew up, Marilyn unconsciously attributed her own memories to her child, even though Jennifer herself was never abused. Marilyn then reacted to what she saw as Jennifer's "abused-child" characteristics with inner rage. She confided her discomfort about the then seventeen-year-old Jennifer to Gwen one day when the two sisters were talking alone. "Why doesn't Jennifer say 'No'?" Gwen remembers Marilyn asking. Or, in reference to a friend's aggression, "Why doesn't she fight back? She's big. She doesn't have to lie down and take it."

In Marilyn's mind, Jennifer's developmental stages reflected Marilyn's own development. Marilyn told *People* that when Jennifer reached the age of five, "I'd tell Larry, 'I don't love her anymore.' It would take ten years for me to understand that in Jennifer I was seeing myself as a five-year-old." Marilyn had remembered her abuse long before this point in Jennifer's life, but her projective-identification defense prevented her from seeing the obvious link between herself at five and her daughter at five.

Marilyn also gave a striking example of projective identification in her Kempe Center benefit speech. "When Jennifer was about eleven," Marilyn said, "she fell asleep in our bed. Larry leaned over to try to scoop her up in his arms. She was growing fast, and her arms and legs were long and dangling. As he picked her up, I was flooded with overwhelming feelings. I was enraged at her. How could she allow herself to fall into a deep sleep and not know what was being done to her? She didn't even know someone was picking her up."

Marilyn had projected her own childhood tragedy onto her husband and child. Projecting a lost experience onto another person makes the memory clearer, the way a bright light clarifies dark film. But by attributing the experience to somebody else, it also becomes distanced and disconnected. With projective identification, Marilyn simultaneously conjured up and defended against her night child's memory.

Marilyn used other objects besides Jennifer for her projective identifications. As a child, she hated dolls and would not play with them. To Sally Jessy Raphaël she confessed, "I hated dolls because you can do anything you want to a doll and the doll has no power." In many ways, other people's suffering was more real to Marilyn Van Derbur than her own. Other people's plights—even a doll's plight—come with intact beginnings, middles, and ends. Marilyn's own story never seemed to line up that way.


On a Saturday morning in May of 1992, I drove down to Hillsborough to talk to Marilyn's older sister. Gwen Mitchell, tall and relaxed in a tailored dark-blue oversize blazer and a pair of wheat-colored slacks, did not have any memories that ran like films, even though she had always remembered her ordeals with her father. Gwen did keep a number of mental photos, however, in her album of episodic memories. "I have a photograph like a click in my mind," she said. "I know what I felt and exactly what was in the room the first time my dad abused me. My grandparents—my father's parents—owned a ranch up in Fairplay, Colorado. And in summertime, as children, we—one or two of us—would go up there and spend some time. I was about seven—though this is a little hard to pinpoint. Seven is a guess." She paused a moment, seeming to inspect her memory. "It was a second-floor bedroom. The head of the bed was against a wall. And then, if you were lying in the bed you faced a window looking over a roof on the porch below."

Gwen Mitchell connected her own precise placement in space with her memories of the most shocking moment of her childhood—her initiation. She was "about seven"—an unspecific age. Age is a vague

part of childhood memory. During our early years, we do not think of
ourselves as a certain age—just as a certain size, or as in a certain
grade in school, or as living in a certain house. Physical placement, on
the other hand, is very exact in memory, especially in memories
formed under terrifying circumstances. To defend yourself to the
death, you do not need to know exactly how old you are—just your
approximate size relative to the threat—but you *do* need to know
your own position. Your position helps you to plot defensive action or
a retreat. Your position can save your life.

Little Gwen Van Derbur woke up in Fairplay, Colorado, utterly
surprised and confused. "I awakened," the sixty-year-old exhaled a
long sigh, "in the middle of the night as I was, uh, working toward,
um, an orgasm."

Gwen turned to me, asking whether children actually have
"those." She laughed in discomfort. Here was a Van Derbur family
trait—the Van Derbur women apparently had trouble saying specific
words related to sexual matters. I told her that children do have
orgasms of a kind. Particularly if introduced to sex by adults or older
children, very young children may get "hooked" on the increasing
motions, the pressures, and the rhythms that build to release. Otherwise, most very young children fiddle with themselves a bit but are
not totally committed to orgasm.

"I woke up feeling an accelerated feeling," Gwen continued. "And
my father was manipulating me with his fingers. And when I understood what was happening—ah, uh, a horrible feeling went through
me. I knew instantly, even though I was young, that this was *wrong.*
This was *bad.* I shut off my feelings, just like that. And I have to tell
you that the shut-off has had a lifelong impact on my ability to have
an orgasm with a man."

"How did you manage to shut off?" I wanted to understand what
had happened at age seven or eight to Gwen.

"I just *stopped,*" Gwen said. "I closed down. I went rigid, I'm sure.
And, um, I've never forgotten it. I don't know if this was the worst
moment of my life, but it sure had an effect on everything that followed."

Gwen dissociated precisely at the moment she felt herself gathering sexual momentum. She dissociated far more precisely than her
younger sister must have done. Only one particular circumstance
triggered it—moving toward an orgasm. As a result of choosing

exactly when to dissociate, Gwen did not forget much—just the final stages of her father's sexual activities with her. And as a result of this precise timing, Gwen Van Derbur did not go "glassy" elsewhere. She never blanked out by day. She did not lose her feeling of being alive.

Virginia Woolf, a victim to her two half brothers in turn, dissociated so much of the time that for most of her life she felt disconnected from others and from her own body. In "A Sketch of the Past," Woolf observed, "My natural love for beauty was checked by some ancestral dread. Yet this did not prevent me from feeling ecstasies and raptures spontaneously and intensely and without any shame or the least sense of guilt, so long as they were disconnected with my own body." Woolf dissociated enough to be noted as distant by others and to be quite unresponsive to sex—or, for that matter, to the death of her beloved mother. With the same kind of provocation, however, a little platinum-blond girl almost half a world away and a couple of generations removed picked only the most specific kind of dissociation and reserved it for only one special kind of moment—impending orgasm. Defenses are interesting groupings. But the individual variants inside these groupings are what make them especially interesting.

Gwen Van Derbur could almost always tell exactly when to expect a sexual session with her father. The anticipation must have been one of the factors that made it possible for her to use such pinpoint dissociation. Francis S. Van Derbur would play the piano and then have a drink before approaching his oldest child. "I was very alert when I knew he had finished playing that piano"—Gwen laughed—"and having his drink. I would wait for the door to open."

Two girls, each waiting for the door to open. But one child must have blanked out almost from the moment the door widened. She became a nighttime persona, a different girl. She saw things through a haze. The older girl bided her time before making her escape. She was more curious. More adventuresome. She wanted to see first what would happen. She anticipated every step. She knew she could get away later. Once the door opened, Gwen let herself stay aware. Her father tried most of the standard sexual things with his hands and mouth. She even remembered his penis. "He felt flabby," she recalled, "and he would rub himself against you. I don't ever remember a real, hard erection. But maybe, now, that happened after I turned off." She laughed again.

Gwen fled from the preorgasmic state by willing her mind to drift away from what was taking place. She diverted her attention before the final escape. When she had had enough, she simply "went away."

"I can describe the wallpaper in a lot of different rooms," she said. "Venetian blinds, too. I remember really detailing things that were there. I would concentrate on something else. I remember ceilings. Counting flowers. At fourteen I thought I had escaped him for good by slapping my mother and being sent away to boarding school in Kansas City. But then we had these 'parent weekends' once a month, and Dad would come and take me off to his room at the Muehlebach Hotel. And I got to know the wallpapers and the ceilings there, too. It was just god-awful. So I reset my goals for eighteen. And at eighteen I never went back."

Gwen used a second defense while her childhood memories of incest were forming—denial in fantasy. This is an important developmental defense, first described by Anna Freud in her 1936 book *The Ego and the Mechanisms of Defense.* The child attempts to surmount pain arising from the outside world by creating a meaningful piece of pretend. The fantasy transforms reality to the child's purposes. Children use "denial in fantasy" to cope with homicides they have witnessed in their families. I found this to be a common defense among children who saw the *Challenger* explosion; many of them told me that for days, even weeks, they had daydreamed that the shuttle astronauts had landed on a desert island or on the moon. By "denying in fantasy," children do not avoid labeling perceptions as significant. Instead, they deliberately misinterpret their perceptions. This defense does not ordinarily block memory—rather, it puts a new slant to memory.

During sex with Francis S. Van Derbur, Gwen planned to murder him. She spent hours of foreplay devising his death. "I think I would have gotten weapons," she said, "if it was today. I told myself how at eighteen I'd be able to get outa there. I was home free at eighteen, and nobody would ever have to know. *He* wasn't gonna tell anybody. And I sure wasn't gonna tell. And so I'd think, 'It virtually didn't happen. No damage done. I'm fine.'"

Gwen thought her murderous and escapist thoughts while being fingered, fondled, and poked. She planned hundreds of getaways. Most of her memories were registered, stored, and available for retrieval—even the memories she put into fantasy. Gwen thinks her anger kept her alive, but she also regrets the anger. Like Marilyn, she loved her father.

Gwen's mother, too, denied because she loved Francis Van Derbur. Boots used "denial of external reality," a defense that probably blocks memory at the short-term to long-term transfer point. The two kinds of defensive denials affect episodic memory very differently. In one, the memory is registered, stored, and later retrieved with its fantasy slant. In the other, the memory may not be fully stored. The event is perceived but may not be weighted with enough significance to move into long-term memory. Mrs. Van Derbur refused to pay attention to her husband's preliminary piano recitals, to pick up the sex smells on her husband's body, to grant any import to his absences from their bedroom. In the article in *People,* she confesses to having little or no recollection of the routines that signalled attack in her daughters' minds.

Gwen's angry thoughts were inspired by physical batterings as well as by sex. "He ran the place with an iron fist," she recalled. "He punished me for a bad attitude. I didn't even have to *do* anything bad. Just my 'attitude.' He kept a wooden dowel over every door in the house, and he'd reach up, get that dowel, and whale the tar out of me. And I was the oldest. So he would be certain the other kids saw it. Everybody was pretty intimidated.

"On occasions, I'd go stay with Grams and GaBa [her maternal grandparents]. There was one time when they were going to call the police because of the welts on me. And Mother prevailed on them not to do it. But my mother knew I was being beaten. And my grandparents knew. And obviously nothing was going to be done about that. I just had to make it through."

Gwen has no memory of penile penetration, but she thinks that it happened, because when she was fourteen her father took her to an abortionist. Gwen sighed as she was telling me this—the sound of a deep, deep sadness. "I was in junior high," she said. "I missed a couple of periods. He found this out because my mother told him. He took me to a backstairs doctor. He said, 'The doctor's going to examine you. I've told him you were raped in the back of a bus. You go up these stairs. And you go see him. He's going to see if you are pregnant.' So I went. I remember that. And I wasn't. So we got through that one."

Gwen can remember her visit to the abortionist. And she can

remember her conversation with her father. But she cannot remember exactly what her father did to her that caused his concerns. Gwen covers for her lost memory by thinking things through. From the beginning of her incestuous relationship with her father, Gwen dissociated as the sex heated up, and therefore could not retrieve memories of what ultimately happened between them. In the matter of the abortionist, she compensates for this lack of memory by joining bits of actual memory to bits of reasoning.

It is difficult for many of us to distinguish what parts of a memory are really remembered and what parts we have reasoned through. Gwen distinguishes between these two things quite well, and she has concluded that she must have had intercourse with her father. This may be a false conclusion.

Gwen's assumption that her father had to have been erect and had to have penetrated her does not necessarily explain her actual memories. Her father could have failed to ejaculate but mistakenly thought that he had. Or he could have thought that his spirited, rebellious daughter was pregnant by some boy her own age. Since Gwen has no real memory of being penetrated by her father, we cannot reconstruct any more from the episode with the "backstairs doctor" than is already there. When we apply "thinking it through" to old, poorly formed memories, we may not get anywhere. Or we may come up with false memories.

Gwen asked me if she could show me something before I left. She laughed a little as she told me of a lifelong habit—a "thing" about tea towels. She got out a pale-green damask towel and twisted it between her third and fourth fingers. "Tea towels send me into orbit," she said. "Just touching the fabric. Twisting it. Napkins are good, too. I rub them between my fingers. At dinners I'm always disappointed when the napkins are paper."

Everyone in the family knew about Gwen's habit, she said. Everybody teased her. "I've got calluses. Look!" I felt the pads between Gwen's fingers. The skin was very rough. "When I twist the towel," she said, "I do it as hard as I can. With both hands. It feels really good. It gives me some kind of little—" Gwen seemed to want to say the word "thrill," but, as in the instance of "orgasm," she could not get it out.

Gwen used tea towels as a displacement—the defense that involves diverting one's attention away from something strongly felt to something less strongly felt. I immediately wondered if there were towels in Gwen's childhood bed. Trauma symptoms can be surprisingly literal.

"Did you ever take a towel to bed?" I asked.

"I wet my bed till I was pretty big," she answered. "Maybe that was one way of keeping somebody out of my room, out of my bed. People woke me up at night to take me to the bathroom. So I would tie myself to the bed with fabric, telling myself nobody was gonna get me up. I could have gotten strips of rags—I don't remember. And I tied them to my bed. And I would twist the cloth, twist it, twist it. It still feels good today. I sometimes still twist in bed with my sheets."

I knew we had found one of Gwen's ways to stop a very specific kind of memory—the memory of orgasm. She had found a substitute excitement, and one which might also connect strongly to her adult sexuality. Gwen diverted her attention to her hand. At age two, she had lost the tip of a finger in Grams's icebox door. Her hand was very important to her. And her genitals were important, too.

"I'll tell you something else, as long as we're on this subject," Gwen said. "If I'm going to fantasize and have a good sexual experience now, the best way is [to pretend] I'm in bondage. It's being done to me, and I can't help it. So it's O.K. for me to feel good about it. You know, my father was dedicated to making me feel something in my childhood. And he did. But I managed to keep the old control by making some of it go my way. The bondage fantasy just—It just came to me. I don't know when. But my bondage has to be with a soft cloth. Maybe a tea towel."

Marilyn Van Derbur Atler wrote in her *Rocky Mountain News* "diary" that she suspected sometime after her memories came back that her father had also abused one of her friends from school. And indeed, the friend phoned to talk about it after Marilyn made her Kempe Center benefit speech. Gwen is certain that another sister also suffered unwanted sex at the hands of her father, though Gwen does not know exactly what happened. Carol Kreck wrote in the *Denver Post* that three, or maybe all four, Van Derbur girls were abused. On May 3, 1992, referring to Marilyn's Kempe Center revelations, she says, "Later other Van Derbur sisters said they, too, had suffered their father's assaults, each believing she alone was the victim."

Gwen remembers that one of the middle sisters, whom she would not identify, told her once, "though she would deny it now," that sex with Francis S. Van Derbur had been "the kind of event Margaret Mead might have reported about—some social more, some rite of passage." "I have never forgotten it," Gwen told me. "She said he was gentle and kind to induct her through this rite of passage. 'Well, that's neat,' I said"—Gwen laughed. "'If that works for you, that's good'"—Gwen laughed again. "But I was amazed."

If Gwen's memory is correct, one of her middle sisters rationalized and ritualized her mental representations of her father's acts. She managed her feelings with intellectualization—another defense. In Gwen's account, the sister pays undue attention to the details of courtesy and niceness shown by her father. She does not attend to the whole. When you intellectualize, you mask disturbing instinctual wishes or external stresses with excessive abstraction or rationalization. Although this process helps to avoid conflicted feelings, it usually does not block memory—although, in theory, any defense can.

The young daughters of Francis S. Van Derbur apparently used at least six different defenses to deal with their common problem. They used splitting, dissociation, projective identification, denial in fantasy, displacement, and intellectualization. One of these, dissociation, was used by the youngest and the oldest girls quite differently. And their mother employed yet another defense—denial of external reality.

At sixty, Gwen is outgoing and energetic, a dynamo. She has a great sense of humor. Marilyn, on the other hand, does not come far into the open. She says she frequently has to force herself into bravado. Marilyn shares Gwen's enormous energy—and perhaps she has even more. But she struggles when she has to use it. The ancient Greeks might have described Gwen Mitchell's demeanor as hubris; the Jews would have called it chutzpah. And any culture would have recognized Marilyn as shy. Shyness has threaded throughout Marilyn's life. Despite the image of bravery she presents to the world, Marilyn has been—to paraphrase her quote from Holmes—dying with her music still inside. Marilyn's and Gwen's character differences are no doubt innate, and these differences probably account not only for their different choices of defense but for their very different uses of the same defense—and for the difference in their memories today.

• • •

Pictures don't tell a whole story. Knowing what I know now, I once again pick up the 1951 newspaper photograph. It shows the most photogenic family you could ever hope to see. Teenagers without frowns or pimples. A man aging gracefully. But I look deeper into the picture.

Where is the wife? Why is she absent? She didn't take the picture—it is a professional shot, taken for the newspaper. Boots is nowhere to be seen. I think I know why. She cannot face the incest in her family. She will not allow herself to perceive what is going on. She needs to preserve her relationship with her Adonis.

The father sits on the arm of the couch looking down at his very special daughters. He looks possessive and powerful. He owns them.

A blond teenager in black laughs in the direction of her dad. A darker girl sits farther away from him, and she, too, smiles. One of these two pretty girls misunderstands what is between herself and her father, perhaps even imagining in her bright young mind that he is helping her to adjust to the frightening world of men.

In the middle of the picture sits a bony, tall girl in profile. Only half her face shows—the half brightened by the photographer's flash—exemplifying the amputation of one side of her persona. We see only the "day child" of Marilyn Van Derbur. Seven years away from being Miss America, this child is painfully tight. Pin curls not quite combed out. Gloves clutched firmly on her lap. Her control makes no difference. Her father is quite used to her. He has already had her for eight whole years.

Next to Marilyn sits a girl with white-blond hair—a woman really, nineteen years old. Gwen wears a smile and looks straight up at her father. She wanted to murder him for years, but the murder wish does not show on her face. What I see, instead, is relief. She has escaped. Francis S. Van Derbur no longer owns Gwen. Perhaps he never did. She's "outa there."

# 6

## The Child Star's Tale

The tapes were of good quality for copies. Much better than what I produce with the coupled VCRs set into my kitchen wine rack. Considering that both times he taped the child, Officer Dorman of the Oklahoma City Police Department did no more than put his videocamera into a fixed position and turn up the lights, what I watched was a small miracle. On the screen, Officer Dorman sat in sharp-focused profile. When he glanced down, as he frequently did, at a short stack of what must have been cue cards, a small sweaty bald spot glistened at the top of his head. At center screen facing him sat the "subject," a ten-year-old girl with a blond ponytail who had come to accuse two doctors of sexually abusing her. On her forehead not a single drop of sweat caught the light.

Some of the girl's words were lost to the tape recorder that rested on the table between her and the policeman. Some of her gestures were obscured by two oversize anatomically correct dolls—a yellow-haired boy doll and a carrot-haired girl doll—positioned in no apparent relationship to each other on the table. But anyone would have overlooked these technical flaws in Officer Dorman's tapes. What was most compelling was the subject herself.

How did Ingrid Bergman look at ten? I wondered. Cheryl Tiegs? Julia Roberts? Were they as physically beautiful as this child? But it was not her beauty alone that put this girl into the child-star category. It was her love affair with the camera. She rarely looked at it, but that meant only that she instinctively knew how to handle it—as if no one had had to tell her what every neophyte needs to know: "Don't look directly at the lens."

The girl used her hands, shoulders, neck, face, and even her silky ponytail to gesture. Her smiles were freely given to the interviewer, with no apparent effort or self-consciousness. She cocked her head and nodded with great charm. On the first tape, she wore a dark-purple oversize sweater, a white blouse, and a silver chain around her neck which caught the light whenever she twiddled it with her index finger or tossed her head. On the second tape, she wore a short-sleeved lilac blouse over a long-sleeved white T-shirt. In both outfits she was as "cool" as ten-year-olds come. Her hands frequently offered a prettily gestured accompaniment to an "I don't remember" or an "Um, yes, that's it!" or a "No, I'd never do that." Her voice revealed an expressive little crack with every other phrase or so. A slightly whispery quality distinguished it from the piping juvenile tones you hear from ordinary child actors on television. This girl was a TV natural. And these were crucial "shows."

The tapes I was watching were four years old. Shortly after they were made, Phil Greene, an auto mechanic, and his wife Karen pressed criminal child-molestation charges against two mental-health professionals, Drs. Edward Riley and Sarah Allston, on behalf of their ten-year-old daughter Lua. Without seeking an indictment, the Oklahoma City District Attorney's Office dropped the criminal case, for lack of evidence. But before the charges were dropped, the Greenes filed a civil suit against both doctors. They also launched a publicity campaign aimed at revealing the atrocities that had allegedly been committed upon their child and the failure of the community to respond. Karen Greene accompanied Lua wherever she had to go to make a complaint, take a psychological test, or be examined. The suit became a full-time job.

Dr. Riley, an educational psychologist, and Dr. Allston, a child psychiatrist, had been friends since college, and they shared a large suite of offices with a couple of other therapists. Lua had been Dr. Riley's patient for four years; his assignment was to work with her potentially serious personality problems: low self-esteem, habitual lying, a constant need for attention, and difficulty getting along with her mother. Phil and Karen Greene had two children, and the older one, a boy, was clearly the family favorite. Lua, it seemed, could do no right. The girl and her mother were constantly at war; the child talked back and would not mind. She needed help with her homework yet fought off her mother's attempts to help her. Lua's brother, on the other hand, maintained an "A" average and performed dazzlingly at sports. At school and at home, everybody liked him.

Dr. Allston, the first professional to evaluate Lua, told her attorney that she had diagnosed the child as suffering from attention-deficit/hyperactivity disorder, a serious problem characterized by inattention and poor concentration, and, as Lua grew, prescribed increasing doses of methylphenidate (Ritalin), a major psychoactive drug that aids a child in focusing and learning. Dr. Allston occasionally dropped into Dr. Riley's consulting room, to write out a new prescription or check on Lua's progress. Dr. Riley, according to his testimony, used a combination of play and talking therapy with the young girl. On occasion, he provided Lua's therapy in exchange for Mr. Greene's work on several old cars that he owned. Before the child-abuse charges were made, he and the Greenes socialized a bit, too. They spent a few Thanksgivings together and sometimes got together on a Saturday night.

It was late—eleven o'clock—and beyond my brightly lit kitchen the house was dark and silent. I had been asked to watch these tapes by Sarah Allston's defense attorney, Tom Blackburn, who had first contacted me by phone from Oklahoma City; I became interested in the case mainly because child psychiatrists, and especially women child psychiatrists, are hardly ever accused of sexually abusing their patients. This doctor was being sued for three million dollars, yet until the moment of the accusation she had enjoyed a fine reputation both as a therapist and as an expert courtroom witness throughout the state.

Tom Blackburn wondered whether I would think Officer Dorman had suggested things to Lua. "Is this kid being brainwashed by the authorities?" he had asked me. "Is somebody feeding her a story?" I listened carefully to Officer Dorman's questions. Were they leading? There is a great deal of difference between saying, "Tell me about your day" and asking, "Did you get caught cheating today?" or even "Did you have a nice day today?" Children's sensitive antennae easily pick up subtle attempts to exert influence. They quickly perceive and seek to avoid the desire to control that lies behind pushy, authoritarian inquiries. *Where Did You Go? Out. What Did You Do? Nothing.*

That old book title captures the spirit of many an unproductive inter-generational exchange. Leading questions may cue the child subject into a false response. Some children stop talking when asked such questions; some offer false details or entire false memories. This may not be "on purpose," as one would define a lie. But whatever the child's motivation, his answer to a leading question may turn out to be untrue.

Suggestive or leading material does not have to be put in question form in order to influence a memory. Remarks, announcements, even casual changes of wording can divert people from what their own minds tell them and steer them in the direction the interviewer expects them to go. Nods of the listener's head, winks, postures that lean toward or away from the subject—these are all powerful means of altering a person's story.

The psychologist Elizabeth Loftus and her colleagues at the University of Washington conduct "misinformation" experiments in which the subjects (mostly college students) are led to believe that they have perceived one thing while having actually registered something else. These experiments create false details of remembered perception. The act of leading can be successfully accomplished in any phase of the memory process—perception, storage, or retrieval. Subtle changes in questioning technique or subtle attitudes and hints from the interviewer can elicit enormous differences in the subjects' responses.

Dr. Loftus's subjects are shown simulated accidents and crimes in movie form. They are also given misinformation at some point in the memory process. At the time of presenting the material or afterward, through a seemingly inadvertent slip of the experimenter's tongue, the suggestive information is planted. A difference as slight as, "Did you see *the* dent in the car?" instead of "Did you see *a* dent?" can result in a mistake. In a plenary speech entitled "The Reality of Repressed Memories," delivered at the American Psychological Association Annual Meeting, August 1992, in Washington, D.C., Dr. Loftus summarized her findings. People who saw a pickup truck can be made to believe through suggestion that they saw a small car or a station wagon, she said. People who watched a crime committed by someone with straight hair can be made to think that the hair was curly. After watching a bucolic country scene with no defining features, people can be misled into thinking they saw broken glass, tape recorders, or a barn at the site. Dr. Loftus and her co-investigators can even get individuals who have seen Mickey Mouse to think they saw Minnie.

Had Officer Dorman used leading techniques with Lua? I would have to watch and listen for them as well as for Lua's own biases. If she had decided at some point in her therapy that she hated her doctors, for instance, this attitude could have colored her recollection of everything that happened before that point. In 1971–72, the cognitive psychologist Baruch Fischhoff, of Carnegie Mellon University, did an interesting experiment along these lines, asking 251 college students to predict the outcome of President Richard M. Nixon's upcoming trips to China and the Soviet Union. A year later, the students were asked to write down what they had predicted. Most of them wrote down the actual outcome of President Nixon's trips, whereas in fact a much smaller group had predicted it. Hindsight had altered their memories. A good many "I told you so"s must arise in the same way.

One could resolve, on the basis of this kind of experimental work, never to ask a leading question and never to slip an outcome to anybody. The problem with questioning children, however, is that you may have to lead them a little, in order to get them to say anything of substance at all. Sometimes children of toddler and preschool age need verbal or picture cues before they can get out the words to express what they remember. Young children are relatively new to words and need help in framing their memories. I do consider anatomically correct dolls far too suggestive for investigative use, however. They force a child to deal with the doll's genital apparatus, which is its most prominent feature. The eyes, for example, have no glass, no brows, no lashes, and no movable lids. But the genitals come complete with yarn pubic hair, openings, and folds.

School-age children often feel that being asked for their memories is an invasion of their privacy. This, too, interferes with free recall. The psychologists Gail Goodman, of the University of California, Davis, and Karen Saywitz, of UCLA, set up an experiment to investigate how children function as eyewitnesses. They arranged for two groups of children—each group consisting of thirty-six five-year-old and seven-year-old girls—to have a complete pediatric exam at the Harbor Hospital clinic, in Los Angeles. The girls in one group were given genital and anal examinations. The girls in the other group

were not. Several days were allowed to pass before the children were interviewed. First, each girl was given a chance to tell on her own what had happened. Then she was given an anatomically detailed doll with which to act out her experience. Finally the investigators asked each child a series of leading and misleading questions.

In the interview's first stage, the girls who were not examined genitally or anally freely described everything that had happened. No child in this group gave a false demonstration with the anatomically detailed doll. But when leading and misleading questions were added, two of these girls offered wholly false reports. One child went so far as to say that her doctor had used a stick that tickled her anus.

Of the group given the anal and genital examinations, only eight girls volunteered this information at the outset, the younger girls being slightly more forthcoming than the older ones. But when offered the anatomically detailed doll, six more children came forward and told; and upon being asked leading and misleading questions, the majority of the girls indicated correctly what had occurred. They were not misled by the suggestive questioning; they told true stories. But they needed strong cues.

Did Lua Greene need such cues? The problem is how to elicit the truth from a child without cuing the child. Interviewing a ten-year-old about sex is tricky. I was interested to see how the policeman would manage with his young "child star."

Officer Dorman began by giving the girl a choice between using "Lua" or "Amy," her middle name. "What a strange thing to ask," I thought. It seemed almost as though Officer Dorman would have preferred Lua to call herself "Amy."

The child chose "Lua" and smiled. When I spoke the next day with Tom Blackburn, I learned what everybody in the Greenes' circle, including the girl herself, already knew. Phil and Karen Greene, on vacation in 1978 in Mexico, had celebrated long and late one night with Kahlua, the national coffee liqueur. The child they accidentally conceived in the afterglow was named "Lua" as a reminder. Did Officer Dorman disapprove of drunkenness? Debauchery? With his very first line of inquiry, the policeman had shown himself capable of the leading question.

Lua told Dorman, in answer to a question about her school, that she was in the fourth grade.

"Oh, you can multiply then?"

"Sort of." A coy smile.

"What's seven times seven?"

"No, I can't do that one." The child looked entirely unruffled. "But I know nine times eight. That's harder."

"What's the answer then?" The officer took the child's bait.

"Seventy-two."

Dorman looked satisfied. So did Lua. But the girl had begun to establish herself, too. She could lead. She could evade. And she could handle adults. Nabokov's Humbert Humbert might have found Lua as fascinating as his twelve-year-old Lolita.

The tape whirred on. "We have a report from your parents that something happened to you," the police officer stated.

"Yes." The child went silent.

"Do you know there are good touches and bad touches?"

"Leading," I thought—especially in the light of Dorman's abrupt shift to this subject.

The child said nothing.

"Do you know the names and places of private parts? Can you show me on these dolls?"

The child shrugged, smiled, and tossed her blond hair. There would be no anatomically-detailed-doll demonstrations today. But she did state her names for the sex organs, a compromise that she and Officer Dorman seemed to have worked out without saying a word. "Boobies," Lua said, that cute catch in her voice carrying considerable charm. "Vagina. Butt."

"What do you use these parts for?" the officer wished to know.

Giggles. Head bobs. Shrugs. No answer.

"Has anyone touched you?" he asked.

"No," said the child.

"But we understand something happened," rebutted Officer Dorman, sounding petulant.

Dr. Riley was "scary and nasty," Lua answered. She seemed eager to erase the pout from the officer's mouth. "He wanted sex with me. He showed me movies where somebody killed someone. And he's supposed to be a therapist!"

The child went on to tell Officer Dorman that Dr. Riley used a reel-to-reel movie projector to show her "Tom & Jerry" cartoons, adult sex films, and films in which people were killed. When asked whether the actors were naked, the child said, "I don't know. I didn't look." When asked whether Dr. Riley himself had been naked, the child answered that he "took all his clothes off, too, and touched himself as he watched the movies."

"What did his penis look like?" Dorman inquired. This question asked for no particular new information, just elaboration. It was a fine question, I thought.

"I don't know what penises look like," responded the child.

She saw Dr. Riley naked and masturbating, yet she didn't see his penis? Inconsistent. She was also vague. In answer to Officer Dorman's "What did the people do in the sex movies?" she answered, "They had sex."

"What's that?"—a good question, once again, from the cop. "They took their clothes off and touched each other. Boobies and butts touching," the child replied. Is that sex? This was a surprisingly naïve observation from a child supposedly exposed to adult sex films and male masturbation.

"Did they use their mouths?" Now Dorman appeared to be planting information, conveying to Lua that the mouths of adults can be used for sex.

"No," the child answered, holding her own.

"How *did* they have sex in the films you saw?"

"They made babies."

This is no answer. Regardless of how much this prepubescent beauty charmed, she had entirely evaded the officer's question.

Lua might have repressed the whole sexual experience with Dr. Riley, I thought. Or she might have repressed parts. She might have dissociated into a dreamy daze of unreality while it went on. She might even have split herself into "the bad Lua" in attendance and "the good Lua" somewhere else. But once her memory returned— which it apparently had, because she had come forward with an accusation—she should have known something. A snippet of memory perhaps. But something.


The case of Lua Greene is positioned at the eye of a storm called the false-memory debate. A false memory is a strongly imagined memory, a totally distorted memory, a lie, or a misconstrued impression. Often such memories have been suggested to the rememberer by an outside agent. At the extremes of false memory one finds nefarious lies and out-and-out brainwashing. At the central, more common ground one finds those people who come to believe, through their therapists' suggestions and interpretations, that as children they suffered sexual abuses that they have completely forgotten. A number of mental-health professionals have lined up at one end or the other of this debate. One side says that people can't be made to recall sexual abuses that didn't happen, and that attempts to disprove these abuses are attempts to victimize the already violated. The other side says that false memories happen all the time: people are remembering what their therapist or their self-help group suggested to them. In fact, this argument goes, hypnotism and Amytal interviewing should be stopped altogether, because these forms of therapy are far too suggestive.

Many of us in the mental-health professions are intensely concerned about whether therapists are creating false memories in their patients. Are therapy groups and self-help groups influencing their members' memories? Is the media encouraging people to create false memories by presenting sensational stories with which people feel impelled to identify? Some therapists, in their eagerness to help, wholeheartedly accept their patients' stories without putting them to rigorous tests of internal and external confirmations. A recent study of fifty-three women with incest memories showed that when they made a serious effort to obtain confirmation of their memories, most of them succeeded. But therapists frequently come to conclusions before proofs are unearthed. Often they tend to look for proof of their patients' memories rather than seeking to disprove them, as a scientist would.

A false memory is even more likely to come about when the therapist is an acknowledged expert in trauma who sees incest victims almost exclusively. Here the patient expects from the beginning to retrieve incest memories from childhood in the course of treatment. The problem becomes more exaggerated if both therapist and patient believe that treatment won't work unless traumatic memories are uncovered. In clinical practice, patients are not particularly enthusiastic about therapists who appear skeptical of their memories. But the patient is better off with a therapist who says, "Let's look at these memories, before we start using them in therapy or in your decisions about your life." The success of treatment does not depend on the retrieval of memories the way the success of a fishing expedition

depends on the catching of fish. One does not have to uncover a buried memory in order to feel better and perform better.

A suggestive technique used on a suggestible patient may wreak all kinds of havoc. Paul McHugh, the chairman of the Department of Psychiatry and Behavioral Sciences at Johns Hopkins University, has expressed concern in an article he wrote in *The American Scholar* (Autumn 1992) that therapists may actually be "giving" their more suggestible patients MPD; the prevalence of this diagnosis, he says, is the modern-day version of the Salem witch hysteria. He writes of five patients who were so strongly influenced by their psychotherapists that they developed signs of the disease, although they actually suffered from entirely different disorders. Lawrence Wright, a journalist, has written a long account in *The New Yorker* of the case of Paul Ingram, a man who confessed under self-induced hypnosis to participating in satanic rituals involving his two daughters. Later, after being sentenced to twenty years in prison, Ingram recanted. He said that he had been wrongly influenced by his interrogators—two policemen, a psychologist, and a pastor—and that they had assured him he would be able to remember his abuse of his daughters once he had confessed to it.

One way to determine whether someone's memory is false is to look for symptoms or signs that correspond to the remembrance. If a child is exposed to a shocking, frightening, painful, or overexciting event, he or she will exhibit psychological signs of having had the experience. The child will reënact aspects of the terrible episode, and may complain of physical sensations similar to those originally felt. The child will fear a repetition of the episode, and will often feel generally and unduly pessimistic about the future.

If, on the other hand, a child is exposed only to a frightening rumor or to the symptoms of another victim of trauma, the child may pick up a symptom or two, and even, perhaps, the whole "story"— but will not suffer a cluster of symptoms and signs. For instance, I know a little girl who, despite the fact that she was not present when her older sister was eviscerated in a freak accident in a swimming pool, "saw" in her own mind what had happened. Winnie had heard the tale of Holly's accident from her older brother and sister, both of whom had witnessed it. These two siblings, however, suffered from symptoms—many, many symptoms. The boy played at building swimming pools; the girl played with strings resembling intestines.

Their stomachs ached. Their sleep was "murdered." But Winnie her-self had no symptoms. She hadn't been there. A horrifying tale alone does not cause the mind to malfunction. Even if the tale is inserted by the most adept of brainwashers, the child will exhibit no symptoms to go along with the "memory." Winnie's account of her memories was in no way a lie. As I see it, her tale was an entirely false memory, albeit innocent.

Not all false memories are deliberately false. Nor are they all delib-erately planted. Much of the controversy today about false memories has nothing to do with whether the people harboring—or instill-ing—these memories are innocent or not. It has to do with whether well-meaning people can inadvertently receive well-meant sugges-tions from their therapists, their friends, their families, or the police, or pick up notions from the books they read and the movies and the television shows they watch, and come to believe that they have expe-rienced something that never happened.

I remember seeing a woman once—let's call her "Anne Blanken-ship Huffman"—whose late father had been a real name in politics and philanthropy. Anne Huffman came to me to ask how to handle her daughter Viveca, age thirty-two, who had started therapy and almost immediately remembered that long ago she had been sexually abused by her famous grandfather. Viveca "saw" her grandfather sexu-ally assaulting her, standing at her feet and putting something painful into her vagina. Her therapist advised Viveca to tell her mother at once, and to consider revealing publicly what her famous grandfather had done.

"I've blown it," said Anne. "I haven't been able to make myself see her, or even *call* her, for three months." Anne Huffman did not believe her daughter. In her own childhood recollections, her father's behav-ior—day and night—had been characterized by benign lack of interest.

Anne gave me a history of her daughter. Viveca's only medical problem as a child had been a "giggle bladder." The little girl invol-untarily "made a puddle" whenever she laughed, sneezed, or lifted something relatively heavy. When she turned three, Viveca was taken to a urologist. "The surgeon kicked me out of the room," Anne recalled. "He said he was going to put an instrument up Viv. I guess it was pretty painful. She was mad at me for days. But the doctor said she had a membrane in the way of her urinary stream and everything would be O.K. after that."

"What did the doctor look like?" I asked her.

"He wore a green scrub suit," Anne replied. "Had a beard. Tall. Dignified. My God, come to think of it, he looked just like my dad!"

In psychotherapy, Anne's daughter had truly experienced the return of a repressed memory. It was of a real event. It was not Viveca's vagina but her urethra that was "attacked." But how would a three-year-old have known that? Viveca's only problems had been with her three-year-old naïveté, her misidentification of the perpetrator, and her misattributions of motivation.

When the great Swiss child psychologist Jean Piaget was two years old, he was deliberately misled by his governess; he later published what has become a famous example of a wholly false memory. To impress the wealthy Piaget family, Jean's governess told them that an attempt had been made to kidnap Jean and that she had rescued him. When Jean was fifteen, the governess took her story back. But until then he had a clear memory, replete with details, of this nonexistent event. What Piaget does not tell us is whether he ever suffered any mental symptoms because of his imagined abduction. I would guess that, like my little friend Winnie, he did not. False memory does not come complete with the findings of psychological trauma—returning perceptions, behavioral reënactment, trauma-specific fears, and futurelessness. Wholly false memory is just a story. It may be internally consistent and laced with details. But it is a story nonetheless.

The reader may notice that I use the modifiers "wholly" and "entirely" when I write "false." One of the biggest problems in the false-memory field is how various researchers and clinicians define false memory. Elizabeth Loftus, for instance, tends to use the phrase to describe a misreported detail inside a memory. A grade of "B–" is an "F," as far as Loftus and a number of her fellow experimentalists are concerned. In my view, a visual misperception, a chronological mistake, or a mistaken motivation does not make a memory false.

My study of the Chowchilla school-bus kidnapping demonstrated that a significant number of the kidnapped children later remembered incorrect details about their ordeal. About a third of the 153 randomly selected eight-year-olds and fifteen-year-olds I interviewed after the *Challenger* spacecraft exploded made mistakes regarding the details. No one doubts, however, that the Chowchilla children were indeed kidnapped from their school bus, and nobody debates the fact that the kids who described the *Challenger* disaster were exposed to it.

False details distort a memory. But many real remembrances are distorted, though essentially true.

If, for instance, an eight-year-old came home from school saying that the class had spent the whole day visiting the science museum, Mrs. Dodge drove, and they finished up with ice cream, would a parent believe that the child was telling a falsehood if the teacher later reported that they had been to the natural-history museum, spent half a day there, Mrs. Whitcock drove, and they ended up with frozen bananas? I would consider the eight-year-old as having offered his mother a real memory, distorted—as so often happens—with minor misperceptions and childhood misunderstandings. But if the eight-year-old comes home and describes a whole day at the science museum and the teacher later calls to say that the child miserably failed a test on the times tables that day, the child is caught lying. He may have offered his wholly false report as a diversion from parental questions about the test. If the child later began to believe in the reality of the made-up event, this would be what I call "wholly false memory"—a full remembrance constructed out of nothing.

Many wholly false memories carry the potential to create tragedies. Lua Greene's memory certainly did. Two doctors stood accused and were in danger of losing everything. We have had a number of "wholly false memory" tragedies in the American family courts. Beginning in about the 1970s, divorce attorneys started arguing cases in which a child accused one divorcing parent of sexual abuse. Often the child in such a case was not given the chance to volunteer a full, undirected account. In a study of eighteen children who had made such accusations in divorce battles, the psychiatrists Elissa Benedek and Diane Schetky found that the majority of these children had given false reports.

Political advocacy groups, however, such as the False Memory Syndrome Foundation, have garnered so much publicity for their cause that this cause is being confused today with a diagnosis. A therapist asked me at a recent meeting whether a patient we had discussed suffered from "false-memory syndrome." There is no such disorder. It is just a name taken by an organization representing parents, uncles, grandfathers, and siblings who believe they have been falsely accused. Now there is an advocacy group of "recanters," too. And something called "false lack of memory," a jibe coined by accused parents, to make people wonder why these accused parents have no memories of abusing their own children. These are catchy phrases, but they are not psychiatry. The debate has become far too politicized.

Only a series of strong clinical studies on adult memories of confirmed incidents of childhood abuse will resolve the false-memory controversy. We will need long-term follow-ups of children with proven abuse in their backgrounds. Until these definitive studies are accomplished, each case must speak for itself. The facts of a case will settle the debate on an individual level. Each case must be assessed and diagnosed for its particular truth. Each patient must be checked for specific symptoms and signs. Adult patients must be willing to look not only for internal but for external confirmation of newly returned memories. Lack of external confirmation does not negate a memory. But many more memories lend themselves to such confirmation than one might think.

As I watched Lua Greene on videotape that night in my kitchen, I saw that she was different from my young "subjects" kidnapped at Chowchilla or exposed to the exploding *Challenger*. While the Chowchilla and *Challenger* kids stuck to exactly the same general series of events or actions and varied from one child to the next as to their details, Lua stuck to her details while drastically varying the actions in her account. Although I don't believe that a story can be assessed in a vacuum, Lua's story—all by itself—was hard to believe. Had some therapist she might have seen after she was taken away from Dr. Riley inadvertently planted it?

And just how did Dr. Sarah Allston enter into Lua's account? Dr. Allston was Tom Blackburn's client, and she was the reason I was watching TV so late at night.

"What did Dr. Allston do?" Officer Dorman demanded of the child, bringing me up sharply in my chair. "Did she come into Dr. Riley's office too?" I leaned forward for the young girl's response.

"Sarah came in." Lua smiled. "And she saw the bad, bad movies with dead people in them."

"Did Dr. Allston say anything?"

"No. She didn't say anything." The child went silent.

"That's all?" Officer Dorman slumped back in his chair.

The child rose to the policeman's nonverbal lead. "Well, sometimes Sarah would say, 'Ed, shut those movies off! You should talk to your patient, not keep playing bad movies!'"

The beautiful child fingered her glimmering necklace. Dorman looked tired. "Do you know what a lie is?" he asked.

"Yes," she responded with perky confidence. "You get in trouble for a lie." In this child's mind, lies were practical matters—matters of strategy between oneself and another person. A lie was to be defined by another's response. By the age of ten, most children have come to think of lying as an ethical problem or, at the least, a problem between the child and God. Lua Greene's moral development was slow, late, and flawed, I thought—and her overactive antennae seemed to sense something amiss, even though that "something" was fifteen hundred miles away and four years into the future. *"This is all the truth!"* she exclaimed, staring straight at the camera, dramatic emphasis underlining each word. And then Lua smiled at me. The tape went blank.

An instant later it came alive again. This was Part 2. Officer Dorman began by announcing the new date, two weeks after the first. He then told Lua he would ask about a list of sexual offenses that, he said, Lua's mother had prepared from the things Lua had told her. How had this list come about? Had a therapist become involved in Lua's case after Riley and Allston were dismissed, and then written up a list of sexual activities for Karen Greene? Did this therapist originally suggest these things to Lua? Or did Karen Greene draw up the list after somehow suggesting things to her daughter by herself? The list in Officer Dorman's hand strongly implied some sort of adult influence over young Lua Greene.

The policeman asked about eleven kinds of activities, and Lua agreed that each had taken place, except that nude photos had never been taken of Dr. Riley. The girl in the lilac shirt agreed that she had been hypnotized and then tied up while Edward Riley and Sarah Allston had sex. She agreed that she had been given drugs, and that Dr. Riley had taken nude photos of Dr. Allston. Videos had also been made, Lua added—this apparently was something not on the list. She said that Dr. Riley had used rubber gloves to touch another young female patient, who had posed with Lua for "nasty pictures." Dr. Riley had had sex with other women in his office. He had made "nasty" movies of Lua while she was hypnotized. He had threatened to kill her.

This list, of course, was entirely leading, because the child was asked item by item to respond to each act. But Lua's elaborations were interesting nonetheless. When Officer Dorman asked her about being hypnotized, she yawned twice, deeply, in response. Then she stretched and said dreamily, "I can't remember it all." She said she did remember going to get coffee for Sarah Allston while under hypnosis. The two doctors would then tie her up, sip their coffee, and have their sex.

This led to another interesting elaboration—or, rather, a failure to elaborate. "They'd have sex?" Officer Dorman asked. "How?"

"They'd just *do* it," Lua replied. Again she seemed unable to describe adult sex.

"Show me with the dolls."

The child picked up the yellow-haired boy doll and the orange-haired girl, and placed the girl doll face down on top of the boy doll. The policeman commented in a puzzled voice, "The girl is on top of the boy?"

"Oops," chirped the child. "The *boy* should be on the top." She changed the dolls to suit Officer Dorman's taste, and then she left them alone.

Neither doll moved. No flexible cloth knees rose to accommodate a thrusting cloth body. No carefully stitched genitalia received its stuffed counterpart. Sex, in young Lua Greene's eyes, was a purely static arrangement of male and female.

"It says here that Ed and Sarah kissed [each other's] privates," Dorman read from his list. I thought back to the suggestive question he had asked two weeks earlier—"Did they use their mouths?"—and that Lua had answered in the negative. Was the child suggestible enough to have begun incorporating oral sex into her memories?

Lua smiled. "That's embarrassing," she said. "Sarah did it, not Ed. . . . Just sometimes. . . . Their clothes were on."

"Hmm," I thought. "Difficult to 'kiss privates' with your clothes on." The child had apparently put her own imagination to work on a planted notion. And she didn't get it. No one had adequately described the experience. "Clothes on" sounded O.K. to Lua.

It was now time for the policeman to put his mother-made list aside. He wanted to know if either Sarah Allston or Edward Riley had ever touched Lua sexually. He began to ask the question in just about every kind of way he could, but the child repeatedly denied being touched or penetrated in any way. Dorman would not let the matter go, however. "Tell everything. Everything," he said forcefully. Here was heavy influence indeed.

Lua finally bowed her head. "Yes," she said. "Ed touched my private parts. In the old office. No, maybe the new one. I'm not sure. It was near a holiday. Christmas. Sarah was there. He just touched me in my privates. My clothes were on." She delicately gestured between her legs for the camera.

This was a new crime, one with big penalties. "What about Sarah? Did *she* touch you?" Dorman asked.

"Yes, at Easter," Lua said.

"Christmas" and "Easter" go together in the same way as the words "dog" and "cat" or "football" and "baseball" on a word-association test. "Easter" sounded like an answer of convenience, not a serious attempt on Lua's part to figure out when a terrible event took place. "It happened lots and lots of times," the child said, quickening her pace. "Really a lot. . . . I was tied in handcuffs. Sarah touched me more than once. . . . They took all kinds of camera pictures. A lot. Really a lot. Thirty times I saw pictures of [here Lua named another patient] and of somebody I don't know with their clothes off. Ed kept the pictures and camera in a model sailboat he made of toothpicks. He also kept his drugs in there."

"Tied in handcuffs?" "All kinds of camera pictures?" "Drugs?" "Thirty times?" The details in Lua's stories were a medley, not a tune.

"Why didn't you tell your mom and dad?" Dorman looked ready to put away his cue cards and go home.

"Because Ed and Sarah said they'd kill me," Lua said. The tape ended. Flickers and static drove me from my chair and up to bed.


For years now, psychologists have conducted hundreds of fascinating experiments to try and find out whether, how much, and at what ages children's memories can be accepted as valid. Stephen Ceci and his developmental-psychology group at Cornell University tell stories to children and then, several days later, give them false information about these stories. If another child plants this false information, most children tend to forget it and remember the story as it originally was told. But if an adult plants the false information, most children add this new material to their memories. This experiment demonstrates not only that children's memories can be modified in storage but that adults are far more influential over these memories than are other children.

Ceci and his co-investigators conducted a fascinating indoctrination study on 164 preschoolers of mixed ages. The study gauged the reaction of the children to an allegedly clumsy adult named "Sam Stone"—played by one of the researchers—who paid a visit to the preschool. The children were divided into four groups: one group was told about Sam Stone's clumsiness before his visit; one group received the misinformation after his visit; one group was indoctrinated both before and after the visit; and the fourth group received no indoctrination at all.

Twice a week for a month, the kids slated to receive the previsit indoctrination were told tales of such things as how Sam Stone once borrowed someone's Barbie doll, ran up the stairs, tripped, and broke the doll's arm. Then Sam arrived at the preschool. He did almost nothing while he was there. He stood around, patted a few heads, and left. But the advance publicity had its effect: the children who had been "programmed" never took their eyes off him. Some called out, "Sam, don't touch anything here!" or "Sam, watch out!" After Sam's visit, the two groups that were to receive indoctrination after the fact were given suggestive misinformation for twelve weeks. They were asked leading questions, such as "Do you remember when Sam Stone ripped the book at school—did he do it on purpose, or was he just being silly?"

After the twelve weeks were over, each of the 164 children was asked by a newly introduced investigator, "I wasn't there when Sam Stone came. Can you tell me what happened?" Following an undirected narrative from the child, the investigator prompted about the specifics in the child's story, such as torn books, soiled teddy bears, and broken Barbies.

It turns out that the three-year-olds in all four categories made many more memory errors than did the corresponding five-year-olds. But if you said to a three-year-old after the free narrative, "Did you see all this with your own eyes?" the number of inaccuracies immediately went down. If you gently pressed further, "Oh—come on. Really?"—these very small youngsters tended to abandon their false stories altogether. Only one in five clung to them. When confronted with the "Oh, come on" question, fewer than one in ten of the five-year-olds persisted in believing the planted misinformation about Sam.

When you compare the power of the various influences on the chil-

dren's "Sam Stone" memories, it appears that the combination of pre-
and post-event suggestion was the most powerful influence. Next
comes post-event suggestion alone, followed by pre-suggestion. With
no suggestion at all, one might think, all memories would come out
true. But a few three-year-olds in the group that received no suggestive information changed their stories on retrieval after "Oh, come
on" kinds of questions from an adult. Adult authority influences very
young children.

Dr. Ceci's studies raise the concern that a combination of parents'
comments and psychotherapy can influence preschoolers' memories.
Cognitive misunderstandings and social influences can combine to
misdirect and misform children's memories. But preschoolers are not
the only group with the potential to be influenced. Will a combination of influences make an older child, like Lua Greene, think that
something happened when in actuality nothing did?

What I saw in my late-night session with Lua's videotapes were
several potential adult influences—Officer Dorman's leading questions, of course, but also whatever went into Lua's mother's eleven-
item list. Perhaps this list had come from a new therapist. Perhaps
Lua had some kind of access to a pornography shop or an X-rated TV
channel. Because Lua's memories seemed false to me, it became
important to know how these memories got in. And who planted
them? Her mother? Her brother? A therapist? Who?

I phoned Tom Blackburn in Oklahoma City the day after I
watched the tapes, and asked him if Lua had seen any other therapists
after leaving the care of Drs. Riley and Allston.

"There were six," Blackburn said. "And that doesn't count a so-
called expert on satanism."

"And how many therapists did she see between the dismissal of
Riley and the making of the tape with Officer Dorman?"

"One, who didn't find any signs of abuse," Blackburn replied.
"And another who thought she was abused, but came up with no specific symptoms." Blackburn wasn't sure what reading materials, pictures, and videos had been available in the Greenes' home around that
time. But it was something he planned to investigate.

I told Tom Blackburn that I could not believe Lua Greene's videotaped statements. Her story was detailed yet inconsistent, and Officer
Dorman had led her much too far. And perhaps her mother had led
her, too. Or one of the therapists, in an excess of zeal to find out just

what Ed Riley and Sarah Allston had done. The eleven-item list sounded suggestive, I said. But there was one thing in the tapes which carried the marks of an actual experience. Lua had described a vibrator. She said that Dr. Riley had used one in her presence. "It was white," she said. "There were high, low, and medium settings. Ed touched it to his private parts dressed and undressed. And to his muscles, too." Here was a story for which the child offered consistent verbs and corroborating detail. Unless this girl had seen or used a vibrator somewhere else, there was a good chance that Ed Riley had exposed her to one—and Sarah Allston's case would be imperiled if only one small piece of Lua's story was true. The vibrator piece sounded "true," I told Dr. Allston's attorney. We had to find out what lay behind it.

Tom Blackburn said that he would send me a box of medical and psychological documents, copies of depositions taken in the case, including Lua's, and some audiotapes that Lua's mother had made with Lua. The box, a huge one, arrived in a few days. I was now part of *Greene v. Riley & Allston.* Blackburn told me he would take this case before a jury. Sarah Allston had refused to consider the Greenes' offers of a cash settlement. She stood falsely accused, vibrator or no. The case was going to trial.

What juries use and what psychiatrists use to ascertain the "truth" of a memory are basically the same. Does the witness show a number of findings—internal signs—that he or she went through the described experience? Is there supportive evidence for the story? I spent hours reading the papers in Tom Blackburn's overstuffed box to find proofs or disproofs of Lua's memories.

The notes of the six therapists who saw Lua after Drs. Riley and Allston were dismissed recorded very little behavior or symptomatology that corroborated Lua's dreadful accusations. The notes also revealed nothing that would confirm or deny that any of the therapists had exerted an influence over Lua's memories. The girl had told her therapists of a few fears, including fear of the dark and fear of being alone in her own bed at night. But any child can experience such fear. Lua also suffered a few nightmares. But these were vague and nonspecific. She lit candles in her room. And she threatened to run away from home a couple of times. But what of it? Where was her fear of other doctors? Of sex? Of handcuffs? Of hypnosis? Of coffee? Of rubber gloves? And where were the physical pains and behavioral reënactments of sex that often occur in victims of child abuse?

Lua's symptoms were nonspecific. This nonspecificity characterizes the "symptoms" of people who have no memories of childhood sex yet see themselves as victims of such abuse. *The Courage to Heal,* by the California therapists Ellen Bass and Laura Davis, a popular self-help book for adults who experienced childhood sex abuse, lists a number of symptoms that sex-abuse "survivors" suffer. All are genuine findings in abuse victims, but many of them are so nonspecific that they could well be signs of other kinds of emotional problems. "Do you feel that you're bad, dirty, or ashamed?" Bass and Davis ask. "Do you feel powerless, like a victim?" Their list includes feeling "different," feeling as if "there's something wrong with you deep down inside," feeling "self-destructive or suicidal," hating yourself, having "a hard time nurturing" yourself, and fearing success. The authors make things even worse: "If you are unable to remember any specific instances . . . but still have a feeling that something abusive happened to you, it probably did."

Good clinicians base their diagnoses of early trauma on very specific post-traumatic symptoms. Survivors of childhood sex abuse generally have specific problems about sex. They have specific problems about control, often falling under the influence of others, such as their friends, teachers, camp counselors, and, ultimately, lovers. As children, they play strange games of imagination, often with a sexual tinge. They get aches and pains in the lower abdomen or on the skin. They develop bothersome anesthesias of sexually related anatomy. They feel intensely ashamed. They do not plan on having children of their own, or, if they do have children, on raising them well.

Because defenses come into play in true memories, these memories often sound fragmented—especially if the abuses or other traumas went on time after time. On the other hand, true memories cannot ordinarily be distinguished from the false by the amount of detail that comes out in the telling. People who have dissociated away their terrible childhood memories can pick up false details from TV, the print media, or suggestive therapists. Moreover, a memory coming from a person who massively dissociates, be it true or false, will probably sound peculiar. You can't tell from a story alone whether a memory is true or false. Every case must be individually evaluated for corroborations.

"Having a feeling" about something does not make for a diagnosis, either. When we studied the thyroid gland in medical school, we all had the feeling that we suffered from Graves' or Hashimoto's disease. When we studied the liver, it was hepatitis or hepatoma. But none of us really developed any of these diseases in school. It is not enough simply to suspect old sex abuse; there must be something specific that points to it, or a number of specific things, before the possibility becomes real.

I did find one specific sign of adult sexual influence over Lua in Tom Blackburn's box of evidence. It echoed Lua's probably true memory of a white vibrator. When the child was nine years old, Karen Greene unexpectedly walked in on her while Lua was applying a vibrator to her genitals. Mrs. Greene later concluded that Lua's use of the vibrator had evolved from her traumatic experiences with Dr. Riley.

"What did Karen do when she discovered Lua?" I asked myself. I found the answer in Karen's deposition. She stated that she had immediately said, "Put the vibrator back in the drawer where it belongs!"

Karen Greene could have said, "Put that back where you found it!" or "Give that to me," or "That's mine. You're not supposed to touch that!" But she had responded to her child's use of the vibrator as if it were a perfectly ordinary household object. How long had Phil and Karen owned this vibrator? And was the vibrator white? Three-speed? Now I knew how Lua had been able to describe a vibrator. She had used one at home! I wondered where she got the idea of using it on her genitals. It could have been from Dr Riley, but it also could have been from seeing her parents use it or hearing about such activities from her older brother.

I was saving the audiotapes for last—for one thing, my tape recorder wasn't working. But Tom Blackburn was not concerned. "Get through all the papers before your deposition," he told me. Plunging further into the files, I found that Karen Greene had personally engineered the huge publicity campaign that accompanied the Greenes' civil suit, writing letters to a number of prominent public officials and reporters to complain that Lua's case had not properly been pursued. There was so much Greene-initiated publicity, in fact, that the Oklahoma City media freely referred to Lua by her first name and often included the full names of her parents.

Two years after the child made her videotape with Officer Dorman, she served as a witness against Dr. Allston before the State Board of Medical Licensure and Supervision. (Edward Riley had earned his doctorate in educational psychology and did not meet the requirements for an Oklahoma clinical psychologist's license. He therefore had no licenses the board could take away.) By then, Lua's story had expanded and become more detailed. Dr. Allston now wore black leather straps "under the boobs" and black leather pants with no crotch. Dr. Riley wore the male counterpart of this costume. Dr. Allston drew blood with a knife. The board did not allow effective cross-examination of Lua, and Sarah Allston was placed on probation. Dr. Allston applied to practice medicine in the state where she was born. But somebody tipped off that board, and her license application was turned down. She then applied for a job at a state mental hospital in the Midwest, in a state where temporary licenses for doctors working with underserved populations are almost automatically provided. Her application was accepted, and Sarah Allston was back at work as a psychiatrist.

What Lua Greene said in her sworn deposition against Drs. Riley and Allston and in her testimony before the state medical board veered on accusations of satanism. Lua had supposedly witnessed bloodletting with a knife. The doctors wore black. Sex and hypnosis were used together. Other children were brought in, too. I could not believe Lua Greene on these points. She showed no confirming signs. She reported no confirming symptoms. So who had given her her ideas? The so-called satanism expert? Karen Greene had written the letters publicizing her daughter's plight. And she had put together the eleven-item list Officer Dorman used to examine the child. I needed to get my tape recorder repaired. Or borrow another one. It would be interesting to listen to this child talking with her mother.

The trial would take place in Oklahoma City in October. A few months before that, Lua's attorney took my deposition. The attorneys for Drs. Riley and Allston also came to San Francisco, to witness this preliminary testimony. When we broke for lunch, Tom Blackburn told me what he had learned about how Lua's lawsuit had come to be filed. A little more than a month before Officer Dorman made his videotape of Lua, word got out in Oklahoma City gossip circles that Edward Riley was being sued. The suit alleged that he had become sexually involved with a married woman whom he was treating. The client had previously been treated by Dr. Allston, who had referred her to Dr. Riley. Within a short time, the woman and her husband reunited and filed suit against both doctors. When news of this suit got out, three other lawsuits were filed against Drs. Riley and Allston by former patients. They claimed sexual misconduct on Dr. Riley's part and negligence on Dr. Allston's part. There was either a devilish conspiracy by the two doctors or a contagious need to sue on the part of the women. At this point in my assessment of the case, I favored the latter explanation.

Karen Greene first heard about these legal actions against Riley and Allston through a girlfriend. "Let's go read the complaints," the two friends decided. They visited the county courthouse, where civil filings are matters of public record. They found the complaints and immediately seized on the horrible possibility that since Lua had been Dr. Riley's patient for the previous four years she might also be one of his victims.

Here, then, was a problematic mother-daughter relationship (favoring of the brother on the mother's part; bickering, lying, and attention-seeking on the daughter's part) that had suddenly acquired a new focus—Dr. Riley's supposed sexual misadventures. When my deposition was taken, I told Lua's attorney and the attorneys working for the Riley-Allston defense that the child's tale was most likely false. I didn't think of it as a lie, but more as an unconscious restitutive attempt on Lua's part to attract Karen's full maternal attention. This child desperately, but probably unthinkingly, needed to repair their relationship. Almost like a child with "Münchhausen by proxy," Lua seemed to want to take her mother's suspicions and run with them. With a story the Greenes could bring to court, the girl would become as important to her parents as was her accomplished brother. At last people could love Lua. Respect her. Watch her. Keep her in mind.

My deposition did nothing to settle things in *Greene v. Riley & Allston*. Six months later, I came to Oklahoma City for the trial. The proceedings were already well under way, having begun two weeks earlier. A jury, made up primarily of blue-collar workers, had already heard from most of the psychologists and from the Greene family, with the exception of Lua, who would testify immediately before I did.

During those first two weeks of the Greene trial, I, too, had been hearing something—albeit in San Francisco. I had obtained a good recorder and was listening to the audiotapes Karen and Lua had made back at the time of Lua's original accusations. Tom Blackburn and I decided to set out strategy for my upcoming testimony based on these tapes. We would use six sessions, four of them prior to Officer Dorman's first videotape and the others prior to his second. Lua's attorney had considered these audiotapes useful enough to his side of the argument that he had already played parts for the jury, so they were now in evidence. Blackburn and I would replay them for the jury, but this time in full. We would play an audiotape, and then I would give the jury my interpretation of it. Another tape, more testimony.

It was these tapes, which Tom Blackburn and I played once again on the night before I came to the trial, that convinced me that Lua's memories were wholly false and that they had been transmitted by Karen Greene. For in the chilling exchange between mother and daughter, I heard a demonstration of brainwashing so florid and undisguised that I could not help thinking of John Frankenheimer's classic thriller *The Manchurian Candidate*. Karen Greene expertly used techniques more commonly associated with torture chambers and the few childhood homes that resemble these. Brainwashing is the combination of suggestion, misinformation, and conditioning (associative learning). It is more extreme than anything that is done clinically or in the experimental setting. By using this technique, Karen Greene had succeeded in getting her daughter to come forward with "memories" of events that had taken place only in Karen's mind.

Karen Greene decided to question her ten-year-old child downstairs, in the below-ground part of the house where she and her husband slept. She chose this area, she said, because Lua suffered from severe attention problems. There would be no distractions there. Karen turned on the recorder. And Lua was trapped.

To start, Karen told Lua that Edward Riley had done a number of "bad things" to his women patients. She also told the child that Ed carried several sexual diseases. (This idea appears to be unique to Karen Greene. It was not alleged, to my knowledge, in the other lawsuits.) These were strong advance suggestions, much worse than anything Stephen Ceci's preschoolers ever heard about "Sam Stone." In order to protect Lua, Karen said, she needed to know "everything"— every single thing that Dr. Riley had ever done. Lua's first taped responses to her mother, and her usual responses thereafter, were "Nothing" and "No." At first she protested that she liked "Ed," but these feelings quickly changed.

Karen seemed to play fast and loose with the truth even on minor matters, telling Lua, for instance, that she could skip school the day after making a tape and stay, instead, with her grandparents. "But they [Grandma and Grandpa] worry when I'm not in school," Lua argued. "What?" Karen sounded nonplussed. "Well, we'll tell them [the grandparents] your school has vacation that day."

"Oh, Mommy," the child sighed. You could literally hear her dismay.

Karen referred to herself and the tape recorder as "us." Yet Karen never told Lua what she intended to do with the tapes. The child had every reason to believe she was alone with her mother. "Tell us about it," Karen would say. Lua corrected her once: "Tell *you?*" Karen backed off for a moment. "Yeah, well, tell me and the microphone." Later Karen said, "Would you like to talk to the microphone by yourself? Privately?" Lua penetrated this deception at once. "No thanks," she said.

Once, Lua told her mother, "Stop the tape!"

"Why?"

"Because I want to talk to *you!*"

"Promise not to tell Daddy anything," Lua begged at another juncture. "O.K., I promise," said Karen Greene. Did Karen cross her fingers behind her back? Her child was destined to have no privacy whatsoever.

Deliberately planting false information requires more than lies. It requires absolute authority in the person doing the planting. In *The Manchurian Candidate,* the character played by Angela Lansbury symbolizes herself as the powerful Queen of Diamonds for her poor adult son, played by Laurence Harvey. Karen Greene conveyed this same sense of control to Lua; not only was she a parent, but she appeared to be a mindreader.

KAREN: O.K. Did Ed ever take any [photos] of you with your clothes off?

LUA: Yes. No. This is what I hate. It's what gets me into a bad mood.

KAREN: I'm reading your body language.

LUA: [Loudly] Well Mommy, I'm telling you everything.
KAREN: O.K., don't yell at me.

If a mother insists she knows everything about you, you feel you have nowhere to hide.

KAREN: You're acting kind of silly.
LUA: I'm helping.
KAREN: Are you telling me the truth, though?
LUA: Yes, I am.
KAREN: Because lots of times you get jumpy when you don't want to tell the truth.
LUA: I'm telling you the truth.
KAREN: O.K. I can tell when you're not telling the truth, you know.
LUA: I know.

Karen presented herself as the supreme authority. "I'm telling you," she said to her daughter, "moms know a lot more than kids think."

Conditioning is one important factor that puts brainwashing in a different category from the usual misinformation experiment. Karen Greene used positive conditioning with the hand of a master. She promised the child that if she told more sex stories, Mommy would let her sleep in Mommy's bed. She offered Lua snacks, bubble gum, and candies in exchange for tales. Lua liked the family typewriter, that was clear. "You can use it later," Karen promised her, with the tacit understanding that the child tell "us" more first. Skipping school was an incentive. Going shopping with Mommy. Bonuses. But there were even more subtle and more important rewards on the table between young Lua Greene and her mother. "Mom's gonna love you even more after you tell it all," Karen promised. "You're gonna make me proud for being able to tell it all." The jury recognized the new infusions of warmth in Karen's ordinarily tight, dry voice.

Karen used repetition. She asked the same questions four, five, and six times. She emphasized identical points. The child said "No" much more persistently to her mother than she did to Officer Dorman. But still, by the fifth or sixth asking, the youngster's position usually crumbled. "Damn it, Lua," my mind screamed, as I listened to the tapes. "Don't give in!" But each time the child collapsed.

There was no escape. "My stomach hurts," the child tried. "O.K. Well, don't get angry. . . . Relax. The sooner we get through all this . . . the quicker we can go about forgetting." The child pleaded fatigue. No good. She pleaded hunger. "We'll go upstairs and get you half a sandwich you can bring down here."

Entrapment is the hallmark of the POW camp, the torture chamber, and the home that imposes captivity. Lua tried to spring the trap by pleading insanity. "Well, you're driving me crazy, too," Karen snapped.

Karen barked out "Truth!" too many times to count. "Truth," in fact, was Karen's favorite comeback—almost like a signal—when she did not like a "No." Karen demanded more, more, and more. "All right. Let's tell everything there is to tell, O.K.?" She pushed her young daughter mercilessly. "I told a mile-long tape already," pleaded Lua. But they taped until mother, not child, had had enough.

The events in Lua's memories changed because the events that Karen suggested changed. It was a wonder that Lua did not pick up sexual behaviors even more peculiar than the ones she had testified to before Officer Dorman and the state medical board.

> KAREN: Did Ed ever take a pencil or anything like that and touch you?
> LUA: No.
> KAREN: O.K., I'm just asking. I've got to cover all the bases.
> LUA: You're crazy.

Karen Greene first mentioned Sarah Allston's name in the fifth audiotape, and Lua's response did not satisfy her.

> KAREN: Was Sarah ever in the office with Ed and you?
> LUA: Yes.
> KAREN: Tell me about it.
> LUA: She was real nice.
> KAREN: O.K., let's go back over it.

By the time Lua finished her final taping, Karen had managed to transform Sarah Allston in Lua's mind. Karen had asked her hundreds of questions about watching adult sex and about being looked at and touched. She had questioned and cross-questioned Lua about Sarah Allston. Then, too, mother and child had uncounted opportunities to talk between tapes.

> KAREN: You said something [away from the tape recorder] about Sarah Allston and I want to know what you had to say.
> LUA: *Sar*ah Allston, you mean? *Ms.* Allston? Sarah *All*ston. [Lua's emphases held all the mockery of the schoolyard.] Um. She told me that she would tie a rope around my arms if I didn't settle down and let her and Ed do what they wanted to do.
> KAREN: What did they want to do?
> LUA: They wanted to pull my pants down and look. She did.
> KAREN: She did? Did this happen more than once?
> LUA: Yes.
> KAREN: Did she pull your pants down and look?
> LUA: Yes. And I didn't want her to, but she forced me.

People sometimes do self-defeating things with tapes. Richard Nixon did. Karen Greene did. Her tapes were made to nail Drs. Riley and Allston. What they actually accomplished, however, was to nail Karen—at least, before that Oklahoma City jury. Karen's tapes provided me with the framework to demonstrate the inculcation of false memory in a way that any juror could understand.

Lua herself sat stiffly on the stand and showed little to no emotion as she spoke of the horrors she had endured. Her story was inconsistent with her depositions and her testimony before the State Board of Medical Licensure and Supervision. When she was cross-examined, her story was inconsistent with what she had said moments before in her direct testimony.

In his final courtroom summation, Tom Blackburn talked about Lua Greene's lack of specific symptoms related to sex abuse and her lack of emotion in speaking before the jury. He reminded the jury that Lua had said under oath that she felt she had to "come out with the truth" before her mother and father would be able to start their lawsuit. Lua had told too many stories, and varied them too much over time, to be telling the truth, he said. Blackburn summarized my testimony about suggestion. He also recalled testimony that an estranged friend of the Greenes had given, to the effect that a stack of *Penthouse* magazines consistently sat on the back of the Greene toilet.

No wonder Lua knew so much about porn, posturing, and leather. She'd grown up with it.

Edward Riley's attorney, in his summation, took the prize for brevity and drama. He simply stood up, walked over to the plaintiffs' table, and pointed at Karen Greene with a big, meaty index finger. His eyes alight with Oklahoma holy fire, he intoned, "*Shaaaame* on you, Karen Greene! Shame on you!!"

The jury cleared Edward Riley and Sarah Allston of any wrongdoing or negligence. Afterward, various members of the jury told Tom Blackburn's legal team that they were convinced that Lua's story was entirely false.

I could not speak with the other witnesses while *Greene v. Riley & Allston* proceeded. But I did learn after I testified that the couple who first sued Edward Riley and Sarah Allston won a verdict against Dr. Riley for alienation of affection in the amount of $77,000. Riley had landed on his feet this time, however, and was continuing his professional life in another state. All of the other civil cases were ultimately dismissed. None of the decisions went against Sarah Allston.

Dr. Allston's reputation was damaged, regardless of her ultimate victories. I learned more than a year after the trial, however, that she had received a major promotion at the Midwestern state hospital to which she had gone when she was almost run out of Oklahoma City. Good doctors are good doctors wherever they go.

I eventually talked with Sarah at a psychiatric conference. She was a bright, pleasant woman, not at all embittered by what a child's false memory had done to her.

The only time I ever saw the child star "live" was on our day in court. I sat in the anteroom of the judge's chambers as I waited for Lua to finish testifying. From this vantage point I could watch her but couldn't hear her words. Lua had just turned fourteen. She was attending modeling school, and already had a portfolio of photos in readiness for her career. She was indeed beautiful. But something had changed. The teenager's platinum streaks, her starchily permed hair, her neon "off-and-on" smile, struck me as false. She had been a full-blown star when she was young. Now she was a starlet.

As I write these words, I ask myself whether Lua lost her case. She made no money out of her multimillion-dollar lawsuit. That was a loss. But she did win a mother. Winning a mother is an important victory for a rejected kid. Toward the end of the tapes, there's a telling exchange.

KAREN: You think maybe we can have a better relationship, get along better, because you're not—?

LUA: Yeah. I'm glad it's over.

KAREN: You've been afraid to be friends with me, haven't you, and to be close to me, because you were afraid of telling me. Is that it?

LUA: Afraid you'd suspect?

KAREN: Uh-huh.

LUA: So I haven't been talking to you?

KAREN: O.K. So now we can get past all that, can't we?

LUA: Uh-huh.

KAREN: We can be good friends and have talks and understanding.

LUA: Yeah.

# 7

# The Black Dahlia's Son

Every so often I browse in the mystery section of a bookstore. Especially when I find myself alone in a big city, I head for the mysteries and invariably feel at home. When I was a kid I read Agatha Christie, Ellery Queen, Conan Doyle, and Poe. I must have taught myself to read for detail from the mystery novel. I spent considerable eleven-year-old enthusiasm trying to solve Agatha Christie's murders before the writer herself would offer the solution. This forced a very peculiar style of reading, shuffling back through parts I'd already read and comparing various sections for clues. I read mysteries, in other words, the way an educated layperson might use a medical text to find a diagnosis.

One evening a few years ago, after my first book was published, I gave a reading at Bay Bridge Books, in Oakland. When I'd finished I felt a postadrenaline letdown and walked over to the store's mystery section for comfort. The manager paused on her rounds to talk.

"So you love mysteries," she commented, a good book-lover's opening. "Have you seen the new James Ellroy novel, *L.A. Confidential?*"

No, I hadn't. I hadn't spent any time with the Ellroys, because they looked more like crime than mystery.

"You'd be interested," she said, aware that I had studied writers who were traumatized as children. "I've heard that Ellroy's mother was murdered when he was a boy. He'd be a fascinating study for someone like you."

I scanned above eye level for the "E"s. Ellroy. *L.A. Confidential* must have been up front with the newly published hard covers, but here were three paperbacks—*Clandestine, The Big Nowhere,* and *The Black Dahlia.*

The "Black Dahlia," I remembered, was the name of a real murder case—one of those famous crimes that turn up in any number of movies. The Dahlia was an aspiring actress who was murdered in Los Angeles some time in the 1940s. She had been tortured before she was killed, and then dragged to a vacant lot near a busy street corner, where she was found. Her jet-black hair had probably inspired the first part of the name she was given in death, but I had no idea what the "Dahlia" part meant. As far as I knew, her murder was never solved.

All four Ellroy titles sounded like they were set in the Los Angeles of the 1940s—the old Los Angeles of James M. Cain and Raymond Chandler. The writer probably lived there, I thought—now, or at one time. Was there some connection between James Ellroy's murdered mother and the Black Dahlia? I took down the book and riffled through it, stopping at the dedication page. The format was so symmetrical that it looked like the lettering on a tomb. "To Geneva Hilliker Ellroy," it read, "1915–1958, Mother: Twenty-nine Years Later, This Valediction in Blood." The copyright date was 1987, twenty-nine years after the author's mother died. Evidently there *was* a connection in the author's mind, but what was it? I bought *The Black Dahlia* and took it home—but the first order of business was to find out more about Geneva Ellroy's murder.

My mother, Esther Cagen Raiken, a very attractive octogenarian who lives in San Francisco, is a professional librarian and a dogged researcher. I phoned her the next morning. "Mom, would you go to the main public library and check out the *L.A. Times* files of 1958 for a news story on the murder of a woman named Geneva Hilliker Ellroy? She had a son, who would have been nine or ten years old at the time. No obituaries, unless you find a big long one. Stick with the news, instead."

"Sure Len. How soon?"

"As soon as you can do it."

Several days later she called my office while I was treating a little boy. "Lenny," she said, her voice excited. "I found a murdered Jean Ellroy, not a Geneva. But this Jean—she had a ten-year-old son. And it was 1958. Should I go ahead and copy it?"

"Yes, O.K. And thanks. I think you've got the right one," I said, and turned my attention back to my young patient, having been careful not to say "Mom" on my end of the line.

The *L.A. Times* of June 23, 1958, told one of those gruesome stories you'd rather not read, let alone contemplate. A woman named Jean Ellroy, a nurse, was found strangled in the Los Angeles suburb of El Monte early one Sunday morning. Her partly clothed body was discovered on a lane close to Arroyo High School by a group of young boys on their way to play in a Babe Ruth League baseball game. Her torn print dress had been hiked up above her waist and her underwear removed; her brassiere lay in the ivy, near her body. She was barefoot. One stocking had been pulled down to the ankle, and the other was wrapped around her neck. The lower part of her body was covered by a woman's navy-blue overcoat. Her pearl necklace had broken, scattering loose pearls all over the ground. On her finger, she wore a large fake-pearl ring.

Mrs. Ellroy had been garroted with a thin, strong cotton cord; it was clear from the marks on the victim's neck that the stocking was not the murder weapon. She had fought hard against her killer and had broken a fingernail. On her left hip was an asphalt mark, indicating that she had been dragged along the ground. Because it did not match the pavement near the school, the police concluded that she had been murdered elsewhere and then driven to where the body was found. There was no purse or any identification on the body. Radio news broadcasts asked the help of citizens in identifying her and gave a description of the victim—bright-red hair, hazel eyes, 5 foot 6 inches tall, weight about 135 pounds. Several hours after the corpse was found, Mrs. Ellroy's landlady phoned the police. They brought the fake-pearl ring to the landlady's home, and the identification was subsequently made. The police told the *Times* that on the Saturday night she was killed, Mrs. Ellroy had been seen leaving an El Monte bar with a blond ponytailed woman and a dark-haired man. Nobody at the bar knew who these two people were. And no one knew of a preexisting relationship between the murder victim and the two strangers. The victim's car was found parked in the bar's lot after her body was discovered and identified. The newspaper article ended by noting the fact that "Jean's" marriage to Armand Lee Ellroy had ended in divorce four years earlier, and that the Ellroys had one child, a ten-year-old boy who had spent the weekend visiting his father.

The date and the last name were correct, even though the woman's first name was off. I assigned my mother another job, asking her to call the *L.A. Times* and the LAPD to see if the Ellroy murder case had ever been solved. The newspaper had no more in their files than what we had. The police confirmed that Mrs. Ellroy's murderer had never been found.

What interested me about James Ellroy was, of course, the obvious question about how a boy comes to fashion his life around a shocking tragedy. But what interested me even more was the question of Ellroy's memory. Here was a situation in which I had, thanks to my mother, the external confirmation in hand—a rather lengthy news account of a grisly murder. Would Ellroy's recollections be as complete as the paper's? What would he have added or subtracted from his memory?

I wrote to Ellroy in care of his publisher, saying that I would like to interview him for a book on memory. I wanted to talk to him about what he recalled of his mother's murder—to learn about it from a child's point of view, if possible. It would be interesting to learn what influence he thought these memories had exerted on his life and writing. I told him that I intended to read each of his published novels, and that I would then want to hear what he thought about what I thought. I proposed an exchange of ideas. But most of all, I wrote, I wanted to assess his memories.

I was curious to know whether James Ellroy had any ideas about who had killed his mother. He brought considerable expertise to the quest for a solution, not only because he had written nine crime books but also because he knew his own family. Had he unraveled the crime on his own? Could Ellroy remember the full story through the eyes of a ten-year-old child? Writers are often able to recapture childhood memory in a more living, breathing way than other people. Had the story been reworked in Ellroy's mind? Perhaps he had altered his memories to fit his emotional makeup. Had his memories been woven into the various murders in his books?

Ellroy finally phoned me late one afternoon in the spring of 1991, eight months after I had first tried to contact him. I was surprised; I'd almost given up. Yes, he would see me. He and his wife lived not in Los Angeles but in Connecticut, and he did his writing in the basement studio of a widow's house in Eastchester, New York, about a half an hour away from his home. He would see me at the Eastchester studio. We made an appointment for the very next week—just time enough for me to read *The Black Dahlia.*

Before I hung up I asked if I should call him James. "Just call me Dog," he said. "My friends call me Dog. And I hope you don't mind dogs yourself. I keep a big one named Barko at my place." Dogs do tend to frighten me, especially big ones. But I wasn't about to let that stop me, and I told him I didn't mind at all. "Goodbye," I said.

"Arf, arf," said Ellroy.


The basement studio wasn't so bad. I found it a roomy, comfortable space looking at grass level into a nice Eastern backyard. Once I had clambered over a fence that had been left closed to keep Ellroy's dog in, the crime writer greeted me without barking and waved me past a cowhide-covered daybed to a big oak desk that looked like it had seen hard use, where we set up my recorder. Framed covers of Ellroy's nine published books lined the walls. Barko, a formidable-looking English bullterrier, lay fast asleep on the cowhide bedspread. Ellroy was formidable himself. He was somewhere in his mid-forties and several inches over six feet tall. His gangly frame was clothed in a plaid flannel shirt and an old pair of blue cords. The effect was casual, but his countenance, with its large dark eyes and prominent bones, seemed haunted.

I was staying with friends in Connecticut, who had suggested that I take along their portable phone. They thought that Ellroy—his history, his profession, his basement, his dog—sounded downright dangerous. I had refused their telephone, but I kept the warning in mind. "Dog" offered me a cup of tea and took one for himself. So far, so good. I turned on the recorder, and he started his narrative.

"I was born in Los Angeles in 1948," he said. "My father was fifty years old when I was born. And he was the handsomest man my mother had ever seen, she told me. My mother was thirty-three. She was a registered nurse. He was an ex-Army officer and a womanizer and an inventor who never made much money. He usually worked as an itinerant accountant."

Both parents had affairs, and his father moved out when James was six, by which time the boy was well aware of the extraordinary tension at home. "There were fights, yelling, and screaming," Ellroy recalled. "No physical violence, though." Ellroy's father was born in

Massachusetts. His parents died young, and he was raised from the age of five in an orphanage. Ellroy's mother came from Tunnel City, Wisconsin ("a cabbage town," according to Ellroy). Her people were German and Dutch farmers. Her parents named her Geneva after the Wisconsin lake, but as she got older her friends took to calling her Jean. She had a sister named Leoda, whom Ellroy had not seen in years. Nor had he seen her two daughters, his cousins.

"Is there a reason for that?" I asked.

"The reason is that Aunt Leoda believed that my father had my mother killed."

"Your family in Wisconsin thought your dad was the murderer? Or that he paid someone else to do it?"

"Yes."

Myths play a big part in family life, and in James Ellroy's immediate family there had been two. There was his mother's Dillinger story and there was his father's Rita Hayworth story. "My mom had gone to a nursing school in Chicago," he said. "One of her favorite stories— and it's a crime story—was that she had been in Chicago in 1934, when John Dillinger was gunned down outside the Biograph Theater. My mom saw it happen. Yeah, she was a witness to the Dillinger shooting. She did not go into detail. I wish to hell she had. It would have made a better story. As it is, this isn't much of a family legend.

"My dad was in the First World War." His voice had changed— there was a touch of pride in it. "Amazingly, if you can believe this, he chased Pancho Villa in Mexico. Won a Silver Star overseas. My father was also a tremendous bullshit artist. This is a classic story about my father. I am fourteen years old. We're lying around the pad. 'You know,' he says, 'you know, I used to fuck Rita Hayworth.'"

I burst out laughing, remembering that famous shot in *Life* of Rita Hayworth kneeling on a bed in a satin nightgown. Barko's eyes stayed shut, but he curled his lip and showed his teeth. Then he rolled over and gave a deep dog sigh. I would have to keep my volume down, I thought. No need to disturb such an animal.

"I said to my father, 'Fuck you, Dad, you never fucked Rita Hayworth.' And he said, 'Yeah. I fucked her. You know, I was her business manager in the late forties.' Well, O.K. You know, I never thought about it again. Then he died, in 1965. In 1975, I'm in Westwood Village in Los Angeles. I see a Rita Hayworth bio in the window of a bookstore. So on instinct I go in, and I look up my father's name in the index. There it is—he *was* her business manager in the late forties. O.K., that's true. Maybe he even had something going with her. But the old man also told me he was Babe Ruth's business manager. *Nooo,* Dad, unh-unh."

Ellroy shook his head, wistful now. "Yeah, he was a man with a great deal of promise who never found his niche," he said. James Ellroy still loved Armand Lee Ellroy—you didn't have to be a psychiatrist to tell that. "There he was with a real Silver Star, and still he was making up more medals than he had. If he'd won all the medals he said he had, he would've been the World War One equivalent of Audie Murphy."

So Armand Lee Ellroy had trouble telling accurate stories about himself. In some instances, he got it right. In some, he got it wrong. His personal narrative had been fraught with exaggerations and inaccuracies.

In his 1992 book *Retelling a Life,* the psychoanalyst Roy Schafer attempts to debunk the commonly held idea that tales of personal experience refer to one single and unified concept of the self. "The so-called self exists in versions, only in versions, and commonly in multiple simultaneous versions," he says. If our own versions of ourselves vary from minute to minute, how can we get our own memories exactly right? Armand Lee Ellroy may have been serving up false memories to his son. Perhaps lies. But perhaps, too, Ellroy's father had distorted his versions of himself in his own eyes. An objective biography would say that he was a successful soldier, a relatively unsuccessful itinerant accountant, and a relatively successful ladies' man who was fond of his son. His own personal narrative might feature instead "fucker of Rita Hayworth and war hero supreme."

Schafer asks—alluding to the process of listening to patients in psychoanalysis but perhaps referring to all personal episodic memories one hears—"Which self stories are now being hinted at or disclosed or are now in the process of being constructed or revised and for which purposes?" As for James Ellroy's versions of his parents, Roy Schafer's questions also apply.

Ellroy still harbors a number of memories from before the age of three, when he lived in West Hollywood. "I recall a Hopalong Cassidy knit short-sleeved shirt I wore all the time," he said. "It itched." Ellroy evidently remembered the itchiness better than the "Hoppy" craze. "I also remember from—I would say, the age of three or four—

ramming my bicycle into a light pole. I remember thinking, 'Wow, I'm going to run into that light pole!' It was a tricycle rather than a bike. On my tricycle. And thinking—I can remember feeling giddy about it—'Wow!' And then hitting it. And, you know, cutting my forehead up and being surprised it hurt as much as it did."

Ellroy's story has a nice spontaneous ring. His emotions shift from glee to terror in the last two sentences. But is this the way our memories first enter our thoughts? They might look more like a picture—heading for the pole. Or feel more like a sensation—the surprise of the pain. But most of the time they don't line up like stories. Later we put them together that way. And when we line them up, they lose a little of their historical truth. They do not become false memories, but they deviate in small ways from what actually happened.

Very early memories, from before about age five, often represent the upsetting things, the scary things that occurred in our young lives. Most of us tend to retain as our earliest recollections the self-defeating decisions we made, the scares, and the surprises. This does not mean that childhood is terrible. It just means that emotion-laden materials are easiest for young children to remember. James Ellroy's itchy shirt and his surprise at the light pole ('Wow! Ouch!') are typical of first remembrances. Ecstatically happy, or annoying, or frightening—our first episodic recollections are usually of things that stirred up strong feelings. I once asked a professional group with whom I had been working at the Albert Einstein Cape Cod Seminars to write down their earliest childhood memory and a few associations to it, and pass it along unsigned. The majority of these earliest memories were of frightening events. A significant number told of happiness. Some were bland. But when a memory itself sounded bland, the memory-holder's associations to this memory usually placed it in the class of intense emotional moments from early childhood.

Affect drives much of the episodic memory we retain or later retrieve. It may be that the neurotransmitters released with strong emotion (perhaps a neuropeptide corticotrophin-releasing factor or the neuronal stimulant serotonin) aid in fixing our long-term memories of emotional events. On the cellular level, these chemicals are probably activated at the time an affect-laden memory is planted. They may be released on retrieval of the memory. We do not know which chemically active brain substances cement these earliest memories. But we do know that early memories are very well cemented.

Later, defenses come in to cover some memories and make them less accessible to retrieval. But it takes practice to defend, so the earliest and the strongest emotional memories may remain available while the conflicted memories of later childhood are lost to us.

James Ellroy remembers his parents' separation and divorce very well. He was six years old at the time. His painful memories of this part of his childhood are full of details. "I remember my mother telling me that she and my father were getting divorced," he said. "And I remember crying. I knew from watching a popular TV show called 'Confidential File' that divorce was a big thing. It was something on the level of a 'social issue,' or whatever they called it back in the fifties. I remember doing a little boo-hoo number about it. And I remember going downtown to Superior Court, or Municipal Court, or whatever it was, when my presence was required for their custody fight. My father had detectives stalking my mother, trying to find her in bed with guys. I don't think they ever succeeded, because she got custody of me." A look of sadness came over his face.

"Ah, in any event," Ellroy continued, "my father didn't see me for a while. Once when I was away on a holiday with my mother, my dad snatched me up and took me into a men's room, figuring he'd be safe in there. He could have a little chat with me."

Like an expert magician, "Dog" had managed to divert my attention, moving us swiftly to the semi-comic setting of a public men's room immediately after bringing up two painful subjects—his mother's sexual escapades and the outcome of the custody battle. I put a mental tab on the moment. Diversion—or displacement, as it is known in psychiatry—focuses attention away from important conflicts. I thought it might figure somehow in Ellroy's memories.

"And the dear lady"—Ellroy was obviously unable to say "Mom" or "Mother" now—"she is fiery-tempered and has fiery red hair. She stalks into the men's room, and I can still remember, there is a guy standing there at the urinal. He was going, like, 'What the hell is this?' I can still see the guy's face."

Faces, like positions and postures, label our very early memories much better than do time perceptions, our ages when the event took place, or people's names. Many times a memory is just that—a face, a simple action, and a posture. It may not take form until a narrative is put to it, and the narrative may not be entirely accurate. The psychoanalyst Donald Spence writes that the narrative part of a memory easily diverges from its historical truth. "The very act of talking about the past," Spence writes, "tends to crystallize it in specific but somewhat arbitrary language, and this language serves, in turn, to distort the early memory." And when therapists add narrative bridges to the memory fragments their patients give them, they detract considerably from the accuracy of the remembrance. This gloss comes from the therapist's imagination and not at all from the patient's original perception. In therapy, memories can become more distorted than they were when they first arose in the patient's mind.

James Ellroy was extremely disconnected from other children as a child. He says that he suffered from intense loneliness. He persistently begged his mother for a dog, but she would not give him one. Once in 1956, when James was eight, Jean Ellroy took him to a drive-in theater where the Dean Martin–Jerry Lewis film *Hollywood or Bust* was playing. "In it"—"Dog" started to chuckle—"Jerry Lewis by himself is driving on the Pennsylvania Turnpike or something. And he has a giant Great Dane in the backseat. He hits a bump, and this Great Dane puts his paws on the steering wheel and starts to drive the car. Like this."

The crime writer gestured at this point to show me how a big dog drives a car. He laughed so heartily that Barko woke up and leaped off the daybed. Barko raced over to me and vigorously sniffed my lap, but he seemed friendly enough. I tried to ignore him. Ellroy was lost in his own childhood wonderment at a different dog, a different time, and he mindlessly patted the animal's back. "I laughed at that dog," he said, smiling at something only he could see. "A Great Dane driving a car—I thought it was the funniest thing I'd ever seen. I howled. Urinated all over myself. I laughed in spastic fits for the ensuing week.

"I laughed far too much," he went on, beginning to sound regretful. Barko lay quiet but alert at Ellroy's feet, listening almost as if it were a dog story, not a story about a boy. "My mother took me to see a child psychiatrist—or psychologist, or whatever. It was a woman. And she gave me some blocks and stuff to play with. And little toy soldiers and Indians, or whatever the hell they were. And what I did was, I put the Indians and soldiers right in the middle of a desk, and I built a very, very high wall around them. The psychiatrist said, 'Well, why do you think these Indians and toy soldiers need to be protected so much? Why are you building your walls so high? Do you want to keep people out, or yourself in?' and all that. That's what I recall. And that's my first experience with a shrink. I wanted out. That was it. I didn't go back. My mother decided it wasn't worth the money."

Ellroy puts this identical psychiatric sequence into one of his books about random murderers, *Killer on the Road*. James did not like the psychiatrist his mother chose for him, but the adult Ellroy knew that this woman had been right. "There *was* a wall there," he said. "I *had* separated myself from other people."

Ironically, however, there were only tissue-thin walls between James and his beautiful mother. After the divorce, James watched Jean's men come and go. He watched her body, too. "She was open about, you know, her nudity," he said. "She was a zaftig redhead. I had a thing about zaftig redheads for a long time. She was *very* attractive. And, you know, I recall dawdling—and it's funny—I can see, you know, the house where we lived. In the bathroom I used to dawdle and go around and around and float in the bathtub, just on the off chance that she would have to come in and take a pee. Sometimes she'd pee naked. So I would wait."

I have a photo of Ellroy naked from the waist up in a bathtub; it appeared in the October 19, 1992, issue of *People,* in connection with the magazine's review of his tenth book, *White Jazz.* He squints and spreads out his fingers in a monsterlike array, looking the very soul of intensity. His chest is covered with hair. In this pose, Ellroy forces the viewer to assume his old role as a child voyeur dawdling in a bathroom waiting for something to happen. It is not a comfortable picture to look at.

Geneva Hilliker Ellroy was too seductive for her own good. She obviously hurt the boy with it. She was probably killed because of it. James wished passionately to go live with his father. "She" was much too much.

In 1956, Jean and her son drove down to Mexico for a short vacation. While there, the boy developed an earache. Jean packed up and drove to a Mexican pharmacy and then came back to the car and gave James a shot. She headed north for home. "It must have been morphine or something," Ellroy remembered. "I drifted into the most amazing haze in the backseat of the car. And I stayed in this state all the way home." Ellroy writes this scene into the end of *Clandestine,* his second and his most autobiographical novel. Michael Harris, the boy protagonist, is drugged with morphine by his father. He lies in the backseat of his dad's car and is driven to visit his mother. His father kills his mother while the boy drifts past consciousness. He is his father's alibi.

"How'd you think of that?" I asked, alluding to this apparent reworking of his own mother's death. "It just came to me," he answered.

James was continually overexcited. As a ten-year-old, he exposed himself to other kids. He masturbated "a lot." Ellroy manages to insert this wild, childhood-bound overexcitement into his mysteries. Dogs are oversexed; his dog characters are named Barko and Night Train and Rape-o. Rape-o, a pit bull in *The Big Nowhere,* mounts everything and anything. But children, too, are oversexed in the Ellroy crime novels. In *Clandestine,* Michael Harris exposes himself to other children and masturbates compulsively. The men in most of the Ellroy books are unstoppable voyeurs. They are trapped with the sexual compulsions of a boy of eight to ten who lives alone with his gorgeous uninhibited mother.

Are James Ellroy's memories of life at the age of eight typical in their abundance and richness of detail? The developmental psychologist Robyn Fivush, of Emory University, has studied how well young children remember at different ages. She concerns herself with three aspects of children's memories—the amount of memory, the accuracy of memory, and the consistency of memory. Children as young as two years old are asked for their versions of confirmable events—such as vacations they took, or a day's outing with Fivush's researchers to the museum—and the accounts are compared for accuracy and extent with those of parents and researchers, and for consistency with those the children give at later times or to different interviewers. Dr. Fivush and her fellow researchers have found that while age has no bearing on the accuracy of children's memories, older children— eight- to ten-year-olds, say—are able to include more details in their memories and are more consistent. They recount their memories steadily over time, with beginnings, middles, and ends. Toddlers, however, offer one part of the memory at one time and another part at another. They often need cues and prompting from the person asking for the memory in order to retrieve anything at all. It is as if the youngster of two or three must learn from the questioner how to organize a memory before he can spontaneously do so.

James Ellroy's memories from ages eight through ten of his impossibly sexy mother and of his own sexual habits sound accurate, although we cannot check them with a second observer, as Fivush does. Ellroy's early memories also internally conform to his adult behaviors—"I'm still sex-crazed," he told me—and to his writings. The memories are relatively full, and they are quite detailed. They make up what Dr. Fivush and other psychologists call a canonical narrative—a narrative that meets the requirements of conventional storytelling. Children of two and three cannot do this. When we try to retrieve our memories from ages two or three, the two- to three-year-old immaturities of narrative style still prevail. Ellroy's "itchy shirt" memory is one such example. He cannot remember where he was going or what he was doing when he was wearing his prized Hopalong Cassidy shirt, or who was with him when he put it on and went out in it. Even though most writers can elaborate seemingly without trying, Ellroy does not elaborate on this very early memory. It remains frozen in non-narrative form.

By the time James was nine or ten years old, his mother had gone too far with him. The boy wanted out. Four months before Jean Ellroy was murdered, she and her son moved from Santa Monica to the blue-collar suburb of El Monte. Their small rented house was "a dump," Ellroy recalls. The ten-year-old boy was forced to leave his small private school for a lower-middle-class, largely Hispanic public school. The move also required a complicated two-hour trip by cab and bus to visit his beloved father. This infuriated James. Was this move a way for Jean to punish Armand Lee? To make it hard for James to visit his father on the weekends? Jean made up for the move by at last allowing her son to have a dog—a tiny, neurotic dog, to be sure, but a dog all the same.

By now James was overlarge and overdeveloped for his age. He smoked his first pot in a vacant lot in El Monte. He knew nobody and felt entirely alone. The "walls" grew higher. He concocted nonexistent literature for his fifth-grade book reports, reviewing elaborate plots of his own making. One might say that these nonbooks are the Ellroy juvenilia.

Another of Ellroy's memories from this period remains strongly associated in his mind with his memories of his mother's murder. Fragments of memory surrounding horrible surprises very often become part of the mental representation of that surprise. They "condense" with the event, and, if personally meaningful, become permanent appendages to the memory. In El Monte around the time of his tenth birthday, James Ellroy was offered a choice by his mother. "Which parent would you rather live with? Children in California get to decide at ten." This is not so, but Jean may have believed it. In any case, the boy immediately made his selection. "I want to live with Dad," he said. Mom reacted fast. A brutal slap jolted the boy's face. The child stung with pain, shock, and outrage. He could barely contain himself. Ellroy remembers that at that moment he made a silent vow: "She will never, ever slap me again." A couple of months later, Geneva Hilliker Ellroy was murdered.

On the night following the discovery of his mother's body, James Ellroy moved to his father's "pad," a few blocks south of the Paramount Studios, in Hollywood. Drugs, part of his experiences in an El Monte vacant lot and on the way home from Mexico, became an almost daily part of his adolescent behavior. Lies and fakery, which had been the stuff of his El Monte public-school life, came to characterize his teens. The dog, that puny and far-too-belated gift, became his alter ego. "Call me Dog," Ellroy says to his friends. "Woof, woof," he says as he picks up the phone. Most important, however, the boy's innocuous vow that "she'll never slap me again" became a key component of his memories of his mother's murder. It served as a powerful "omen."

I discovered omens when I was working with the kidnapped children of Chowchilla. After the kidnapping, the Chowchilla group found belated significance in several items that had preceded the kidnapping by seconds to weeks, months, and years. For instance, an eight-year-old Chowchilla girl resented her parents' refusal to take her on an adults-only camp-out in the Sierras on the same day as the kidnapping. If she had gone to the mountains with them, she figured, she wouldn't have been kidnapped. A five-year-old girl blamed herself for having stepped in "a bad-luck square." A boy, age nine, thought the kidnapping had occurred because he was thinking "nothing ever happens to me" a short time before it happened. An eleven-year-old blamed himself for failing to answer a question his father had asked him a few years before, as they watched a scene in the film *Dirty Harry* in which the killer hijacks a Marin County school bus. "What would *you* do if you got kidnapped like that?" his dad had asked, interrupting the exciting action on the screen. The boy brushed the question off. He later believed that his failure to read "the signs" had got him in trouble.

I found that by five years after the Chowchilla kidnapping, nineteen of the twenty-six victims had appended mental representations of earlier or later events into the memories of their ordeals. One eleven-year-old girl, for instance, told me that a crank caller who phoned her house several times had predicted the kidnapping, although the calls had actually been made after the event. "I'm sure it was before," the girl said. "It seemed like a warning." Five of the kidnapped kids considered their parents responsible for failing to read "the signs." Ten went so far as to say that they themselves might be able to predict the future in other situations. Omens create mental mistakes. But they do not create wholly false memories. They cause memories to stretch, creating longer beginnings and later endings.

Omens are formed in the child's struggles to find a turning point in a surprisingly intense, sudden, and inexplicable event—a point at which everything could have been avoided. In the search to assign meaning to the meaningless, the child may land on something only remotely connected but nonetheless linked in some irrational way. Items may be linked because both of them are big, say, or because both of them make the child angry, or because their names are similar. They may be linked only on the flimsy ground that both are emotionally significant. This is why James Ellroy linked his "coming of age" vow to his mother's murder. The link was not logical. But it remained operational.

The UCLA psychiatrist Robert Pynoos, who studies childhood trauma, calls these appendages to memory "cognitive reappraisals." He means approximately the same thing that I mean when I use the term "omens." Neither term is quite right, though. "Cognitive reappraisal" assumes too much deliberate thought. Some of what goes into a memory is unconscious, primitive, and almost somatic, even though it adheres to the conscious mental representation of an event. And the word "omen" is not without its problems, since in my usage it is retrospective, not prospective.

There are other kinds of condensations that occur between real memories and other related thoughts or events. Cognitive psychologists have shown experimentally that if a person is exposed to several similar episodes, these episodes tend to merge in the mind. A child under the age of five who has undergone a relatively long emotion-laden event or a series of emotional events, stands a particularly good chance of condensing several episodes into one memory.

For instance, a twenty-seven-month-old toddler I'll call Muffy sat keening for two weeks outside the closed door of the bedroom where her mother lay dying of a viral infection. Muffy had a beloved governess, Ella Mae, who was fired a year later by Muffy's new stepmother. But Muffy—eleven years old when I met her—did not fully separate these two events in her memory. In response to my asking her to "tell me any awful things that have happened in your life," she responded, "I was sitting on a floor outside a closed door." She believed that this memory connected to the time her mother died. When I asked shortly afterward, "What happened to your governess?" she said, "Ella Mae died before my mother. I think she left before—no, after—no, before my mother died. Wait. I think Ella Mae died. No, I don't think she died after"—here Muffy broke into nervous giggles—"I think Ella Mae left after. No. No. Before my mother died."

A boy I'll call Sylvester also condensed two relatively long-lasting events in his developing memories. When he was three-and-a-half, Sylvester and his younger brother, "Clint," twenty-eight months old, were kidnapped by their father, a popular movie actor, from the park where they had been playing in the care of their nanny. For the next two weeks, the father flew the boys to Chicago, Switzerland, and Africa, every day or so jetting somewhere else just an hour or two ahead of their mother's detectives. About half a year later, he took the boys to Manhattan for the Christmas show at Radio City Music Hall, where he put them on stage, each dressed in a tiny tuxedo. I saw Clint when he was seven years old. By that time, he did not remember the snatching at the park. He had been at the borderline age for narrative remembrance when it happened. But he did fully remember his stage appearance at Radio City. Sylvester, on the other hand, remembered both events. But his anxiety had caused him to condense the two memories into one story. And the fact that the two stressful events were relatively lengthy aided in this condensation.

At age eight, Sylvester's memory of his most terrible moment in life went like this: "There was a frightening trip once. I went to Chicago, Switzerland, and maybe Africa. I was three then [all this is correct]. It was—I think—Christmastime [wrong]. I had a tux—yeah, I did. I wore a baby tuxedo [wrong]. I think I thought my mother was leaving me [correct—I saw Sylvester when he was eventually returned to his mother, and he would not let her out of his sight]. I took lots of planes on that trip [correct]. People were touching me when I was walking [this is probably the Christmas performance]. I remember thinking Mommy had left me [correct]."

Sylvester's mixed-up account is not a false memory. His mother's detectives vouched for the Chicago, Switzerland, and Africa trip, and thousands of New York theatergoers could vouch for the second. However, his account is marred by the inaccuracy of condensation.

At my request, James Ellroy told me his murder memories. Barko lay awake and alert at his feet. Ellroy sounded casual—at least, when he started. After all, the memories, bad as they were, were thirty-three years old.

"Anyway," he said, "the old man did not have a car. It was summer, and we had spent the weekend together. You know, the old man liked to chase women, read, go to the ball game, watch the fights on TV, endure golf—you know, and sit and think. And, ah, it's absolutely no accident that I'm his son." Diversion again. Would James return? I kept quiet. "Sunday night, my dad took me back to El Monte on the bus. At El Monte, he put me in a cab and said, 'See you next weekend.' There at the bus depot we said goodbye. The cab took me to Bryant and Maple, where I lived with my mother. It's slightly altered now—because I was out there last week, and I'm speaking from a recent memory now—but it was two houses then. A landlady's house right here, and our house facing perpendicular in a yard." Ellroy set up the relative positions of the houses with his hands. He certainly did see stressful old memories in terms of the space around him. "When I got there, there were a lot of stern-looking, outsize men— one guy in particular who had light-blue eyes and a gray crew cut."

I could see the scene through the young boy's eyes—the exact positions of the houses, the policeman with the pale eyes and the marine-style haircut, and all the other official-looking men milling about. These were burned-in visual memories; they forced the listener to visualize, too.

"The cab pulled up on the right-hand side of the street," Ellroy went on, without pause. "I could draw an 'X' on the spot where the cab stopped." Ten-year-old James's horror registered clearer than clear. A photo by Ansel Adams. A Vermeer painting.

The reason we remember terrible events with such a marked spatial sense may go back to our origins in the caves. In those days, your survival as you were being charged by a woolly mammoth or a saber-toothed tiger depended on your remembering exactly where to retreat. Those of us who made it into the twentieth century probably come from stock with excellent positional-recognition skills. Positions highlight our episodic memories of stressful events, even though we may not now require these pieces of memory as acutely as early man did.

"The guy with the light-blue eyes," Ellroy went on, "he was the one who took me aside when I got out of the cab. And I knew exactly what he was going to tell me. Exactly."

At this juncture in his murder memories, Ellroy asserts that he knew his mother was murdered before the man with the blue eyes told him so. Most likely, this is unconscious elaboration of the memory—a mistake. His mother could have been raped, or robbed, or wanted for some crime. A neighbor or friend could have been hurt instead. Any of these things would have explained the presence of the police. The boy may well have instantly suspected that something terrible had happened, but later he pushed for even more control over the uncontrollable. He went backward in his mind and reworked his memories. He attributed to himself the power of "simultaneous cognition," a paranormal power. This was an attempt by an overwhelmed child to re-create a sense of mastery. James mentally reached in order to regain control. Of course, in reality it was too late to control anything.

This almost paranormal sense of "knowing" in the wake of a disaster was also in evidence among the children I studied in Concord, New Hampshire, and Porterville, California, after the *Challenger* exploded. Five to seven weeks after the space tragedy, I asked each of the 134 children I saw at that point questions about paranormal experiences following the event. Of the East Coast teenagers—who had witnessed the disaster "live" and thus without warning—four in ten told me that they had had such an experience afterward. Two in ten of the younger Eastern children had had the same sort of experience. Several of the East Coast children had seen "good ghosts." Others had felt a "presence." Many of them experienced déjà vu or telepathy. (This was not a significant finding among West Coast children, who had heard about the explosion before seeing the videotapes on TV.) A year later, with nineteen new children added to the study, fewer than one in six of the Eastern teenage group and one in ten of the younger Easterners claimed to have had such an experience within that year. Paranormal experience, something that apparently comes in the early aftermath of a shocking event, and especially to adolescents, tends to condense with traumatic memories, creating variants of the truth.

"And this is what the man with light eyes did," Ellroy said. "He told me, 'Son, your mother's dead. Where is your father?' And I said, 'My dad's at the bus depot. He's gone back to L.A.' I did not cry." James may have been far too scared to cry. "I felt that time was centered at that very moment. It is the die that was cast. Right there. There was no going back."

Ellroy is aware of a peculiar sense of time in connection with this memory. In the midst of his stress, his past, present, and future had lost their context and relativity. The sense of time is vulnerable to trauma, and traumatic memories show it. A relatively recent evolutionary acquisition, it quickly disappears when a person is under severe stress, or has sustained a head injury, or is on drugs or alcohol. Young James Ellroy felt entirely overwhelmed at the moment he learned that his mother was dead. He "centered" time, losing all temporal perspective. However, Ellroy does not accept the idea that his telescoping of time that night constitutes a problem with his memory. "This is not any kind of revisionist memory," he insisted, as he bored into me with obsidian eyes. "I knew immediately as the cab was pulling up and I got out and saw all those people milling around—I *knew* my mother was dead."

Distorted time sense adds inaccuracies to memory. Five years after the Chowchilla kidnapping, four of the youngsters said that the event had seemed to take a much shorter time than the twenty-seven hours it actually took. Two Chowchilla children confused day and night. Seven others skewed time, reordering their memories of events following the kidnapping into a time preceding it.

Memories frequently suffer inaccuracies from time distortion, omen formation, and visual misperception. These mistakes may infect the memory of a single event, even if this memory subjectively feels clearer than clear. The infection lasts into adulthood. There is little opportunity for correction. Consider the example, for instance, of a well-known singer who a few years ago was named by a syndicated gossip columnist as having been involved in a nasty contract dispute with his manager. The singer could not get over the horror of having his personal business exposed in the press. He found himself dwelling almost incessantly on another situation—a much older situation—in which his story had also hit the papers. This was an incident he had put out of mind but had never forgotten.

In the singer's memory, he had been nine years old at the time, and his mother and he were leaving a market in the gray light of a small-town summer evening when a stranger grabbed him, dragged him into a nearby park, and orally raped him. The man let him go after a while, and the boy returned home. Despite his strong objections, his mother insisted that he tell the local police what had happened. The boy wished only to be left alone and to forget, but he did go to the police. A few days after the rape, the stranger was arrested. The boy testified. The man went to prison on a long sentence.

But the boy felt exposed. He left town for a New England boarding school, because he felt sure that the account about him in the town newspaper would reach everyone he knew. He recognized and dwelled upon this very same sense of exposure when, as an adult, his name appeared in the gossip column.

Shortly after seeing his name in the column—and because of it—the singer felt impelled to go back to his hometown and confirm his old memories. They had never been repressed, but he wanted to see what had happened from a more objective point of view. In the sleepy town, he went to the library where he had borrowed his first books. The back issues of the town newspaper were kept on microfiche. He sat down and checked all the issues that had come out when he was nine years old. There was no story. Age ten? No. Age eleven? Yes, there were a couple of articles. The singer had thought he was nine when he was raped. Age, part of chronological memory, had been distorted. He looked at the top of the page for the date. It was February, the dead of winter. Far from the balminess of summer, the temperature that day had been 31°F. Again, time was out of joint.

The singer thoroughly read the articles about his attack. The newspaper reported the name of the stranger who had raped him—a name he had forgotten. But there was no mention of his own name. The reports said that a boy had been kidnapped from his mother and sexually assaulted. They never used the terms "fellatio" or "oral sex." Anyone reading this small-town newspaper would have had to guess not only his identity but the nature of the sexual assault.

After conducting an external check of his old memory, the man was greatly relieved. His mortifying experience was probably known only to the few people he had originally told—his mother, the police-man, the judge—and, of course, to the perpetrator. The more recent but far less terrifying exposure of his legal problem with his manager was, he realized, "no big deal" either, even though it had been broad-cast far more widely. The singer relaxed and started working on his new repertoire. He was sorry he hadn't known the facts sooner. The library had brought him solace.

Even if a person remembers a horror consistently for years, as this man did, the attendant perceptions are not necessarily accurate. The principal events, however, are generally accurately remembered. It would be highly unlikely for a man who had been orally attacked to remember it as an anal attack, for instance. It would be highly unlikely for him to remember being taken from his father or from a friend rather than from his mother. And it would be unlikely for him to believe that his attacker was a woman. The gist of the memory stays true, but the details sometimes go "off." That's why the extreme polarization of the false-memory controversy does not make sense to me. People who say that their accusers are completely fabricating may be missing the essence of how traumatic memories manifest them-selves. Parts are true—often the gists. Parts are false—sometimes details in the descriptions of the perpetrators.

When memories of repeated events are repressed, dissociated, split off, or displaced, they are not necessarily more inaccurate when they return than are single-event memories that were always remembered. They tend to be more fragmentary, however, and they tend to be more condensed. If the perpetrators are clearly seen in these memories, their identifications are usually correct, because they were familiar people in the first place. After all, in repeated events, perpetrators are usually not strangers, who can be misidentified. But when massive dissociation or splitting prevents clearly "seeing" the perpetrator in memory, then descriptions of the perpetrator may be inaccurate. Often there are no "omens" in long-standing or repeated traumas. Once abused, a child uses more energies on prevention of feelings and thoughts than on retrospection. This prevention can interfere with looking at the face of the perpetrator and thus later accurately remembering him as Grandpa, brother George, or Uncle Joe.

We reëvaluate our memories as we get older, and their emphasis sometimes shifts in the process. When he was kidnapped at age three by a stranger, a boy I'll call Alan Bascombe blamed his mother for giving him up. But by age eight, Alan had shifted the internal emphasis of his memory. "I already know what it's like to die—to be killed," he told me. "I realize now that the man who took me could have killed me, [and] I know he had a gun on Mom and he would've killed her. Now I feel better about Mom, but a little worse about me."

We reappraise our pictorial memories with new advances in our thinking. The pictures last, but the captions change. Alan Bascombe had realized by the time he was eight that the man who kidnapped him was "two inches bigger than my dad." That piece could not have been part of his language as a three-year-old. Alan also had originally thought that the man's gun shot arrows. "I know now," he said at eight, "it was a real gun with bullets."

I wonder if an elderly blue-eyed cop in Los Angeles even knew that he appeared in two well-respected crime novels by James Ellroy. In *Brown's Requiem,* Ellroy's first book, the protagonist muses about a powerful older man, "There was nothing but the pale blue eyes, but it was enough." In *Suicide Hill,* a villainous L.A. cop named Gaffaney finds that an evangelistic wino's "blue eyes singed him in his sleep. . . . The blue eyes . . . were always a half step away, ready to pounce just when he thought everything was going to be all right." James may not have registered the color of the policeman's eyes correctly. But he certainly retained their meaning.

"They took me to the police station," Ellroy went on with his memories. "And somewhere in there they told me my mother was murdered. I'm not sure how they told me, or when. That part is fuzzy." The police strongly suspected Armand Lee Ellroy of killing his ex-wife. He had a motive—child custody. But the police had no choice but to believe the young boy's insistent account. His father had been home with him all the time. There had been no babysitters. He had not been aware of someone coming or going during the night. Saturday night had been just like any other night at his dad's apartment.

At my request, Ellroy recited what he remembered of the June 23, 1958, *L.A. Times* article reporting his mother's killing, though he told me he had read it only once, when he was ten. (Was this true? He asked me to send him the article after our interview—he said he didn't have one of his own.) I was later taken aback to find that Ellroy closely paraphrases this article, even dating it June 23, in *Clandestine.* He also includes a small part of it in *Brown's Requiem.* The use of the

details of his own mother's murder struck me as coldblooded—
though post-traumatic repetition can often be disturbingly literal.
Ellroy misstates one small detail in his recital to me and in the novel-
istic paraphrases of the *Times*. The boys who discovered Jean Ellroy's
body were not Boy Scouts but Babe Ruth League baseball players.
Much more important, I think, is a blank spot in his memory of the
article. In his paraphrases, he forgets the stocking that was wrapped
around his mother's neck. He forgets the asphalt mark on her hip. In
other words, he has entirely put from mind the fact that the killer
tampered with his mother's corpse.


When I met Ellroy for the second time, in late August of 1991, he
was living in a rented house in Los Angeles—a two-story rustic hide-
away owned by a French countess—and working for the summer on
screen treatments for a German film company. I had read all his books
by then, and I wanted to discuss their psychology with him. *The
Black Dahlia* had intrigued me enough to warrant two readings; I
knew that this book was particularly significant to Ellroy. In *The
Black Dahlia,* a cop named Bucky Bleichert falls in love with the dead
Dahlia upon beginning to investigate her grisly murder (here, the
novel reads almost like nonfiction, because Ellroy includes so many of
the actual details of the Black Dahlia case). Bleichert meets a Dahlia
look-alike named Madeleine Sprague, and they begin an affair. But
Bleichert pines for the dead Dahlia. Suddenly his partner and best
friend turns up murdered in Mexico. And Bleichert, at a loss for
friendship, begins spending more and more time with the Sprague
family—Ramona, Madeleine's bohemian mother, and Emmett
Sprague, her father, who is a successful real-estate developer. At the
end of the story, Bleichert discovers that it was Madeleine who killed
his partner. He also discovers that Ramona Sprague helped the murderer of the Black Dahlia to torture the doomed actress before she
died. The girl's murderer is a weird hermit who lives in a house
owned by the Spragues; he is Ramona Sprague's secret lover and the
utterly deranged natural father of the psychopathic Madeleine.

Ellroy picked me up at the airport the morning I arrived in L.A.
and took me home to work, pausing in Beverly Hills to show me the
big brick house with its oversize front window, through which Bugsy
Siegel was gunned down by Lucky Luciano's hitmen in 1947. Ellroy

clearly loved mid-twentieth-century urban history. Figures like John
L. Lewis, John F. Kennedy, Marilyn Monroe, Micky Cohen, and Walt
Disney peopled his conversation. Ellroy's house, a wood-shingled
overfurnished place nestled in a dry oak-filled canyon, was exactly the
kind of place Californians dread, especially in August. It was a wonder the countess had been able to lease it at all.

"My dad started buying me crime books right after my mother was
killed," Ellroy told me when I turned on the tape recorder. "I started
stealing crime books right away. Within a year of my mother's death,
I got myself all involved with the Black Dahlia murder case."

On January 15, 1947, the body of a twenty-two-year-old would-be
actress named Elizabeth Ann Short was discovered just off the side-
walk in a vacant lot at the corner of 39th Street and Norton Avenue,
in South Central Los Angeles. The body was completely cut in two at
the waist. Cigarette burns, knife cuts around the breasts and thighs,
broken knees, and rope burns at the ankles indicated that she had
been tortured for about two days before she was murdered. Her
mouth had been sliced from ear to ear in a hideous smile. ("I knew I
would carry that smile with me to my grave," says Bucky Bleichert.)
The *Los Angeles Herald* dubbed Elizabeth Short "the Black Dahlia" the
day after her body was discovered. In the investigation's first twenty-
four hours, eighteen people falsely confessed to the killing. There was
something about Elizabeth Short in death that attracted the public,
normals and weirdos alike. She was depicted in the papers as an innocent girl who had come to Los Angeles to become a movie star and
changed within a short time into a black-clad, man-hungry femme
fatale.

Despite one of the biggest, most political, and most visible murder
investigations the Los Angeles police ever carried out, the Dahlia's
torturer, killer, and postmortem mutilator was never discovered. I
made a note of James Ellroy's "involvement" as an eleven-year-old
with this sexy but long-dead murder victim. "Displacement" was a
possible defense that James Ellroy—at eleven—had begun to employ
in order to avoid his memories of his sexy mother and her dead,
rearranged body.

"I also started walking around late at night and looking in windows," Ellroy continued. "Burglary and voyeurism, that was my
game. I was hot, too, for the Jack Webb 'Dragnet' TV show then. It
was on its last legs, and I loved it."

By the time James turned twelve, he was compulsively playing games of sex and death. "I would shoplift model airplanes," Ellroy told me. "I'd take books on the Dahlia." He stole his favorite, Jack Webb's 1958 salute to the LAPD, *The Badge,* with its long section on the Dahlia and a glamorous photograph of her. "And I'd take a number of pulpier publications that delved more deeply into her life and death. Crime magazines, all sorts of pictures. I made a photo wall of Dahlia stuff. My father worked late nights a lot. And I became a full-blown shoplifter.

"I would build the model cars or planes I had stolen. And then I would want to destroy them. So what I'd do, I would sit down on the curb at Beverly and Irving, where we lived—a busy spot late at night. And I'd wait for 2:00 A.M., when all the bars on Western Avenue let out. People would be highballing it west on Beverly. Then I would put these little cars, model cars, out in the street. And I would squeeze the glue—you know, the glue from my model-airplane construction—all over them. And squeeze a little trail of glue over to the curb and get some matches. Then I would either set the car or the trail on fire. I would watch the model car explode. I'd try to time the explosion to the arrival of an oncoming car. One day I put my model car way, way over the double yellow line. The oncoming car saw the fire and swerved at the very last minute. It went up on the curb on the other side of Beverly Boulevard and hit some bushes and stalled out. And I raced inside my house as fast as I could," Ellroy chuckled.

As a kid, James had come pretty close to being a killer. I could see myself in that car on Beverly Boulevard, stalled out and breathing like a steam engine, thanking my lucky stars that nobody had been coming up the street from the opposite direction. James Ellroy had indeed been "playing with fire," a murder—a real one—undoubtedly driving his actions.

James's preteen games with fiery model cars brings to mind the play of another creative and traumatized boy, Stephen King. In an interview in the April 1982 issue of *Penthouse* King said that he made up a game he played on his own for years as a child. He called it "Sodom and Gomorrah," and it involved bolting from imagined fire and brimstone raining from the sky. When King was four, he and a young friend were playing by the railroad tracks and a freight train hit and killed his friend. King writes in *Danse Macabre* that he remembers nothing of that terrible incident, and maintains that it does not account for the tenor of his work. But King writes mechanical monsters into much of what he does. He occasionally uses train metaphors to express nonmechanical horrors. The trains in the films *Stand By Me* and *Silver Bullet* literally loom up before our eyes to argue against King's protestations. Sudden devastating death lies behind both King's and Ellroy's childhood play. Their horrible memories also set the themes, consciously or unconsciously, for their adult play—their writing.

One of the factors that may distort what a child tells you about his or her long-term memories of a terrible event is how close to a life-threatening danger the child actually was. Robert Pynoos and Kathleen Nader, his colleague at UCLA, studied a number of free remembrances of L.A. children whose elementary-school playground was attacked by a sniper. The man unloaded several rounds of ammunition at them. One little girl was killed. The nearer a child was to the dead girl, the more likely the child was to minimize or completely omit that fact when asked to describe what had happened. These children may have been too embarrassed about nearly getting killed to bring it up spontaneously. On the other hand, a child safely inside the school was more likely to exaggerate the risk. It may have been safe to brag a little under such circumstances. This study reflects no problem with spatial sense, which usually is amazingly good in traumatic memories; it rather reflects what a child chooses to tell of his terrible memories. It is another reason that a certain number of specific questions must be asked of a child before a full memory can be obtained. These must not be strongly leading or misleading questions. The interviewer of children must carefully walk the line between eliciting free and cued recall.

"I always thought the cops were going to stake out the Franklin Life Building looking for some kid who dropped burning model planes from the tower." Ellroy looked rueful, thinking about his uncelebrated escalation of the Beverly Boulevard road game. But the police almost inevitably disappointed young James. The L.A. County Sheriff's Department never found his mother's killer. They never located him as the teenage menace of the Franklin Tower. And they never found the murderer of his love, the Black Dahlia. As far as James was concerned, the cops couldn't find out about anything.

High school offered no improvement in the life of this unhappy boy. Along with his one and only friend at Fairfax High, a Jewish boy who defined himself as a Nazi, he organized the Nazis of Fairfax. The two pals did not attend any official Nazi Party functions, but they offended their virtually 100-percent Jewish peer group by announcing their so-called Nazi Party meetings on the school's P.A. system and using their classrooms for Party business. The boys' assault on school sensibilities went too far. Before James could graduate, the principal kicked him out. James immediately enlisted in the Army, avoiding problems about his age by getting his father's consent.

Armand Lee Ellroy suffered a series of strokes around this time, and shortly died in an L.A. hospital. At age seventeen, James was an orphan. Within months, he feigned mental illness in order to get himself discharged from the Army. At loose and virtually alone in Los Angeles, he began to drift toward out-and-out depravity. He worked in Hollywood pornography shops. He did drugs in the caddy shacks of L.A.'s ritzy golf clubs. He broke into many houses, sometimes masturbating and stealing unknown women's underwear. He was arrested thirty times for various misdemeanors. Finally the LAPD came through with a substantial arrest. They booked James for burglary, a charge that was reduced to trespassing. He served a jail term—forty-five days. James had never really thought—from his ten-year-old perspective—that cops could catch anybody. Perhaps it helped him as a writer to realize that once in a while they do.

This realization, however, did little to change his behavior. After his release, he spent seven more years in the weird world of Southern California country clubs and porno shops. He caddied at the golf courses he writes about in *Brown's Requiem.* Drugs, alcohol, and making mischief remained his specialties. He says he always knew, however, that he would be a writer. And he also knew that his genre would be the crime novel.

In his early thirties, Ellroy courted a woman who asked him to please go see a psychiatrist. He agreed, and saw a female psychiatrist for ten months. "I think she was turned on by me," Ellroy told me, again indicating that he could not connect well with "shrinks." He may have displaced his early sexual interest in his mother onto the psychiatrist and then projected his own feelings into her mind. Then again, maybe the psychiatrist *was* turned on. It's hard to know now one way or the other.

Ellroy left psychotherapy, but joined Alcoholics Anonymous. It was time to write, he had decided. It was also time to move to the East Coast and away from his addicted friends. Both moving and writing helped Ellroy—as did a couple of years of attending A.A. meetings. His first book was published when James was thirty-three years old. Working steadily, once he started, James had his tenth book, *White Jazz,* ready in manuscript form by the time I interviewed him in L.A. ("Would you read it?" he asked, with disarming diffidence.)

I must tell one more story of James Ellroy's youth before completing our exploration of his early life. It is the tale of his obsession with "The Black Dahlia." From age eleven, young James could not get enough of her. He felt totally committed to her, totally "in love." She was—*is,* perhaps—the love of James Ellroy's life. After his mother died, James diverted himself entirely with the Dahlia. It was her picture that he kept, not his mother's. It was 39th and Norton that he visited, not his mother's grave.

By concentrating on a lusty dark-haired girl James avoided his lusty redheaded mother. By fixing his mental sights on the younger woman's death, the boy could evade most thoughts of the more meaningful older one's death. He could dwell on aspiring actresses, not registered nurses. (I found only two nurses in Ellroy's books, alongside eight "Dahlias.") He could pin up pictures of the younger woman. He could read everything about her that he could find. Keep scrapbooks. Even masturbate to his new obsession. This defensive dislodging, or transposition from one object to another, prevented the boy from thinking about "her." This is the essence of the defense known as displacement.

All defenses may be put to the service of forgetting. But displacement is a somewhat unusual way to put a memory out of mind, when one considers the more direct and common avenues of repression and dissociation. In the case of the Black Dahlia as a substitute for Geneva Ellroy, James was able to think, think, and think about the Dahlia's pre- and postmortem bodily tamperings. And in so doing, he was able to forget that somebody had tampered with his mother.

Elizabeth Short was the perfect diversion from Geneva Hilliker Ellroy because she was so much like her. Both women were easy with men, and both came from someplace cooler, cleaner, and far more wholesome than L.A. (The Dahlia was from Massachusetts; she came from a milieu not unlike Jean's in Wisconsin.) Both women moved freely among the late-night crowd. Neither ever had enough cash.

Each desperately wanted something better. And each thought she knew how to get it.

After he learned to travel on his own, James visited and revisited the spot where someone had dumped Elizabeth Short. He did not visit the spot where somebody had dumped his mother until a week before we first met, when a magazine crew from *Rolling Stone* asked him to go along with them while they took pictures of the place. James tacked the Dahlia all over his walls. "Pictures keep the woman young," he writes at the very beginning of *White Jazz*. Focusing on pictures of a forever-young black-haired woman served to defend against memories of the redheaded one. After age ten, James managed to keep his mind off Mom.

"Murder visited my life when I was only ten years old," Ellroy recalled in that parched, oaky California canyon. "It was shocking. It was horrifying in ways I probably cannot fully assess to this day. So I have to pass it along to my reader." That's a defense, too—"passive into active," in which something passively experienced is converted into an action aimed at somebody else.

When defenses work against memory, they don't necessarily block out all of the memory. They sometimes go to work on only one bit—the most painful or the most conflicted part of the story. Repression, the defense so often mentioned in contemporary controversy about false memories, accounts for the full disappearance of some memories but also can cause the disappearance of one tiny piece—the worst piece. I once worked for several months with a four-and-a-half-year-old boy who had spent a terrifying twenty hours stuck alone in an elevator. Nobody knew where little William was. And he could not figure out how to call for help. From the very beginning after he was rescued, William could not tolerate the dark—a behavioral indication that the lights in the elevator had been off. However, when I saw him for the first time, forty-eight hours after the incident, William insisted to me that the lights had been on. His behavior did not match his words. He appeared frightened when he spoke of the lights. As I continued to see him, William sometimes said that they had been on and sometimes that they had been off. But he frequently hid my toy cars in dark places—beneath my couch or behind my desk; this behavior pointed to the lights' having been off during his confinement and also to his anxiety with regard to this subject.

I saw William for a reëvaluation when he was eight. He was

entirely unable, though he tried, to remember whether the elevator lights had been on or off. The darkness now was lost to conscious memory, although it was clear that William did not like to sleep in dark rooms or to be confined. The darkness would have been the scariest part, the part most connected to William's feelings of helplessness and loss of connections with the people he loved.

The Black Dahlia displacement did almost the same thing to James Ellroy's memories that little William's "on and off" shiftings did to his. It created a small hole, a crucially placed one, in memory. What was most painful to James had to do with his mother's body— that "zaftig" body so openly shown to him as a child.

"If I suggested to you that it was too threatening to you as a child to stay obsessed with memories of your mother, so you picked the Black Dahlia instead, what would you say?" I asked.

Ellroy nodded and paused a moment before he spoke. "I'd say you were right," he answered.


Of course, Ellroy, as an avid watcher, student, reader, and thinker about murder from the time that murder visited his life, offers a solution to the killing of his mother.

"This is what I think happened," he says. "And I'm a gifted lay criminologist." We are sipping tea in his Eastchester basement, and our first interview seems about to end.

"I think my mother went out drinking that night. I think she got a little bit high. You know—she's an alcoholic, she's promiscuous. She went with this guy [the dark-haired man] and this woman [with the blond ponytail]. My mother was a caustic woman, a well-read, articulate woman. The man came on to her. She said 'No.' It got out of hand. He was not a habitual sex killer and he was not a serial killer. This is a single murder here. It is not any kind of serial chain."

Ellroy turns to me quickly, as if he thinks I don't believe him on this point. "As a psychiatrist interested in crime you must know that serial killers are just done to death these days. Far too much *Silence of the Lambs* stuff." He is arguing with me, even though I have said nothing. "There are probably fewer than forty real serial killers in America right now. Your odds of running into a crazed junkie are much, much greater."

Must I contemplate how I will be murdered? If Ellroy had been my patient, I would have shown him that he had displaced once again—this time from Geneva Ellroy to me. This is a very specific kind of displacement, defined in respect to psychotherapy or psychoanalysis as "transference." It is a displacement from childhood love objects—parents and other important early figures—to the therapist.

A number of professionals, concerned about the recent rash of accusations of family members by adult children in therapy, contend that transference adds to the inaccuracy of patients' memories. "The recall of the past is hostage to the transference," the psychoanalyst Donald Spence writes. He means that transference can be so intense that patients may tailor their remembered accounts of the past to please or displease their therapists, who must carefully consider this as well as how much of a patient's recall to elicit by cue and how much to elicit as free recall. One of the problems in therapy today is what to do with the small vacuoles in a patient's memory. It is important that the patient, not the therapist, fill these in. Or leave them unfilled altogether. The occasional patient requires an Amytal interview or hypnosis. But these techniques are very strong cues and must be administered with extreme care. At the opposite pole are the entirely nondirective therapies, which provide hardly any cues. In these therapies, many a traumatized person has no way to express the painful bits and pieces that still live in childhood memory. The therapist's nonresponse may unwittingly convey that these memories are insignificant, or too disgusting to discuss.

Ellroy manages to give me his conscious solution to his mother's murder without any prompting or cues from me. "I think the man was an El Monte man but not a habitué of that bar, or he would have been identified." he says. "I think he knew exactly where Arroyo High School was because he lived near it. I think he took my mother's body out and dumped it, and went home to sweat it out for a couple of months. And he got away with it. I think it was the exact combination of the wrong man and the wrong woman and the wrong circumstances. And the blond woman who was with them at the bar—she knows what happened. And she kept her mouth shut."

In Ellery Queen mysteries, Ellery's not-too-swift father, Inspector Queen, usually offers the wrong solution before Ellery gets his chance. Inspector Queen invariably falls for the obvious solution—the one we know will not hold true. Then Ellery, the boy wonder, reveals the key to the crime. I think of James Ellroy as a boy wonder, even though he is well over forty. But like the limited Inspector Queen, he came up with the wrong solution. It did not fit his memories. Nor did it fit his writings.

No matter which of James Ellroy's mysteries you read, you find no solutions involving a dark-haired man and a blond woman working together to pick up a woman in a bar and then murder her. Such a twosome does appear at a bar in *Clandestine* for a couple of moments, but only as a false clue. If James Ellroy really believed in this dark-man/blond-woman solution, why is it nowhere at the conclusions of his novels, where so many other events from his past reside?

Who did Ellroy *really* think had murdered his mother?

Ellroy thought it was his dad. And he thought it was himself. He took responsibility, in his own imagination. He knew he didn't kill his mom. But he beat himself up for it nonetheless. James was asleep the Saturday night his mother was killed, and he never really knew what Armand Lee Ellroy did or didn't do. In fact, James figured out a way that his dad's airtight alibi could have been set up through him—and he explains it in *Clandestine,* in which the "alibi" is drugged and taken along to the murder. If Dad so desperately wanted custody of James and he was brave enough to chase Pancho Villa in Mexico, he could also kill Mom. And if James could swear that "she'll never ever slap me again," he himself would have to be the murderer. Not in reality, but in his own mind.

The killer in *Clandestine,* Ellroy's novel of his own childhood, is his father. In *The Black Dahlia* and *L.A. Confidential,* the killer is the biological but unacknowledged father. In four other Ellroy novels, the murderer is a father figure: three times he is an elderly and corrupt cop with a gang of young men around him; once he is a paternal but villainous psychiatrist.

Ellroy's description of Cathcart, the corrupt older cop and killer in *Brown's Requiem,* matches his description of his father. "He was a formidable-looking man," Ellroy writes, "iron gray-blond hair, sharp features. The body of an athlete at fifty-five." Ellroy does not add, "and the handsomest man my mother had ever seen." But he does—almost—in *Clandestine.* Doc Harris, the father and killer, is described this way: "Sitting across the battered coffee table from me was one of the most impressive-looking men I have ever seen. Six feet tall, close to sixty, with a full head of white hair, the body of an athlete, and a chiseled face." That's Dad.

In six of the Ellroy books, including a few that also feature "fathers" as killers, flawed young men also kill. They are the "sons." In his memories, Ellroy appears to inculpate himself in his mother's death because of his vow. Though he was only ten, his vow felt that powerful.

Since almost everybody in Ellroy's fiction is Ellroy himself, even his oversize, oversexed dogs, it is no real surprise to find that the cops are Ellroy, too. Lloyd Hopkins, a protagonist cop in three of the novels, answers to Ellroy's description: "About forty and very large. Intense gray eyes and dark hair sort of unkempt. Ruddy complexion. His clothes are out of style. He's funny and arrogant and sarcastic." Most Ellroy protagonists are just as flawed as Ellroy is. They have already failed or are currently failing to make it as cops, just as he failed to graduate from high school and grow up with a "clean rap sheet." Ellroy's most important youthful mistake—his silent oath—forces his fictional protagonists repeatedly to cross the invisible line between cops-as-helpers and cops-as-killers.

David Klein, the unsympathetic policeman protagonist of *White Jazz,* kills throughout the novel—both for the Mob and for a killer group inside the LAPD. Buzz Meeks, of *The Big Nowhere,* runs David Klein a close second in killings, yet he manages (just) to hold onto the reader's sympathy. It is clear that in creating a young protagonist, Ellroy knows how to flaw him. And in creating a young murderer, Ellroy usually knows how to evoke some empathy. "More than any other contemporary author, Ellroy gets inside the skull of the sadistic psychopath," the psychologist and mystery writer Jonathan Kellerman has noted of Ellroy's work. Indeed, Ellroy can make the reader identify with a homicidal maniac. This is because the young and crazed serial killers of *Blood on the Moon* and *Killer on the Road* are James Ellroy himself. Like James, these sex-crazed young men peep through women's windows, hang photographs of sex and death on their walls, and masturbate to memories of murder.

It is important to recognize that James's unfortunate young life with his mother did not make him into a killer. It made him *feel* as if he were a killer. "I'm doing what I have to do, so are you, so was Fat Dog," writes Ellroy, in the guise of Fritz Brown (*Brown's Requiem*). "The only difference between us [good guys] and Fat Dog [an arsonist, extortionist, and killer] is that our conditioning was tempered with some love and gentleness. His wasn't." James Ellroy was loved.

He turned out to be a "good guy." He is not a killer, except in his own imagination and in his own memories.

When I remarked to Ellroy that all his major killers are either fathers or sons, he agreed, saying that he had never really thought about it before. Only two women kill in all of Ellroy—Ramona Sprague and her daughter Madeleine, in *The Black Dahlia*. But these two women are not nearly as powerfully controlling as are the men behind them. The quintessential Ellroy woman is simultaneously a seductress, a naïve object, and a victim. Only men are truly capable of murder.

At this point in a mystery, Ellery Queen usually clears up the side issues. What of the tendency in James Ellroy's life to displace as a way to forget? Did I find this tendency, too, in the Ellroy mysteries? Yes indeed. Ellroy's fictional detectives are obsessed with the dismembered corpses that they must investigate. Often they "fall in love" with these corpses. One detective, Danny Upshaw, thinks so obsessively about a group of cadavers that he accuses himself of sexual perversion and slits his throat. Lloyd Hopkins muses so much about the murdered women whose cases he investigates that he loses his wife. Bucky Bleichert has an affair with Madeleine Sprague, the Dahlia look-alike, while he investigates the killing of Elizabeth Short. Teddy Verplanck, the maniac killer of *Blood on the Moon,* carries a torch for Kathy, a girl he knew as a kid but didn't dare approach. To handle his loss, he fancies himself in love with other women, whom he then kills "for Kathy."

Ellroy's bodies almost always are tampered with after they are killed. Their postmortem "arrangements" vary from simply being moved to being raped, gutted, flayed, skinned, burned, sawed into pieces, shot, frozen, scalped, axed, and even heated up to force fast postmortem changes. It is no brilliant feat to conclude that because Jean Ellroy's body was tampered with and dragged to Arroyo High School, her writer son is led to re-create these depradations in his books. Bodily tamperings, more than any other single quality, characterize the corpses that James Ellroy puts into his novels.

The boy's displacements from Jean Ellroy to Elizabeth Short helped him to forget that somebody had violated his mother's dead body. When Ellroy and I speak about his mother's corpse—we are still in Eastchester, with Barko at our feet—I feel the *"POW!"* of his returning memory as it hits the air. It is as big as a *"POW!"* in the comic strips. Ellroy concludes his view of the killing this way: "Let's say arbitrarily that they left the bar together at 11:00 P.M. They had to go someplace. The sex vibe goes down or the sex vibe doesn't go down. The combustion happens. He frets over the body. You know, that the body is there. Much as I imagine the Black Dahlia killer fretting over the body: 'What do we do with it?'"

Who are "we"? The ponytailed blond and the dark-haired man, or James and his father? Or the unknown killers of the Dahlia? "Yes," I say, deciding he must be speaking of the dark-haired man and the blond woman.

"So one guy drives it to 39th and Norton and dumps it"—"Yes," I repeat, quickly shifting my focus to the Dahlia, and wondering if Ellroy will ever put her aside—"after mutilating it hideously. And one man, you know, takes her clothes off. He probably wanted to see her naked."

"Uh-huh." We may be back to Jean Ellroy now.

"And he covers her with an overcoat. And dumps her body in the bushes there by the high school." Ah yes, it's Jean.

Ellroy has mentioned nothing about the killer's postmortem rearrangements of his mother's body—about the broken pearls, the missing shoes, the stocking taken from her leg and placed around her neck. Could the stocking have been used to protect the killer's hands from the taut cotton cord he or she used to garrot Jean? I wonder. Could it have been placed there to divert the police from the real weapon? Was it left around Jean's neck as one last weird inexplicable gesture?

"There was a stocking wrapped around your mother's neck," I say. "The stocking didn't kill her, but it was there at the scene. Right?"

"You know, God—I hadn't thought of that in years!" he exclaims, apparently amazed. "You're right! That's right!"

"You *can't* remember that?" I ask. Those mutilated torn-up bodies in *The Black Dahlia* scream at me for understanding. Here are corpses that resemble Jean's—yet their author does not realize that he has repeated something from his childhood too painful to retrieve. I will later discover that tampering with corpses is a common element in Ellroy's fiction. A few people will tell me that they could not stand to finish one or another of his novels because of all the postmortem mutilations. Yet these cadavers have a reason for being—a surviving boy's need *not* to remember his own mother's body that way. I wonder if I have hurt him by mentioning the stocking.

"Did I put a stocking in any of my books?" he asks.

"Not in what I've read so far," I say. (There are, in fact, no stockings in Ellroy's fiction.)

"It might have been one of *her* stockings," Ellroy says. He is still grappling with it. He doesn't want to remember.

"It *was* her stocking," I say. I devoutly hope that Ellroy will be better off for knowing. It may cause him momentary pain, but in the long run he will be more complete.

"There," Ellroy says. "That was the first chill. The very first chill I've gotten from this interview. And I didn't get any chills from visiting my mother's murder scene with the *Rolling Stone* magazine crew last week."

"But this—about the stocking—you forgot that? I mean you don't remember?"

"Now that you tell me, yes. I remember it now. I know this is true."

Ellroy's defense was displacement. He had displaced from Jean to the Dahlia and had thereby forgotten a key piece of memory of his mother's murder. The unremembered piece was reproduced in novel after novel without any conscious awareness on his part. There were no stockings, but everything else that could be done with a body after death was done. These tamperings were a boy's displacements from one single stocking. Ellroy did not dissociate as a boy, nor did he massively repress, as does his murdering protagonist Dr. John Haviland of *Because the Night*. (Haviland cannot remember anything at all that happened to him as a child in the year 1957.) Ellroy told me, too, that he had never split—though his serial-killer protagonist Martin Plunkett of *Killer on the Road* considers himself to be both "just plain Martin" and "Shroud Shifter," a vicious comic-book character. Ellroy says that splitting is easy for writers: "It's an old device—the Doppelgänger."

Ellroy tells me that these days he is eagerly looking forward to writing novels dealing more with history and less with crime. In fact, over just one year, 1991, he divorced, remarried, changed publishers, and signed a three-book contract. Our two meetings may have been something both of us needed. I know I needed a good story about a boy's memory. And Ellroy may have needed a jolt to get himself out of a rut. Filling up one tiny hole in a ten-year-old's memory gave Ellroy a momentary chill. But these moments can also provide a sense of completion. Retrieving our childhood memories often has the power to release us from old, fixed patterns. Like Ellroy perhaps, we may move on to new adventures.

# 8

## Searching for Corky

There is a letter in my morning mail from a radio-talk-show host in Memphis, Tennessee. But he doesn't want to interview me. He wants to tell me about a quest he has undertaken—for his own memories.

Ross Harriman is thirty-five, he says, is married to a woman named Suzanna, and has two boys—Peter, who is five, and Jonathan, a year-and-a-half. His talk show is broadcast from Memphis on weekday afternoons into four states.

He has read *Too Scared to Cry* twice, he writes. After the first reading, a three-day run-through, he decided to take steps to unearth his past. One piece of his autobiographical memory was missing. He can hardly remember his brother.

"When I was four," Ross's letter continues, "my older brother, six, was crushed to death by a drunk driver. I didn't see the accident, but I was there when Dad broke the news to Mom. I don't remember very much from the days and weeks following Corky's death, and I don't remember much at all about Corky . . . but I can still clearly hear Mom's protests of disbelief when she learned that Corky was gone. . . . Corky was run over by the uncle of one of his classmates while Dad waited in the pickup line. This was a day Dad came home early. So he was there to get Corky. The drunk guy had come to pick up his nephew, and he hit the gas instead of the brakes. All the kids but Corky scattered when they saw the car coming. Corky's back was turned, and he was hit and killed. My dad covered his body with his coat and then came home to tell my mom."

Kent and Lucille Harriman handled the disaster by experiencing "the peace of God," Ross writes. "And it didn't take them long. They had 'the peace of God' when they went to the funeral, and they had 'the peace of God' when they met with that kid's uncle to let him know he was forgiven. Years later my grandfather told me he thought my parents were drugged, they were so calm at Corky's burial. God wasn't the only one to help them, though. I did my part."

After his brother's death, Ross grew up fast, he says. He had been a rambunctious child; now he took the mantle of the oldest son. He was coöperative and responsible. And he made sure that his younger brother, Scott, was kept away from harm. He would tell other people, on the few occasions when he spoke of Corky, that he had had an older brother who was killed. He never elaborated. And he never grieved.

Ross's grief—in essence, memories of his long-buried emotion—came back to him when he started raising his own boys, particularly the older of the two. "I didn't know I had that much sadness in me," he writes. When Ross's memories came back, they were of emotion entirely divorced from events. Memories come back that way sometimes, although less frequently than as events disengaged from emotions.

"I didn't start wrestling with my grief directly, consciously, until Peter, our oldest, started closing in on his fourth birthday," his letter continues. "It seems crazy to me now, but for years and years I believed that when I was four years old I was too young to have known Corky well, to have been close to him, or able to mourn his death. Spending time with Peter at four, and seeing his attachments to my wife and me, to his little brother, and to his neighborhood friends made my beliefs about myself at that age simply incredible."

Peter would be able to remember his brother Jonathan—Ross knew it. His own amnesia about Corky had left a black hole inside of him. Ross cried not just for his brother but for the loss of a part of himself, frustrated by an absence of knowledge about his responses to Corky's characteristics and to events involving Corky. In short, Ross knew he had lost part of his autobiography.

Toward the end of his letter, Ross writes that he has begun a search. He says that he has been writing to people who knew Corky. And he has sent this letter to me. He attends a weekly men's group. At one such group meeting, he openly grieved for Corky. "But I spent time grieving," he writes, "the way Pharoah's army spent time bathing in the Red Sea. One moment I was on dry solid ground; the next I was engulfed by an ocean." And he tells me that he intends to talk with his parents. "I wish to resurrect the parts of me that got buried along with Corky," Ross says. Ross Harriman wishes to resurrect himself.

Ross's letter prompts me to wonder about the lost pieces of autobiographical memory that haunt our lives. How does it feel to have a piece of our life missing? And how does one begin to find these memories? And what kind of "wholeness" or "healing" results at the end of these quests? Perhaps I will learn directly from Ross. I will also turn to the writings of Marigold Linton, a psychologist at the University of Utah, who is an expert at searching her own memories And I will look at a few of my own early memories—even though they are not particularly traumatic—to see how they come and go.

I am five, maybe six. Photographs of me from that period have me looking serious, in curls reminiscent of Shirley Temple's. But in my mind I do not see myself. My viewpoint is from below the waist of an average adult. I hold someone's hand—it must be my mother's. And I look into a kind of cage. That's how I think of the brilliantly lit room I can see from the darkness of a hallway. I look into this room the way one looks into the indoor zoo compartments where lions and tigers are kept.

In the "cage" stands a young woman. She has shoulder-length black hair and wears a dress with a red velvet top and a sweetheart neckline. The skirt of the dress is white and has so much fabric that it stands way out from her slim body. She is surrounded by people telling her how wonderfully she has played. I have just heard this young woman play the Grieg Piano Concerto in A Minor with the Cleveland Symphony Orchestra. And I decide—as I stare into this "cage"—that I, too, will be a concert pianist.

Twice more in my very young life I see this same sort of "cage," but these occasions carry less meaning for me. My uncles marry, and their brides stand in brilliantly lit rooms, too—beautifully dressed in white and surrounded by well-wishers and fussbudgets (the gown, the veil—are they arranged properly?). I do not enter these rooms. For me, they are there to be stared into, not entered. But I make no promises to myself at these thresholds. Only at the doorway to the pianist's "cage" do I tell myself that someday this will be me.

I keep my promise and play the piano in a few concerts myself before I turn twenty. I wear beautiful dresses, too. And friends come back afterward to give me their congratulations. These memories do not rank with the one at five or six years old, however. They are good moments, maybe great moments, but none are epiphanies, as the first was. Now that I think of it, I must already have been a pianist when I recorded my memory of the "cage"; otherwise, why would I have cared so much? I started my piano lessons at five, so I must be six in the memory. But this is reasoning, not remembering.

How often do I think of this memory? Sometimes when I'm in Cleveland it comes to me—especially if I run into the pianist, whose name is Eunice Podis. We became friends when I grew up and joined the same professional music sorority to which she belongs. Eunice still plays occasionally with the Cleveland Symphony and in chamber-music recitals; she has had a marvelous piano career. Hearing the Grieg A-minor Concerto sometimes serves as a cue to my old memory, although no performance ever sounded as good as the one I hear in my five- or six-year-old "mind's ear." Perhaps that is why I have never played that particular piece myself.


At the turn of the century, Freud came up with the concept of "infantile amnesia," to explain an almost blanket cloud that obscured the memories of many of his patients before their sixth or seventh year. He also postulated that some of our early memories are actually "screen memories," hiding emotionally significant events behind trivialities. For example, if Ross Harriman had written to me that he had a clear memory of burying a pet fish when he was seven but not of the earlier interment of his brother, the fish memory would have been a "screen memory," standing for lost memories of his brother's burial.

This was not the case. Corky Harriman's burial was one of the few things about Corky that Ross could remember. "I remember Corky dead very well," he told me later, when I met him. "I remember the funeral. And the crowd of people. And the casket. An open casket. I can remember looking in once. I can remember seeing his face in the casket, way down there. He has very pale blond hair. It feels crowded around me. Real crowded. I feel kind of scared. And I see Corky's body way down there. He's in his church suit. And he looks asleep. And I think there are flowers in the casket. There's no expression on his face. . . . I've seen this before in my mind. I know he's dead in my memory. I have an image of shoes. He's got dark shoes on. I can see that in my mind, too."

Psychologists study the phenomenon of infantile amnesia by asking their classroom students for their first memories, or for anything they can remember from before a certain age. Both approaches reveal that three-and-a-half or so is the age from which the earliest memories can be freely recalled. Ross was four by the time his brother was killed. He should have had memories of the living Corky.

Psychologists make the task of retrieving early memory easier by asking about something specific, such as the birth of a younger sibling. Most people can remember back a little further than the mid-fourth year when they are given a specific category to search. In a 1982 study, for instance, the earliest age at which female college students remembered the birth of a sibling turned out to be three years of age. When a different psychology team asked high-school and college students to produce memories of President John F. Kennedy's assassination, an event that had occurred when these students were between the ages of one and seven, few students who were younger than three at the time could report any information about the event. About a third of the subjects who had been three years old could recall something about the event, as could six out of ten who had been five years old at the time. And more than nine out of ten who had been seven reported memories.

Personal trauma, such as kidnapping, abuse, or the death of a sibling, can sometimes be remembered from slightly before the age of three. I have found bits of verbal memory in some youngsters suffering from trauma prior to the age of twenty-eight months, the cut-off age for full verbal memories in my study of twenty children with documented traumas. One child, a five-year-old girl, told her mother that at the nursery school she attended when she turned two, "a big boy put a stick in my face." The young man in question had been convicted of forcing oral sex on a number of other children from the same nursery school long before this little girl made her comment. Nobody had ever told her about the abuses, hoping that she had been spared. The only thing that an eleven-year-old girl could remember from the day she fell into the running inboard motor of her father's boat and cut her face was being taken into the bathroom and having the blood washed off. She had been twenty-three months old at the time.

These early memory fragments do not tell enough of a story to qualify as full memories. They do not give the gist of what took place. In fact, at first hearing, a "stick in the face" or a face-washing sound as trivial as Freud's screen memories. These snippets are parts of the traumas, however. They are memories of traumatic events which were laid down at the same time as the events. Most people can express their memories of terrors that occurred before the age of twenty-eight months only in bits, if verbally at all—as two- or three-word phrases, for instance. People can describe their very early visual memories in word pictures, of course. But it is difficult if not impossible to construct any sort of narrative.

Children do not appear able to form narrative memories until they become able to construct meaningful phrases. Memories of early trauma take an alternative form in their minds. The youngsters play out these memories, and they fear trauma-related stimuli. If Corky had been killed before Ross turned two-and-a-half, for instance, Ross might have demonstrated his memories entirely in behaviors rather than words. Children respond actively to the horrible things they implicitly remember. One little boy whose mother had slit his throat when he was only twenty months old responded at age three with crazed screaming when an emergency-room nurse blew up her rubber glove "for fun." The little boy was in the emergency room because his leg needed some stitching. His screaming at the blown-up glove reflected a nonverbal but vivid visual memory of another nurse who had done the identical glove trick when the drastically injured boy was too young to form fully verbal memories. This little boy was three years old when he came to my office. He picked out puppets—a rabbit for himself and a lion for me. Before we could even get started playing, a toy airplane came zooming out of my cabinet, its wing slashing across the neck of my lion. The airplane had "remembered" the nonverbal memories of the boy.

There are most likely two memory systems in humans—one awaiting development as an infant's words come in, and another already developed enough to use as the infant focuses his eyes, follows, feels emotion, and responds to other human beings. Daniel Stern, a psychiatrist who studies the mental life of infants, has shown through his experiments with infant puppet theaters that babies retain mental images of flamboyant puppets for several days, immediately responding to them with smiles when they are reintroduced. Babies do not behave this way in experiments with puppets of a more sedate cast.

Later in life—certainly by the time Ross lost Corky—both the verbal and the nonverbal memory systems are working. One can refer to the verbal system, which comes in at around the age of three, as the explicit, or conscious, system. It operates through sensory pathways that lead to the hippocampus and medial thalamus and then run up to the cerebral cortex for associations and long-term processing. Implicit memory is earlier in appearance, different in anatomical distribution, and very reliable. This is why, though we have no words for our infantile connections to our parents, these old nonverbal memories from our infant and toddler stages often predict the strength of our connections to others as we grow older.

In many ways Freud was correct about his infantile-amnesia hypothesis. We have few narrative memories before the age of three. But after three, many memories are retained, especially if they reflect traumas or epiphanies. Here Freud's idea about a blanket amnesia up to age six is not correct. He recognized that many memories from before the age of six are so heavily conflicted because of the Oedipal complex that they are defended out of consciousness—usually by repression. This aspect of infantile amnesia has been supported by countless child psychiatric and psychoanalytic case reports. Ross Harriman's lost memories of Corky, however, did not conform to the Oedipal situation. Instead, the memories were tinged with the trauma of Corky's death. They could have been remembered. They would not have been covered by infantile amnesia.

Some memories are "forgotten" no matter what the age of the child, because they are of repeated assaults against which the child is helpless. In the study I did of twenty singly and repeatedly traumatized preschoolers—cases in which the traumatic events were corroborated by outside sources—those children who had been fully verbal when their repeated traumas occurred retained only partial memories. Those singly traumatized children who endured their trauma after achieving the ability to use words, on the other hand, were able to tell their stories in full.

But Ross Harriman had not been a repeatedly traumatized child.

And for this reason I thought that Corky had a good chance for a comeback in his mind. Ross would have laid down a number of explicit memories of Corky. Perhaps memories already in Ross's consciousness had simply lost their linkages to Corky. Ross could get his memories back, I believed. And he probably knew instinctively how to go about it.

Dr. Marigold Linton has a long head start on Ross Harriman. She has been figuring out for years how to go about eliciting memories. She is a psychologist who studies her own memory processes. Her routine is to write down each day a brief verbal narrative of that day's personal and world events. She then tests her memory of the events at particular intervals. She also tries to record her memories when they come to mind. She watches for thoughts that come unbidden as well as for memories that appear after prompting.

Dr. Linton has watched her mind for her own recollections in a number of ways. She has tried to carry a note-pad or a tape recorder around, so that whenever a memory is retrieved its specific content and other characteristics can be recorded. She finds that this kind of "memory watching" is not at all ideal: if she restricts the kinds of memory topics she will record, she creates an easier task but loses material; if she decides to record everything that comes back to her, she protects herself from missing something, but her vigilance may well slip. Vigilance may produce its own memories—for instance "Today I spent the day memory watching." When does Dr. Linton have time for the present and the future?

General "memory watching" does not work at all well. "After a period of time I simply forgot to keep the records [of the memories]," the psychologist writes. She then decided to record only thoughts that come unbidden." Unbidden memories come while the mind is silent, as byproducts of internal searches for other information or by selecting a topic and then mentally "floating" rather than deliberately searching. Dr. Linton's unbidden memories are relatively simple and embedded in "a kind of crystalline clarity."

Here Dr. Linton comes close to the psychoanalytic process of free association. This is the technique Freud developed early in his career to help patients retrieve previously inaccessible memories and emotions. The couch—that piece of furniture

analysand to look away from his analyst and let his mind float where it will—is not absolutely essential to free association. One's mind can wander in a rocking chair, or in a desert of saguaro cactus. In fact, one's mind can wander while one's eyes follow another person's finger wagging back and forth. These wanderings of the mind can be extraordinarily useful in recapturing old memories, in finding the meanings of dreams, in rediscovering strong early emotions. Contemplating one's own creative product—a poem or drawing, for instance—may have the same effect. Free association brings snippets of old feeling and old memory to mind.

Marigold Linton also uses three types of prompted recall to retrieve memories—"temporal," "categorical," and "cued." When she does a temporally prompted memory search, she asks herself, "What was I doing last January?" or "What happened last year, starting from the beginning to the end?" Experimentally, Dr. Linton has asked herself to remember everything that she can think of from a certain year. She has asked herself for all memory contents from a certain month. In my work with children, I notice that they use holidays, particular times in the school year, and their own birthdays to help them remember important events. Often an early memory is labeled "a little before my birthday" or "when we took the trip to Kentucky." Starting at about age five, children love having their own personal calendars. It helps them to group their memories.

Dr. Linton finds that adult memories older than two years are more easily recalled by categorical than by temporal prompts. She notes that when she searches for her older memories she often pairs a category—work, say—with a date. In doing a personal memory search into one's childhood, the question one might ask would be "Remember the teacher from first grade? What happened in that class?" or "Remember the neighbors on Adams Avenue?" When questions involving category and chronology are asked together, the search becomes more manageable.

Cued recall ordinarily comes from outside the individual. Going to places where you once did something brings that something back. Tasting a certain cookie brings back the days when the cookie was first tasted. Good conversationalists bring back memories in the same way—by cuing them. "Remember those steep amphitheaters at the med school?" Charlie Davenport, a friend of mine from the University of Michigan, asks. And suddenly the memory comes to mind

of one of our classmates falling asleep on an aisle and tumbling all the way down the stairs to the professor's feet. We both laugh.

Cued recall is the easiest method of memory retrieval for Marigold Linton. Seeing a picture of what she did last year or reading a brief vignette from her notes often brings effective recognition of the episode itself. Although everything about an episode is not stored in a posed snapshot at the beach or even within a videotaped record of a family wedding, the pictures frequently release a flow of memories. That's why people so often express pain at the loss of their family photos and mementos—as so many did after the 1993 floods in the Midwest, for example. We need these kinds of recognition stimuli to help us retrieve our old memories. Without old memories, we are somehow incomplete. Did Ross Harriman have any old pictures of Corky? Had he gone to his parents' house to look? I was interested in knowing more.


I go to visit Ross Harriman in Memphis. I go because I'd like to meet the person who wrote such a moving letter to me out of the blue. And I go because I'm fascinated with his do-it-yourself search for Corky. How would a person go about trying to know someone who has been dead for thirty-one years?

We meet for lunch in the quiet upstairs dining room at a neighborhood restaurant. No one else is up there with us. Ross and a number of his colleagues from the radio station use this place when they want to do an interview away from the station. But the tables are turned today. I am the talk-show host and Ross is the interviewee. We order lasagna, iced tea, and pecan pie. Ross says the food is good here.

Ross looks like a lot of the radio personalities I meet in my career as an author. Not as handsome as TV journalists, they are uniformly pleasant-looking and blue-jeans casual—nobody has to wear a tie on the radio. They're also bright and easy with words. Ross is all of these things. He is carrot-topped, freckled, and lean. He looks very young. His smooth face may easily escape the razor two out of three days. Once in a while during our lunch, his bright blue eyes fill with enough tears to "drown Pharoah's army." Ross has opened an old wound. On the subject of Corky, the talk-show host is almost at a loss for words.

Ross grew up in the Washington, D.C., area, first in Georgetown and then in Silver Spring, Maryland. His father wrote for a major Washington newspaper. The first time Ross remembers crying over Corky was when he was twenty years old. During his sophomore year at Williams College, he had come home to Silver Spring for the weekend to learn that his younger brother Scott had fallen in with a religious cult in Thailand. The family's church—a Baptist congregation—set up a prayer meeting for Scott. "You know," Ross says, "it's O.K. to be real religious, but not *that* kind of religious. Everybody in the church was praying real hard for my brother to come back. I was overwhelmed with emotion. So I got up and went out for a walk. But I just wailed when I got outside."

Who was Ross really wailing for—Scott or Corky? And was he also wailing for himself? Obviously, the first person for whom he cried was Scott. But Ross let go, also, about Corky. The second brother's loss stood in part for the first. And it also stood for important but unrecognized losses in Ross himself.

Mrs. Harriman hired a detective to find Scott. They traveled together to Thailand, and with the help of the American Embassy they brought him home. The echoes of Corky quieted in Ross' mind. But that year he became more and more uncomfortable at Williams. He tried Buddhism and grew long hair. Confused about his identity, he sought help at the college counseling center. After four sessions, Ross's therapist told him that he was moving to Hartford and Ross would have to switch to another therapist. As Ross prepared to depart (having once more been made vulnerable by an unexpected loss), the counselor said, "There's much more to your brother's death than you are recognizing."

"I remember crying when he said that," Ross tells me, as he downs his first bite of lasagna. "And then it was, like, *pffft*—gone. And I didn't go back for treatment, and that was it. But I was surprised at how close to crying I again felt about Corky."

Ross had been hit with another flood of emotion—not only about his loss of a therapist and a brother but also about the loss of part of himself. Toward the end of his sophomore year, he informed his professors that he was leaving college—"I really flamed out of there." He took the next year off, traveling to Asia for a few months, painting strange pictures at home, and working. The next year he transferred to St. Olaf's College, a small school in Minnesota, where he met

Suzanna. He graduated in 1979 and then completed two years of graduate work in communications at Duke. He and Suzanna married in 1981, and he took a job doing a radio call-in and disk-jockey show in Fort Myers, Florida. Four years later, he established his own talk show in Memphis. His boys were born. And suddenly, when Peter entered his prekindergarten year, Ross realized what he was missing. Peter told almost daily stories about his friends. He tattled on the babysitter. Once, Jonathan ran from the backyard out into the street, and Peter fetched him. The older boy talked about it more than once. Peter would remember things like the death of his sibling, Ross realized. There must have been something wrong with himself as a child.

Having children is a potent cue to one's own childhood memories. In a photograph from *National Geographic,* an Afghan baby is sucking at his mother's breast. The woman, in turn, sucks on a blanket slung over her shoulders and head. Mother is graphically "remembering" what it was to be an infant. Truly experiencing her own infant helps her to reach, if only in part, her own distant childhood.

Not long after Ross Harriman decided to search for his memories of Corky, a fragment of memory came to him as he sat in his den in Memphis trying to think. "I got this brief image of sitting on my bed as a kid," he tells me. "It was our house in Georgetown. It must have been the night Corky died, or the night after. And I remembered looking over and seeing an empty bed. And feeling this real sadness.

"So recently I phoned Chattanooga, where my parents have retired," he goes on. "And I asked Mom how the beds were set up in our room. You know, what was it like? And so Mom describes basically what I was seeing in my memory. They were two parallel twin beds. And she says, 'Yes, there was an empty bed in there for several nights.' . . . And Mom said that at the funeral one of our relatives came up, and somehow they started talking about the sleeping situation and the empty bed. And this relative was aghast and said, you know, 'How can you have Ross sleeping with this empty bed?' And my mom, once it was brought to her attention, she went, 'Of course, of course.' I think I was moved down that night to the nursery, where my younger brother Scott was sleeping. And eventually they moved Corky's bed out. And then I moved back to my room."

Ross knew he had recovered a true memory; his mother had confirmed it. The twin-bed memory is not a screen memory, standing for something related to an internal conflict of childhood. It is, instead, a fragment of a real and traumatic experience—the death of Corky.

Marigold Linton does not use furniture-placement prompts as one of her own strategies to remember the past. But it would be helpful. I find that having my patients make maps of old rooms or old back-yards or schoolrooms brings back many of their memories—particularly, traumatic ones. One man drew a map of a scene he had always remembered; when he had been a toddler, his father had threatened to throw him off the balcony of their apartment. As he made the drawing, he recalled for the first time that his mother had been present. He could see the horrified look on her face. She had been there! And the man hadn't realized it. He found the thought of his mother's response comforting. Ross, too, captured something of his buried past by mentally mapping out the bedroom he had slept in when he was four. It is a very effective technique.

Memories of our placements in space are among the best entry points we have to our old memories—not just memories of shocking events but also of the more ordinary episodes from childhood. Reconstructing our old rooms in our minds lets us "see" that empty bed next to ours, that open door, or that standing figure. The neuroscientists Bengt Gustafsson and Holger Wigström, of the University of Göteborg, have shown that spatial memories are handled by relatively simple presynaptic and postsynaptic connections in the hippocampus. Spatial memories may be processed, in fact, in the very same hippocampal cells that handle episodic memories. We can literally map out on paper or mentally follow our childhood selves, as we trudge up trails, into fields, over to school, and back into our old kitchens. It is possible to rediscover many real memories and real feelings from our own remembered placements.

I can say to myself, for example, "picture the bedroom where you slept between ages five and twelve," and I can see my twin bed shoved against the left wall of the room. As I look up from my pillow, I see a pink bedroom, with cherrywood furniture. There is a small bedstand between my sister Bobby's bed and mine. I can recall the feeling of slipping my foot into the cool dark crack between my bed and the wall. I can see Bobby and me using the bed for a trampoline. I can see my brother Robert when he was less than a year old, doing "acrobatics" above the bed with Bobby's and my "help": "Up in the air with the greatest of *eeez-a-Heee's* a Superbaby, *Heee's* a Superbaby." I can still hear the cadence of that chant. And I remember, almost as if the association slips in sideways, Bobby and me bumping our heads together on that bed, and throwing ourselves against "my" wall, and making up a secret language that neither of us could understand even then.

My bedroom memories are the ordinary stuff of childhood. But as Ginny, the narrator and protagonist of Jane Smiley's 1991 novel *A Thousand Acres,* lies down for a moment to rest in the Iowa bedroom where she grew up, the memories that crop up in her mind are far from ordinary. Ginny is now well into the middle of her life. She surprises the reader. "Lying here, I knew he had been in there to me, that my father had lain with me in that bed, that I had looked at the top of his head, at his balding spot in the brown grizzled hair, while feeling him suck my breasts. That was the only memory I could endure before I jumped out of the bed with a cry." These memories metaphorically lie in place—in this case, in a childhood bed. Many of our good and bad memories lie in such places.

In 1967, the novelist Frank Conroy wrote an autobiographical book called *Stop-Time,* describing his own difficult and perhaps traumatic adolescence. Like Jane Smiley's Ginny, Conroy uses placement cues and visualization to rediscover his childhood. There is a scene in *Stop-Time* in which Conroy has "the boy" (himself) go to visit a cousin who lives by the water. In February 1992, I heard Conroy describe this scene at a conference on memory held in San Francisco and sponsored by the American College of Psychiatrists. "I wanted to get the boy to a seawall where his cousin is playing," he said. "So the boy rides his bicycle and gets there—I remember the house and the seawall today. So I wrote the scene. And then I didn't know what else to do. It was too abrupt. I still had to finish the chapter. . . . So, concentrating in my mind on the pictures, the visual mental images, I turned the boys away from the seawall to go back to the house. It was as if I had a camera behind them. I watched the boys walking toward the house. And then my mind's eye went to the screen door—actually, the top half of the door. It opened. And nobody came through it! And then the camera panned down to the bottom of the door, where a black cocker spaniel had just pushed it open. 'My God,' I said to myself as I was doing this, 'That's right! They had a cocker spaniel. And it's black, and its name is Shadow.'"

Frank Conroy completes his *Stop-Time* chapter with the door and the dog. But the two images also complete a small chapter in the author's own book of memories. "That's a memory I can trust," he told us. "It's like watching the original event." Conroy also said that before writing *Stop-Time* his past had been "a great blur" to him. "The chronology was all wrong," he said. "The memories were scattered. The discipline and the concentration of writing brought both things back to me."

The act of writing memories down increases their chances for retrieval. Marigold Linton keeps well-documented journals of the happenings in her life. A new set of memories is created by writing or speaking into a tape recorder. This second set of actions—writing, speaking, looking it over—reinforces the original perceptions (and alters them, too, at times). Those who have continual access to journals or sketch pads have a better chance of remembering than those who don't. The more functions involved in what becomes a memory, the more places in the brain that that memory is represented.

The Plains Indians had—and I hope still have—a traditional mechanism of recording and keeping their memories called the winter count. Each winter, an individual would paint on a large buffalo skin something symbolizing what he considered the most striking event of the year. As the years accumulated, the winter counts grew. Years were named on the basis of these winter counts—"the year of many buffalo" or "the year of little water," for instance. But a person from the Great Plains could also remember his own life events by looking at his winter count, through chronological and categorical cuing.


When Peter Harriman turned four, Ross went up to Lookout Mountain outside Chattanooga to hike and to think. He had decided to go visit his parents, who had moved to Chattanooga from Silver Spring after his father retired. Ross had been preoccupied for several months with Corky. Why didn't he know him better? How had they acted together? He had seen a number of family-album photographs of himself and Corky as children, but they had never seemed to call up any narrative memories. This time he would talk, not look at photographs, he told himself.

"I sat up there on a rock and sunned myself," Ross says over our lasagna, "and I thought about what I might say to my folks. I had told them I was going to go up and do some hiking and then stop by

and visit them before I went home. . . . In the woods, my mind
always slows down. I can hear the water and the wind. . . . When I
got down from Lookout Mountain, *I* knew what I wanted to do but
my parents didn't. It was a real set-up, for them."

Ross needed to make his parents' memories his own. He was hun-
gry for memories—even somebody else's. "We started off in a casual
conversation," he says. "Then we started talking, just in general,
about memories of us as a family when Corky was around. And Mom
started talking about some of her memories of the time around
Corky's death." Ross asked his mother what she remembered of his
relationship with Corky. She told him that he had not gotten along
with his older brother. Ross had always pushed to keep up, she said.

"They have this big old dining-room table, and Mom was at one
end," he says. "Dad was at the other, and I was in the middle. At one
point, Mom mentioned that I hadn't cried when Corky died—that
she had been surprised that I hadn't cried. And she recalled that I had
talked about missing Corky only that first night and never again.
And then she said I had probably been too young to appreciate his
death. And I jumped on that, man! I just went, 'No! No! I think I
must have been in shock when he died.' And for me it was a big
thing to be able to say that to her. And, you know, she didn't fight
it—and she fights if she doesn't like something. Mom hadn't thought
I could appreciate Corky's death, and really my whole life—everything—had been built around it. I appreciated it too much!"

Here were two separate stories—Mom's and Ross's. Both were true
memories, real memories. But neither person had heard the other's
perspective and feelings until that moment. In listening to these
vignettes from the Harriman dining room, I could almost feel the
intense emotions. These were three intelligent people with nothing
to hide—no incest, no cruelty, no alcoholism, no fights—yet Ross's
coming home to ask for memories stirred up extraordinary affect.
Ross recognized the potential emotional cost to his parents in dis-
cussing Corky. But his need to know Corky exceeded his need to protect himself and his parents from a painful scene.

Ross and his mother became "misty-eyed" over how much Corky's
death had meant to him, he says. "My dad chimed in, too. He talked
about how, when Corky got hit, he had this overwhelming urge to
get home immediately and tell my mother what had happened. He
said he got in the car, leaving Corky's dead body at school, and came

right home. And I can remember—that is the memory I've *always* had—standing at the far end of the living room and, like, freezing up. And hearing them."

At the dining-room table in Chattanooga, when his father began sharing his anguish at the old memory of seeing his son's crushed body, Ross felt his own emotions welling up. "I could feel this single tear start down my cheek," he says. "And I wondered what the hell Dad would make of this—because this was something new, me crying. But he kept right on talking, and soon, you know, I was into really hard crying. And then it got to be absurd. He went to get some Kleenex. That's Dad—always practical. And soon I had a little mountain of these soggy Kleenexes in front of me."

Ross's father talked faster and faster as his son cried. Ross's mother came around the table and put her hand on Ross's shoulder. But the Harrimans' memories had run out for the moment. They were left with the thoughts to which they habitually reached for comfort—thoughts of Corky alive on some other plane, in God's hands. Ross finally looked up from his tears to realize that his father had disappeared. "Dad just didn't have any more to say," Ross says. "He couldn't stay with us any longer."

A scene like the one at the Chattanooga dinner table doesn't happen too often in the life of a family. Ross stirred up strong emotion in his aging parents in order to hear each of their accounts and compare them with his own. What he found was that each had a separate story. But these stories fit well together. They confirmed Ross's own snippets of recollection. Ross found himself able to begin modifying his parents' versions of how he had responded. He *had* cared about Corky, he told them. He had cared enough to change his whole life as a child. A tough little competitor to Corky had become—almost overnight—a passive little "father" to Scott. Everything changed for Ross. And now his parents knew it. Even better for Ross, he knew they knew.

Although the experience of memory sharing can be strongly emotional, it carries the possibility of external confirmation and the opportunity to rework our memories—to find new emphases and understandings. This is why some therapy groups—particularly those with a specific orientation, such as groups for traumatized Vietnam vets or incest survivors—work so well for many of their members.

While Ross was in Chattanooga, he told his parents about the various ways he was searching for memories of Corky. He told them about his letter writing and his men's group. They agreed these might help, and they gave him a few old photos of Corky to keep. These would help, too. When the professional memory searcher Marigold Linton hunts for her memories, she uses a hierarchal structure. This is quite different from what Ross Harriman was doing. Dr. Linton moves in her mind from mood tone (which she labels as either "negative" or "positive") to themes (work memories, social memories, memories of love relationships), to what she calls "extendures," or labels ("when I worked in Utah," "when I was in graduate school," or "my close friends"). The labeling, Linton believes, is her most useful method of stimulating free recall from adult life. Finally she focuses on the details of an episode already recalled—nuances of color, sound, texture, and exact location.

Marigold Linton, of course, is not looking for traumatic childhood memories—she looks only for the things that have happened to her as an adult. But Ross was not looking for traumatic memories either. He already had them. The terrifying conversation he had overheard in the living room, his memories of an empty bed, Corky's open casket— these are traumatic indeed. Ross was looking for just plain memories of Corky—the kind of everyday, ordinary things that Marigold Linton ferrets out. To do a Linton-style search, Ross would have to think of positive things about Corky—on the "play" theme, for instance, when they had both returned from Hartwell Academy in Georgetown (where Ross went to preschool and Corky went to school) or on weekends. Then he would have had to move down to the details—the who, what, where, and other defining qualities.

In a 1986 article, Dr. Linton explains how she tested herself on the long-term autobiographical memories she laid down between 1971 and 1983, a period in which she wrote down two- or three-line accounts on prompt cards of anything significant that happened to her. She checked her memories once a month, shuffling the cards and then attempting to date the events and describe them more fully. Once a year she tried for free recall of all events of that year. At the end of the twelve-year period, she tested herself on all the events in the dozen years. Linton found that only about one in ten freely recalled memories were of negative events. The rest were either neutral or positive. The memories most likely to be omitted from her free recall were what she considered the "niggling daily items, such as quarrels with loved ones, disagreements with colleagues, the first pained response to a negative review, a broken treasure." She also lost the free recall of certain negative work events. Negative memories, however, did not entirely disappear from the Utah investigator's mind. With recall cued by the prompt cards, she could recapture the dates and unique characteristics of the negative items as readily as the positive ones. In other words, something about free recall blocked many negative items from consciousness. A psychodynamic clinician would say that Dr. Linton's negative memories were blocked by defenses. In a sense, Linton's study of her own memories gets quite close to "proving" repression.

Traumas like Ross Harriman's, of course, are associated with a very special kind of memory. It is highly unlikely that in Marigold Linton's list of memories over her twelve-year period there were any personal traumas: she does not mention any in her 1986 summary paper. Trauma—especially a single unrepeated episode—would have had a far greater chance of surviving in Dr. Linton's memory than "the niggling daily items, such as quarrels." Trauma bursts past ordinary defenses. Ross's trauma did, but what he wanted was the rest—the everyday stuff. It was as if the trauma had blasted out a crater, not where it landed but about a mile away.

Would Ross's memories of Corky stay lost because they were simply too old to remember? The work of Dr. Larry Squire at the San Diego Veterans Administration Medical Center—work discussed in Chapter 4—demonstrates that in people with an organic amnesia very old memories may persist, whereas the more recent memories are wiped out. Old memories apparently "reorganize" themselves many years after they are formed. Ross's memories of Corky, even if they had been repressed by Ross after Corky's death, might have been reprocessed, but they would not have been discarded or lost.

Marigold Linton has observed that her memories change once they are more than two or three years old. "Rewriting" of the memories occurs. She finds "shifts in emphases and wholesale deletions" in her older memories. They now have greater or lesser significance depending on the continuing narrative of her life. The salience of an event— how emotionally stimulating or important it was, and how frequently it was talked about—begins to figure into whether the memory is freely recalled. Negative memories are shoved aside. Amalgams of events begin to break apart after a couple of years, often sending the less dominant items completely out of the range of free recall. Elements and details are lost. What seemed, in Dr. Linton's case, insignificant at first—meeting "a shy scholar"—takes on profound significance years later, as she marries him.

But after long periods of not thinking of them, a few memory items enter the mind "unbidden," Marigold Linton finds. And here was something Ross Harriman might hope for in his quest for Corky.

Ross tells me—as the waitress clears away our lasagna and brings our pecan pie—that his biggest breakthrough in remembering Corky was a letter he received in response to his request for information from Deanna Wood, Corky's kindergarten teacher at Hartwell Academy. "Apparently Corky was real religious," he says. "I think my folks had said that he was religious, now that I think of it. But Deanna gave me details. The day Corky died, they had had an open art class. She had given out straws, scissors, and glue and told the children to make anything they wanted. Corky made three crosses and put them on a little hill. He said the middle one was Jesus. Deanna had also gone around that day asking the kids what they wanted to do when they grew up. And Corky said he wanted to be a pastor. He was going to be a minister."

This was an aspect of Corky that Ross had never known about. Here was his brother alive, not dead, making crosses and thinking about Calvary. The teacher also reported that Mrs. Harriman had had a waking vision in the week before Corky died. She saw Jesus coming to her, not saying anything but opening a gate in a wall.

Ross cannot go on. He is temporarily derailed by emotion. The man who uses metaphor so well understands the meaning of an "open gate." Tears fall. "It's—it's all part of the package deal," he says finally, again commenting on his family's use of religion as a substitute for more realistic remembrance of Corky. If he were to combine his mother's tale with that of his brother's kindergarten teacher he might well create an amalgam, making Corky's death part of the Christ story. But he appreciates the stories for their simpler aspects: here is Corky, very much alive in Deanna's memory.

"Deanna also told me that the week before Corky died the class went to the Washington Zoo. And Mom was recovering from giving birth to Scott that week, so she wasn't able to look after me all the time. So I went along on the class trip, Deanna said. And she wrote in her letter that my mom was having lots of anxiety, apprehensions about us going."

Suddenly Ross stops. "It's interesting," he says. "As I was talking, I just had a memory. I *see* the zoo! I can remember an elephant with a—his trunk came out. And it kind of sucked on my head or something. I can remember feeling scared. But I don't know if that's even the same trip Deanna wrote me about." The memory lands right in the room where we are having lunch. And it startles us a bit.

Ross eats some of his pecan pie and takes a few sips of cold coffee. His orange-red hair might easily attract an elephant, I think. He pulls out an old black-and-white photo of himself and Corky and silently shows it to me. Both are cute little boys in dark-collared striped polo shirts. Both have pug noses, short glossy hair, and big smiles. They stand before a nice old Georgetown house. Corky's hair is so white it looks like a halo.

Ross tells me that he also wrote a letter to the Fords, friends from the days when both fathers were Washington journalists. "And the Fords wrote a letter back and they talked about a trip to the beach—What beach was it?—Virginia Beach, maybe. They talked about Corky and me playing on the sand dunes, with towels tied like capes around our necks, jumping off the dunes. And again, it hit a chord." Ross smiles. "I can see it in a way," he says. "But in my mind I don't see Corky. Or the Ford kids. It's a dune, and it's fun. I love to jump off dunes. I still do it when I can. Do you know Sleeping Bear Dune, up near Traverse City, in Western Michigan? You can fly, if a dune is steep enough."

Now Ross finds himself remembering some primitive sex play he had performed in the basement of his Georgetown house with a couple of older girls from the neighborhood—"maybe five- or six-year-olds."

"How does it feel in your memory?" I ask.

"Bad," he says. "I felt guilty."

Ross had never lost this memory, but at this moment he is able to remember coming upstairs to dinner, "wondering if I'm gonna get reprimanded, if I'll be caught, and promising to myself that I'll never do it again. My folks are there in the kitchen. And somebody else is there—like a child. There's no high chair there, so it's not Scott. The feel is definitely our family. You know, just our family."

I tell Ross that this must be Corky. Corky alive.

Ross looks excited. Yes, this is Corky. Is that enough for a memory? Just the *sensation* of somebody else there?

Yes, of course. That is enough for a memory. Memory, I tell him, is located all over the brain—not just in the frontal cortex but all over. The sensation of a person being present is as good a memory as a mental picture is.

Not all Ross's attempts to recapture his memories worked for him. He tried to push his own mind to remember—"concentrate, concentrate, concentrate," he would say. But the more he pushed, the more his memories eluded him. Memories do not break free upon being attacked with a jackhammer. They float up to the surface as we "think sideways." If a person relaxes and lets the mind drift, the memories are far more likely to come in. Relaxed thinking, visualization, and free association are generally as successful in retrieving memories as hypnosis is. Except in cases of generalized amnesia, questioning under the influence of sodium amytal is generally no more effective than a freely drifting mind in recalling memories.

Pencil and paper—or a computer—is a great aid to memory, both the memories going in and the ones coming out. Ross's letters to Deanna Wood, the Fords, and me were one such device. The journal or diary is another. Writing one's autobiography may be the best way of all—although in such works the dramatic is often emphasized to create interest, and this, of course, modifies the memory. If an autobiography paced itself the way life paces itself, no one would read it. Marcel Proust's *Remembrance of Things Past* homes in on certain memories and then goes on about them for pages. It must have taken Proust all of thirty seconds to eat a madeleine, and yet the memory of the madeleine takes his fictional character, Swann, years to savor. This elasticity of time and of emphasis is the privilege of the storyteller. When we tell our own memories, we are granted these same privileges. But, as I have noted, the story loses accuracy in the telling. It even loses accuracy when we tell it to ourselves.

Many memories will always remain snippets in our minds, unless we expand them through storytelling. Ross Harriman had suddenly seen an elephant, in telling me a snippet about a zoo trip. He had sensed the presence of his brother in the kitchen, in telling me of his early sexual encounter with a couple of little girls. In this regard, I remember a conversation I had a few years ago in a New Orleans oyster bar with Paul Wilson, a Washington, D.C., psychiatrist and old friend. We each recounted a snippet of memory from early childhood. And then we elaborated on the memories, to illustrate how important they really were. I remembered my paternal grandmother trying to force hot liquid into my mouth as I lay in her arms. Paul remembered being carried in someone's arms and staring at the sky as he crossed a bridge. That's all we actually remembered. But then we told each other the expanded stories, which our families had supplied once we were old enough to tell them what we had remembered. And it was these expansions that gave meaning to the actual memories.

I was eleven months old, and moving from New York to Cleveland. My father, a struggling artist during the Great Depression, could no longer support us, and my mother, accompanied by my paternal grandmother, was taking me by train to Cleveland, where her family would temporarily provide us with a home and food. I am told that I behaved terribly on the train. I did nothing but cry. My mother thinks that I sensed I was leaving my father, who even then was my love. To calm me, my Russian-born grandma stuck a spoonful of tea into my mouth—my mother remembers it, too. "Dearila, take tea," she said. Did I understand language then? I don't know. But I still hear a voice saying those words in connection with the memory.

Paul Wilson's memory is far more exotic. Like me, Paul was eleven months old in his memory. But Paul was escaping with his missionary parents and all their worldly possessions across a bridge into a safe part of China. It was 1937, and the Japanese were coming. Paul's family were fleeing for their lives. Yet his actual memory—the fragment of being supine and staring at the sky—is close to my memory of being supine in my grandmother's arms. Both memories involve separation from home. Both involve profound infantile discomfort. One involves great danger. One involves the temporary loss of a parent. Because an infant's mind is so undeveloped and so poorly verbal, the snippets, at face value, seem almost insignificant—two babies looking up while they lie in somebody's arms.

Our earliest memories work the way Paul's and mine did—and Ross's. They are only bits. Often we must tell someone before we can see their significance. And we must also associate to the memory—mentally drift around the idea. Paul and I understood more, as we shared our stories and ate our oysters. (In fact, I decided that day to study infants' traumatic memories, if I could.) As Ross Harriman talked to me over his lasagna and pecan pie, he began seeing the significance of Corky's presence in his already active early memories.

Corky had been there, at the zoo. Corky had been sitting at the kitchen table, too. Ross had simply eliminated Corky from his memories when he died, the way Ramses II eliminated the cartouches of the other pharoahs from their monuments.

Ross has saved for last an incident he once thought he had always remembered but has recently come to doubt.

"It's a memory of my brother and a neighborhood friend, Max Chase, riding their bikes up a hill," he says. "And I'm behind—I was, what? two years younger?—and I'm on my bike shouting at them, 'Wait up! Wait up! Wait up!' It's a vivid memory. I've had it for as long as I can remember." But I was talking to my wife. This past month, it was. And I was kind of revisiting what I had put together on Corky. And Suzanna looks at me a little funny and says, 'Well, you know your mother told that story to us early in our marriage.' I was stunned! I had no recollection of Mom telling that story."

The memory certainly characterizes the relationship between Corky and Ross—confirming the image of a pushy little brother trying to catch up with his older sib. But Ross is so unsure of his efforts to remember that he has given up on this memory. I say to him, "But your mom's story doesn't necessarily make it a false memory of yours. Maybe your mom saw the same thing you did."

Ross looks doubtful.

"Can you remember your position in the memory?" I persist.

"I'm at the bottom of the hill," he says. "They're at the top. I know the street. It's in my old neighborhood, in Georgetown. We're on tricycles—the three of us. It's not a big hill, but, yeah, I know it."

"Can you see what they're wearing?"

"Yes. A striped shirt on one."

"Can you see who's on the left and who's on the right?"

"Hmm, I've never approached these memories with those kinds of questions in mind. Corky's on the left. I see that in my mind. And the Chase kid—he's got the stripes."

"Can you see what time of year it is?" I ask, one last question entering my mind.

"No. No, I can't," Ross shrugs. "I can't see my mother, either. And in *her* story she was there."

"You're asking two boys to wait up for you. Why would your mom be in your memory?"

Ross laughs.

Almost instantly, Ross comes to believe in his remembrance of Corky, Max, and the tricycles. Here is something completely apart from Corky's death. It is a memory of a real moment—but more than that, of a real relationship. And even more—of who Ross was before his trauma made him so eager to please and so sad. Ross's mother's memory does nothing to negate Ross's memory, though her point of view is different. In fact, she confirms it. She was there. But what is most important in this memory is that within it Ross finds himself. He knows who he is. And at last he recognizes himself.

I received a letter from Ross a week after our visit. He has a new memory, he says—another healthy one, full of fun and brotherhood. He writes:

Dear Lenore,

It's Sunday evening, we just put the boys to bed, and I'm listening to the Eagles' "Life in the Fast Lane." The weather in Memphis has been hot and muggy Saturday and today, and the newspaper says they had much of the same up in the foothills. It would have been another fine weekend near the top of Lookout Mountain; only in the mid-seventies up there.

I'm writing to thank you for lunch and for the interview. Our conversation was a good nudge for me to keep plugging away at this stuff. I had figured I would shed a few tears as we talked; I didn't think I'd be salting my lasagna. . . .

It was yesterday, as I was thinking about just who was at the kitchen table at dinner after I had messed around with those girls, when I had another memory. It's not new, I've had it before. But it's been some time since I thought of it. And the memory is different now. The memory is of our living room in Georgetown, and Dad is giving us horsey rides. We are really whooping it up, and I remember feeling happy.

The real kicker is I've always thought of just Dad and me in this memory. But Mom's there too. She's laughing. . . . I'm drawing this blank as I wonder what we were wearing. But I can almost see the big red chair and the big circle Dad is going around on the floor. And definitely lots of laughing. And there are warm happy feelings as I remember the bucking bronco who keeps complaining about how hard we are jumping on him. My feelings almost instantly switch to sadness as I realize Corky is there, too. And the same thing is happening now as I sit here in front of my computer.

I've been looking out the window lost in this reverie and now all of a sudden my old Georgetown address and phone number come back to

me. How easily they surface. I'm feeling confident that other memories
will come, too.

Sincerely,

Ross

I phone Eunice Podis. It is deep winter, and I am in Cleveland, visiting family. I tell Eunice my memory. Did she have a dress with a red
velvet top, a sweetheart neckline, and a big white skirt? Did she play
the Grieg? With the Cleveland Symphony? I confess to her what a
high point the moment was and, even though in the long run I didn't
stick with the piano as a career, how I drew general inspiration from
the memory.

Eunice remembers. "But can you hang on, Lenore?" she says. "I
keep complete scrapbooks of everything having to do with my
career."

I wait for a minute or two, and then she is back on the phone. "I
was nineteen years old when I played the Grieg," she says. "It was
with the Cleveland Pops. At Public Hall. Summertime. It was my
second performance with the Pops. The year before, I played the
Tchaikovsky. Are you sure it was the Grieg?"

"I'm sure about the Grieg. That's what I hear in my mind. Do you
have any record of what you wore when you played the Grieg?" I ask.
"It's an early memory—probably from the summer after I turned six.
Do you remember a dress with a red top, white skirt?"

"It's coming to me now," Eunice says. "When I married Bob, I had
a wedding dress with yards and yards of skirt. We didn't want to
waste the dress after my wedding. And so the summer I played the
Grieg, my mother sewed red sequins all around the neckline—yes, it
*was* a sweetheart neckline—and she sewed a flower on the skirt. So
that my performance gown wouldn't look like a wedding dress."

She tells me the year she was married and it is the year I turned six.
I am wrong about the velvet. But I am right about the red. All
around that sweetheart neckline that I so admired were red sequins,
signalling the color that remains in my mind today. Suddenly I flash
on the flower. It is a partly open rose. My memory has expanded. And
I am suddenly sure of what it tells me.

"Is the flower on the skirt a huge red rose with a long stem and a
few leaves?" I ask.

"Yes," she says.

A memory from age six has been confirmed by a phone call. Some of my details were wrong. But how would a six-year-old have known the difference between the Cleveland Symphony Orchestra and the Pops? And would a six-year-old retain the fine points of fashion? The thrill lies in knowing that the gist of something very meaningful to me from childhood is true and correct. And the thrill lies in rediscovering one buried but very large sequined rose.

When I met Ross Harriman for lunch in Memphis I had just begun gathering materials for this book. After I had nearly completed the manuscript, I phoned him to see how he had managed with his do-it-yourself memory search.

Ross sounds good—more self-confident. His real memories of the living Corky have added a dimension to his personality. His talk show has extended to television now; he has an hour-long show on Sunday mornings. He's interviewing all sort of Southern politicians and cultural leaders.

He says he no longer weeps for Corky. In fact, he has stopped hunting for memories. He feels more attached to his parents—"that talk we had in the dining room worked wonders."

Scott has moved from Chicago to Birmingham, Alabama. He and Ross are close and see each other fairly often. Ross still goes to his men's group, but he's gone on to discuss relationships in his day-to-day life and the politics of work instead of talking about Corky. But this doesn't mean that Ross no longer thinks about Corky. If he wants to, he can "see" Corky ahead of him up a hill in Georgetown, or perched on Dad's bucking back.

Until his deliberate search, Ross's memories of Corky were almost exclusively traumatic—memories of a boy dead in a coffin, of a father's horrifying announcement, and of a mother's protests of disbelief. The bad memories had shoved the good ones aside. Even the slightly irritating ones were gone. Even the ones about self. When Ross felt Corky's presence in the Georgetown kitchen, when he accepted his "tricycle on the hill" memory and recaptured his "riding horsey" game, he once again had living memories of Corky. And of himself. He could begin to see his brother in the context of his own thirty-five years of life. Most of us need only two or three snippets to remember and understand our preschool years. Ross has his now.

Hundreds of scientists—cell biologists, Drosophilists, monkey researchers, chemists, neuropharmacologists, cognitive psychologists, anatomists, neurologists, and psychiatric and psychological clinicians—are working today on various aspects of the human memory system. They will discover many general "rules" about the conduct of memory—rules we may not even be able to imagine at the present time.

But one thing stands clear about the individual's search for his own memories. It will always be a solo search. Each case stands by itself. Though some memories are false, many more are true with false components. And some are altogether true. We must refrain from taking a general stand on the truth or falsity of recovered memories from childhood, even as we learn more and more from the experts. Each case must be assessed individually, by ourselves, and with an open mind.

Like Ross, all of us need our memories and must be willing, at times, to search for them. Even when we have many recollections, we can still look for more. And we can talk them over—not only to tell them but to confirm and expand them. We need our remembrances to understand ourselves—who we are and what we believe. We are our memories.

# NOTES

2  The circumstances surrounding Eileen Franklin Lipsker's first recollection of the murder of Susan Nason are described in E. Franklin and W. Wright, *Sins of the Father* (New York: Crown, 1991). This book, about Eileen's childhood and her adult adjustment, includes a report on the trial. See also the opinion (not for official publication) of Justice William Newsom, Division One, California Court of Appeal, in the case of *The People of the State of California v. George Thomas Franklin, Sr.,* April 2, 1993.

3  "Something whitish"; "some hair that was no longer attached to her body": see the opinion of the California Court of Appeal, p. 8.

4  Eileen's attempts to force her memories "back into a little drawer" are from a personal interview with Eileen. I conducted two two-hour interviews with Eileen Lipsker on August 16 and 17, 1990, and a third interview a year later, September 11, 1991.

    The effects of Eileen's memories on her stomach and heart were told to me in her August 1990 interviews, and are also based on my own observations of her.

5  Eileen's memory cascade is recounted in *Sins of the Father;* see especially pp. 107–12. Some details also come from my personal interviews with her.

5–6     The details of Eileen's first murder memories were recounted to me in interviews and are also included in the opinion of the California Court of Appeal, p. 3. She also discussed her murder memories in a speech before the American College of Psychiatrists, Annual Meeting, February 12–16, 1992, San Francisco.

6       For the initiation of Eileen's repression on the night of the murder, see the opinion of the California Court of Appeal, p. 9.

        Freud stated his theory of repression in J. Breuer and S. Freud, "Studies on Hysteria" [1893–95], in *The Standard Edition of the Complete Psychological Works of Sigmund Freud* (hereafter, *Standard Edition*), vol. 2, trans. and ed. J. Strachey (London: Hogarth Press, 1955).

        Schopenhauer's and Herbart's contributions to the understanding of repressed memory are cited in G. Vaillant, ed., *Ego Mechanisms of Defense: A Guide for Clinicians and Researchers* (Washington, D.C.: American Psychiatric Press, 1992).

7–8     Evidence of clear memory of single-event trauma was first found in the Chowchilla study of 1976–77: L. Terr, "Children of Chowchilla: A Study of Psychic Trauma," *Psychoanalytic Study of the Child* 34 (1979): 547–623.

        The *Challenger* study, "Children's Responses to the *Challenger* Spacecraft Disaster," which also demonstrated clear memory of single events, was presented at the New Research section of the American Psychiatric Association Annual Meeting, New York City, May 17, 1990, and is abstracted in *New Research Program and Abstracts* (1990): 269. It awaits journal publication. The authors are L. Terr, D. Bloch, B. Michel, J. Reinhart, and S. Matayer.

9       Freud's theory of actual seduction can be found in "The Aetiology of Hysteria" [1896], in *Standard Edition,* vol. 3 (1962). His shift in 1897 to internal conflict as the source of his patients' repression and hysteria is first found in his letters. See M. Bonaparte, A. Freud, and E. Kris, eds., *The Origins of Psychoanalysis, Letters to Wilhelm Fliess, Drafts and Notes by Sigmund Freud* (New York: Basic Books, 1954), pp. 215–16; and S. Freud, letter to Wilhelm Fliess of May 4, 1896, quoted in J. Masson, *The Assault on Truth: Freud's Suppression of the Seduction Theory* (New York: Farrar, Straus & Giroux, 1984), p. 10.

        Jeffrey Masson's own views on this shift of Freud's are also stated in *The Assault on Truth.*

10      Pierre Janet's ideas about dissociated memories are summarized in B. van der Kolk and O. van der Hart, "Pierre Janet and the Breakdown of Adaptation in Psychological Trauma," *American Journal of Psychiatry* 146 (1989): 1530–40.

Phyllis Greenacre's papers on recovered repressed memories include "A Contribution to the Study of Screen Memories," *Psychoanalytic Study of the Child* 3/4 (1949): 73–84; "On Reconstruction," *Journal of the American Psychoanalytic Association* 23 (1975): 693–712; and "Reconstruction: Its Nature and Therapeutic Value," *Journal of the American Psychoanalytic Association* 29 (1982): 386–402.

David Levy's key paper on childhood trauma is "Psychic Trauma of Operations in Children," *American Journal of the Diseases of Childhood* 69 (1945): 7–25.

G. Lacey's Aberfan, Wales, study can be found in "Observations on Aberfan," *Journal of Psychosomatic Research* 16 (1972): 257–60. C. Janet Newman's report on the Buffalo Creek flood is "Children of Disaster: Clinical Observations at Buffalo Creek," *American Journal of Psychiatry* 133 (1976): 306–12.

10–11    For the findings in the Chowchilla kidnapping study, see L. Terr, "Psychic Trauma in Children: Observations Following the Chowchilla School-bus Kidnapping," *American Journal of Psychiatry* 138 (1981): 14–19; and the follow-up study, L. Terr, "Chowchilla Revisited: The Effects of Psychic Trauma Four Years After a School-bus Kidnapping," *American Journal of Psychiatry* 140 (1983): 1543–50. The McFarland-Porterville control group is described in L. Terr, "Life Attitudes, Dreams, and Psychic Trauma in a Group of 'Normal' Children," *Journal of the American Academy of Child Psychiatry* 22 (1983): 221–30.

For a summary of what I consider important from my studies on childhood trauma up to 1990, see *Too Scared to Cry* (New York: Harper & Row, 1990; paper ed., Basic Books, 1992).

Type I and Type II childhood-trauma victims are described in L. Terr, "Childhood Traumas: An Outline and Overview," *American Journal of Psychiatry* 148 (1991): 10–20.

11    The study of twenty young trauma victims is L. Terr, "What Happens to the Memories of Early Trauma? A Study of Twenty Children Under Age Five at the Time of Documented Traumatic Events," *Journal of the American Academy of Child and Adolescent Psychiatry* 27 (1988): 96–104.

George Franklin's violent behavior toward his family was described by Eileen Lipsker in her speech before the American College of Psychiatrists, February 1992. See also the opinion of the California Court of Appeal, p. 9.

Mrs. Franklin's hospitalizations for mental illness were recounted by Eileen in her interviews with me and also appear in H. MacLean, *Once Upon a Time* (New York: HarperCollins, 1993),

p. 77, and in *Sins of the Father,* pp. 31 and 58. When asked by prosecutor Elaine Tipton at the trial whether she had ever been hospitalized for a mental illness, Leah answered that she could not remember.

12–13    The idea that both a ground and a cue are clinically important to the recovery of traumatic memories from childhood is a new one as set forth in this book. However, the idea is based on considerable work in the experimental psychology field. See D. W. Goodwin, B. Powell, and D. Bremer, "Alcohol and Recall: State Dependent Effects in Man," *Science* 163 (1968): 1358–60; and D. Godden and A. D. Baddely, "Context-dependent Memory in Two Natural Environments," *British Journal of Psychology* 71 (1975): 99–104. For mood-dependent memory, see G. H. Bower, "Mood and Memory," *American Psychologist* 36 (1981): 129–48; and J. M. G. Williams and H. R. Markar, "Money Hidden and Rediscovered in Subsequent Manic Phases: A Case of Action Dependent Mood State?" *British Journal of Psychiatry* 159 (1991): 579–81.

Verbally cued childhood memory is discussed in R. Fivush, "Developmental Perspectives on Autobiographical Recall," in G. S. Goodman and B. L. Bottoms, eds., *Child Victims, Child Witnesses: Understanding and Improving Testimony* (New York: Guilford, 1992); and in G. S. Goodman and C. Amen, "Children's Use of Anatomically Detailed Dolls to Recount an Event," *Child Development* 61 (1991): 1859–1971.

The cuing of adult memories is described in various papers in D. Rubin, ed., *Autobiographical Memory* (Cambridge: Cambridge University Press, 1986).

13    For Eileen's revelations to her psychotherapist Kirk Barrett, see the opinion of the California Court of Appeal, p. 4.

14    On Eileen's lies to her mother and brother regarding her recovery of the murder memory under hypnosis, see the opinion of the California Court of Appeal, pp. 4–5.

14    For the conversations between Leah Franklin and George Franklin, see the opinion of the California Court of Appeal, p. 10.

14–15    My account of Janice Franklin's 1984 attempt to turn her father in to the police is taken from a personal interview with Eileen. It is also described in *Sins of the Father,* pp. 95–97.

The information about Kirk Barrett's attempts to help Eileen comes from a personal interview with Eileen and from the California Court of Appeal opinion, p. 4.

15    George Vaillant's findings on suppression are described in his *Adaptation to Life* (Boston: Little, Brown, 1977).

16      Barry Lipsker's response to Eileen's revelation and George
        Franklin's behavior in regard to Sica come from my personal inter-
        views of Eileen Franklin Lipsker.

16      Barry Lipsker telephoned the San Mateo County D.A.'s Office
        without Eileen's knowledge or consent: see California Court of
        Appeal opinion, pp. 5–6. The account of their marital relationship
        is from *Sins of the Father* and from personal interviews with Eileen
        Franklin Lipsker.

17–18   The circumstances surrounding the 1969 murder of Susan Nason
        were summarized by Elaine Tipton in her speech at the Annual
        Meeting of the American College of Psychiatrists, San Francisco,
        February 1992.

19      Eileen's statement on "the right of the Nasons to have this re-
        solved": see the opinion of the California Court of Appeal, p. 5.

19–23   On the audiotape of the conversation between Eileen Lipsker and
        Inspector Charles Etter: I made a tape of this phone call while it
        was being played at the Annual Meeting of the American College
        of Psychiatrists, in February 1992. My punctuations are different
        from the official transcript of this phone call in *People v. Franklin.*

23      That Eileen became "too choked up and started crying" when
        asked for the name of the killer, and that Barry told the District
        Attorney's Office, "I guess she can't live with it anymore" can be
        found in *Sins of the Father*, 139 and 122. The "choked up" quote is
        also in the California Court of Appeal opinion, p. 6*n*3.

24      The contents of George Franklin's apartment at the time of his
        arrest were described to me by Inspectors Brian Cassandro and
        Bob Morse of the San Mateo County District Attorney's Office.
        The description is also in *Sins of the Father*, p. 149.

        On George's question upon his arrest, "Have you talked to my
        daughter?" see the opinion of the California Court of Appeal, pp.
        34, 43–45, and *Sins of the Father*, p. 148.

25–26   On the clarity of children's remembered details from horrifying
        events and the mistakes they make, see L. Terr et al., "Children's
        Responses to the *Challenger* Spacecraft Disaster."

27–28   On discrepancies in the Chowchilla children's memories, see
        L. Terr, "Psychic Trauma in Children," and L. Terr, "Chowchilla
        Revisited."

29      For Barry Lipsker's collection of news clippings, see the opinion of
        the California Court of Appeal, pp. 13–14*n*7.

        Barry's arrangements to videotape Eileen for the "Today" show
        were described to me by Eileen in a personal interview. Also see
        *Sins of the Father*, pp. 159–60.

29      Eileen's confusion about the time of day that the killing took

place: personal communication from Elaine Tipton. See also *Investigative Report* of Inspector Bob Morse, San Mateo County District Attorney's Office, May 11, 1990.

On time sense being vulnerable to stress, see L. Terr, "Time and Trauma," *Psychoanalytic Study of the Child* 39 (1984): 333–66.

## Chapter 2. Expert Witness for the Prosecution

35    Eileen's recollections of incest are from my personal interviews with her, conducted on August 16 and 17, 1990, and September 11, 1991. See also E. Franklin and W. Wright, *Sins of the Father* (New York: Crown, 1991) and the opinion (not for official publication) of Justice William Newsom, Division One, California Court of Appeal in the case of *People v. Franklin,* April 2, 1993.

The *Challenger* study is L. Terr, D. Bloch, B. Michel, J. Reinhart, and S. A. Matayer, "Children's Response to the *Challenger* Spacecraft Disaster," in *New Research Program and Abstracts,* Annual Meeting, American Psychiatric Association, New York City, May 17, 1990, p. 269.

36    The books Eileen Franklin loved as a child: A. Lindgren, *Pippi Longstocking* [1950] (New York: Puffin Books, 1977); N. Brelis, *The Mummy Market* (New York: Harper & Row, 1966).

37    Judge Smith's ruling and the opinion on that ruling: see the opinion of the California Court of Appeal, pp. 14–23.

40    Clear, detailed memories over a four- to five-year lapse are noted in L. Terr, "Chowchilla Revisited: The Effects of Psychic Trauma Four Years After a School-bus Kidnapping," *American Journal of Psychiatry* 140 (1983): 1543–50.

41    "She's going to like this, huh, George?": see *Sins of the Father,* p. 228.

Eileen's delay in recalling the true identity of her rapist is also described in *Sins of the Father,* pp. 112, 119, 171, 227–28, and was described to me in her interviews.

42–43  On the anatomy and function of the brain, see, for example, Sir John Walton, *Brain's Diseases of the Nervous System,* 9th ed. (Oxford: Oxford University Press, 1985). The anatomy of the brain is well illustrated in J. de Groot and J. G. Chusid, *Correlative Neuroanatomy,* 20th ed. (East Norwalk, Conn.: Appleton & Lange, 1988). A good source of information on the anatomical location of language is A. Damasio and H. Damasio, "Brain and Language," *Scientific American* 267 (September 1992): 88–95.

44    On the concept of declarative and nondeclarative memory, see

L. Squire, *Memory and Brain* (New York: Oxford University Press, 1987). Squire uses the term "procedural memory" for nondeclarative memory.

44–45    Mortimer Mishkin's experiments on primate memory are found in J. V. Haxby, C. L. Grady, B. Horowitz, L. G. Ungerleider, M. Mishkin, R. E. Carson, P. Herscovitch, M. B. Shapiro, and S. I. Rapoport, "Dissociation of Object and Spatial Vision Processing Pathways in Human Extra Striate Cortex," *Proceedings of the National Academy of Sciences of the United States of America* 88 (1991): 1621–25; and in M. Mishkin, "Cerebral Memory Circuits," in *1990 Yakult International Symposium: Perception, Cognition and Brain* (Yakult: Honsha Co., 1991). For a summary, see M. Mishkin and T. Appenzeller, "The Anatomy of Memory," *Scientific American* 256 (June 1987): 80–89.

45    H. M., the man without hippocampi, was a patient of the psychologist Brenda Milner. Two of Milner's best publications on the loss of memory after limbic-system injury or surgery are W. B. Scoville and B. Milner, "Loss of Recent Memory After Bilateral Hippocampal Lesions," *Journal of Neurology, Neurosurgery, and Psychiatry* 20 (1957): 11; and B. Milner, "Amnesia Following Operations on the Temporal Lobes," in C. W. M. Whitty and O. L. Zangwill, eds., *Amnesia: Clinical Psychological and Medicolegal Aspects* (London: Butterworths, 1966).

46    Dr. John Briere's study was given at the American Psychological Association Convention, New Orleans, August 1989: J. Briere and J. Conte, "Amnesia in Adults Molested as Children."

46–47    The Dutch study is N. Draijer, *Seksuele Traumatisering in de Jeugd (Sexual Traumatization in Childhood)* (Amsterdam: SUA, 1990).

The sociologist Diana Russell's findings appear in D. E. H. Russell, *The Secret Trauma* (New York: Basic Books, 1986).

47    On the importance of rehearsal in the storage of explicit memories, see F. I. M. Craik and R. S. Lockhart's "Levels of Processing: A Framework for Memory Research," *Journal of Verbal Learning and Verbal Behavior* 11 (1972): 671–84; and A. E. Woodward, R. A. Bjork, and R. H. Jongewerd, "Recall and Recognition as a Function of Primary Rehearsal," *Journal of Verbal Learning and Verbal Behavior* 12 (1973): 608–17.

48–50    On the various types of memory, see H. L. Roediger and F. I. M. Craik, eds., *Varieties of Memory and Consciousness: Essays in Honor of Endel Tulving* (Hillsdale, N.J.: Erlbaum, 1989). In this same book is an essay by Robert Bjork alluding to forgetting and entitled "Retrieval Inhibition as an Adaptive Mechanism in Human Memory."

Patricia Goldman-Rakic, of Yale, is a leading researcher on working memory. See particularly her "Working Memory and the Mind," *Scientific American* 267 (September 1992): 110–17.

50–51   Storage strength and retrieval strength are explained in R. Bjork and E. Bjork, "A New Theory of Disuse and an Old Theory of Stimulus Fluctuation," in A. F. Healy, S. M. Kosslyn, and R. M. Shiffrin, eds., *From Learning Processes to Cognitive Processes: Essays in Honor of William K. Estes,* vol. 2 (Hillsdale, N.J.: Erlbaum, 1992). Robert Bjork delivered his views on processes of memory in his talk, "An Experimental Psychologist Considers Six Types of Memory," at the Annual Meeting, American College of Psychiatrists, San Francisco, February 12–16, 1992.

51      Elizabeth Loftus has an extensive and significant list of publications about the "wrong things" people remember, including the books *Memory* (Reading, Mass.: Addison-Wesley, 1980); E. Loftus and K. Ketcham, *Witness for the Defense* (New York: St. Martin's Press, 1991); and G. L. Wells and E. F. Loftus, eds., *Eyewitness Testimony: Psychological Perspectives* (Cambridge: Cambridge University Press, 1984). Although Dr. Loftus does few experiments on children's memories, she did publish a useful review of the literature on this subject with G. M. Davies, "Distortions in the Memory of Children," *Journal of Social Issues* 40 (1984) no. 2: 51–67.

52–53   Linda Meyer Williams's study of a hundred women who as children visited emergency rooms in connection with sex-abuse charges is "Adult Memories of Childhood Abuse: Preliminary Findings from a Longitudinal Study," *The Advisor* (American Professional Society on the Abuse of Children) (Summer 1992): 19–21.

54      On the lack of dreams in certain instances of childhood trauma, see L. Terr, "Children of Chowchilla: A Study of Psychic Trauma," *Psychoanalytic Study of the Child* 34 (1979): 547–623; and L. Terr, "What Happens to the Memories of Early Trauma?" *Journal of the American Academy of Child and Adolescent Psychiatry* 27 (1988): 96–104. I have also written about the content of those dreams that children do remember in "Children of Chowchilla" and in "Children's Nightmares," in C. Guilleminault, ed., *Sleep and Its Disorders in Children* (New York: Raven Press, 1987).

55–56   Stephen King's *Danse Macabre* was published in New York by Everest House in 1981. The story of King's trauma with the train is on pp. 84–85. *Stand by Me,* directed by Rob Reiner, was released in 1986.

See also L. Terr, "Terror Writing by the Formerly Terrified: The Life and Works of Stephen King," *Psychoanalytic Study of the Child* 44 (1989): 369–90.

56      The episode in the coffee shop occurred—after my paper on King
        was published and shortly before the Franklin trial—at the Bev-
        erly Wilshire Hotel, in September 1990. I was debating whether
        or not to introduce myself to King—having to interrupt an
        important conversation among three men—when King suddenly
        stood up, terminated the discussion ("I don't know if we can work
        together or not, but I'll send you a screenplay"), and left.

57      David Spiegel's work on dissociation is best exemplified by
        D. Spiegel and E. Cardena, "Disintegrated Experience: the Disso-
        ciative Disorders Revisited," *Journal of Abnormal Psychology* 100
        (1991): 366–78; and D. Spiegel, "Hypnosis, Dissociation, and
        Trauma: Hidden and Overt Observers," in J. L. Singer, ed., *Repres-
        sion and Dissociation* (Chicago: University of Chicago Press, 1990).
        See also a book coauthored by Spiegel and his psychiatrist father:
        H. Spiegel and D. Spiegel, *Trance and Treatment: Clinical Uses of
        Hypnosis* (Washington, D.C.: American Psychiatric Press, 1987).

59      The California State Supreme Court ruling denying the Franklin
        appeal was reported by Harriet Chiang: "Conviction in Rape-
        Slaying Let Stand," *San Francisco Chronicle,* July 16, 1993, p. 20.

        The circumstances of Barry Lipsker's death and the estrange-
        ment between Eileen and her siblings: personal phone communi-
        cations from Eileen Franklin Lipsker in the fall of 1992. See also
        *Once Upon a Time,* p. 478, for Barry's death, and *Sins of the Father,*
        pp. 221–23 and 304, for the sibling estrangements.


        Chapter 3. A Drunken Woman at the Side of the Road


66      Pierre Janet and Sigmund Freud published their views on hysteri-
        cal amnesia at about the same time. The two men never clearly
        differentiated between the two defenses, dissociation and repres-
        sion. In fact, Freud once used the word "dissociation" when writ-
        ing about what seems to be repression (see S. Freud, "A Case of
        Successful Treatment By Hypnotism" [1892–93], in *Standard Edi-
        tion,* vol. 1, trans. and ed. J. Strachey [London: Hogarth Press,
        1966], p. 122). For Janet's description of dissociation, see
        *L'Automatisme Psychologique: Essai de Psychologie Expérimentale sur les
        Formes Inférieures de L'Activité Humaine* (Paris: Félix Alcan, 1889;
        Paris: Société Pierre Janet/Payot, 1973). Janet believed that disso-
        ciation was based on an innate psychological weakness and was
        seen only in people with disordered conditions. Freud held that
        repression was used by both emotionally healthy and disordered
        individuals. Today the two defenses are generally considered dif-

ferent from each other: the American Psychiatric Association's *Diagnostic and Statistical Manual, 4th ed.* (Washington, D.C.: American Psychiatric Press, 1994) lists the two defenses separately in Appendix B.

67–68   The organic amnesias are covered in Sir John Walton, *Brain's Diseases of the Nervous System,* 9th ed. (Oxford: Oxford University Press, 1985).

69   The psychological amnesias are classified as dissociative disorders in the American Psychiatric Association's diagnostic manual, 4th ed. John Nemiah, M.D., wrote a review chapter on the "Dissociative Disorders" in H. I. Kaplan and B. J. Sadock, eds., *Comprehensive Textbook of Psychiatry,* 4th ed., vol. 1 (Baltimore: Williams & Wilkins, 1985).

69   For those interested in dissociation as it is expressed in multiple-personality disorder, two classics are C. Thigpen and H. Cleckley, *The Three Faces of Eve* (Augusta: Cleckley-Thigpen, 1955); and F. R. Schreiber, *Sybil* (Chicago: Henry Regnery, 1975). A more recent trade book about a killer who probably faked MPD as his legal defense is the psychiatrist M. Weissberg's *The First Sin of Ross Michael Carlson* (New York: Delacorte Press, 1992).

70   The Milan Kundera novel referred to is *The Book of Laughter and Forgetting,* M. H. Heim, trans. (New York: Knopf, 1980). In another Kundera novel, the protagonist muses on how often the soul leaves the body during sex, its attention drawn "to a game of chess, to recollections of dinner, to a book": *The Joke,* M. H. Heim, trans. (New York: HarperCollins, 1992).

70–71   For the connection between hypnotism and dissociation, see E. R. Hilgard, *Divided Consciousness: Multiple Controls in Human Thought and Action* (New York: Wiley, 1977), and D. Spiegel, "Hypnosis, Dissociation, and Trauma," in J. Singer, ed., *Repression and Dissociation: Implications for Personality Theory, Psychopathology, and Health* (Chicago: University of Chicago Press, 1990).

In his foreword to D. Middlebrook, *Anne Sexton* (Boston: Houghton Mifflin, 1991), pp. xiii–xviii, Martin Orne also tells us that he encouraged Sexton to write down her experiences "in order to help other patients." Orne began treating Sexton in 1956. After a few months of therapy, he says, Sexton began to write her poetry. Many of these earliest Sexton poems have therapy-related titles— "Appointment Hour," "One Patient Released Today," "A Foggy Adjustment."

72   The film *Love Letters* (1945) was directed by William Dieterle. The classic 1940s amnesia film is, of course, *Spellbound* (1945), starring Gregory Peck as the amnesia victim and directed by Alfred Hitch-

cock. Others from the heyday of film amnesia are *I Love You Again* (1940, directed by W. S. Van Dyke II), *Crossroads* (1942, directed by Jack Conway), *Random Harvest* (1942, directed by Mervyn Le Roy), and *Somewhere in the Night* (1946, directed by Joseph L. Mankiewicz). William Powell played the amnesic protagonist in the first two of these.

76      I write of how children with Type II trauma teach themselves to dissociate in "Childhood Traumas: An Outline and Overview," *American Journal of Psychiatry* 148 (1991): 10–20.

77      Eugene Bliss has noted spontaneous self-hypnosis in adult MPD patients in "Spontaneous Self-hypnosis in Multiple Personality Disorder," *Psychiatric Clinics of North America* 7 (1984): 135–148; and in E. L. Bliss, *Multiple Personality, Allied Disorders, and Hypnosis* (Cambridge: Cambridge University Press, 1986).

The Philadelphia psychiatrist Richard Kluft has attempted to characterize the childhood symptoms and signs that may eventually go into adult MPD. See his "Childhood Multiple Personality Disorder: Predictors, Clinical Findings, and Treatment Results," and "The Natural History of Multiple Personality Disorder," in R. P. Kluft, ed., *Childhood Antecedents of Multiple Personality* (Washington, D.C.: American Psychiatric Press, 1985).

On dissociation during childhood, see also F. Putnam, "Dissociative Disorders in Children and Adolescents: A Developmental Perspective," 14 (1991): 519–33; and F. Putnam, "Dissociative Phenomena," in A. Tasman and S. M. Goldfinger, eds., *Review of Psychiatry* 10: 145–60 (Washington, D.C.: American Psychiatric Press, 1991).

78–79   On the hidden observer, see E. R. Hilgard, *Divided Consciousness,* chapters 9 and 10, and E. R. Hilgard, A. H. Morgan, and H. Mac-Donald, "Pain and Dissociation in the Cold Pressor Test: A Study of Hypnotic Analgesia with 'Hidden Reports' Through Automatic Key Pressing and Automatic Talking," *Journal of Abnormal Psychology* 84 (1975): 280–89. The chief critic of the "hidden observer" concept is the psychologist N. P. Spanos. See his "The Hidden Observer as an Experimental Creation," *Journal of Personality and Social Psychology* 44 (1983): 170–76.

87      Arata Osada's collection of essays by Hiroshima schoolchildren who survived the atomic bomb is *Children of Hiroshima* (New York: Taylor & Francis, 1981).

88–99   Virginia Woolf on her sensation of "nonbeing" is from "A Sketch of the Past," in *Moments of Being,* J. Schulkind, ed. (San Diego: Harvest/Harcourt Brace Jovanovich, 1985), p. 70. For my biographical information on Woolf, I rely on Louise DeSalvo, *Virginia*

*Woolf* (Boston: Beacon Press, 1989); Quentin Bell, *Virginia Woolf: A Biography* (New York: Harcourt Brace Jovanovich, 1972); and Leon Edel's essay on Woolf in his *Stuff of Sleep and Dreams: Experiments in Literary Psychology* (New York: Harper & Row, 1982). See also L. Terr, "Who's Afraid in Virginia Woolf? Clues to Early Sexual Abuse in Literature," *Psychoanalytic Study of the Child* 45 (1990): 533–46.

## Chapter 4. The Silver at the Surface of the Water

98–100    *Drosophila* memory studies: see T. Tully, "Physiology of Mutations Affecting Learning and Memory in *Drosophila*—The Missing Link Between Gene Product and Behavior," *Trends in Neuroscience* 14 (1991): 163–64; and T. Tully, "Genetic Dissection of Learning and Memory in *Drosophila melanogaster*," in J. Madden, ed., *Neurobiology of Learning, Emotion and Affect* (New York: Raven Press, 1991); and R. L. Davis and B. Danwalder, "The *Drosophila Dunce* Locus: Learning and Memory Genes in the Fly," *Trends in Genetics* 7 (1991): 224–29.

Tully's fruit-fly conditioning experiments have identified four memory phases in flies: short-term (gone in 60 minutes), middle-term (gone in 6 hours), anesthesia-resistant (gone in 2 to 4 days), and protein-synthesis-inhibitor-sensitive long-term memory (lasting more than 7 days). The first three of these memory-phase experiments are described in T. Tully, S. Boynton, C. Brandes, J. M. Dura, R. Mihalek, T. Preat, and A. Villela, "Genetic Dissection of Memory Formation in *Drosophila melanogaster. Cold Spring Harbor Symposium on Quantitative Biology* 55 (1990): 203–11. Research on the fourth phase is currently in progress.

Long-term memory can be interfered with by inhibiting protein synthesis. When protein-inhibiting compounds are administered to laboratory animals, the animals can learn, but they cannot retain their knowledge for more than a few minutes. See S. H. Barondes, "Multiple Steps in the Biology of Memory," F. Schmitt, ed., *The Neurosciences: A Second Study Program* (New York: Rockefeller University Press, 1970).

102–3     Some selected references to the work Eric Kandel's team does on the cellular memory of *Aplysia* are E. R. Kandel and R. D. Hawkins, "The Biological Basis of Learning and Individuality," *Scientific American* 267 (September 1992): 79–86; R. D. Hawkins, T. W. Abrams, T. J. Carew, and E. R. Kandel, "A Cellular Mechanism of Classical Conditioning in *Aplysia*: Activity-Dependent

Amplification of Presynaptic Facilitation, *Science* 219 (1983): 400–5; and E. R. Kandel, "Genes, Nerve Cells, and the Remembrance of Things Past," *Journal of Neuropsychiatry* 1 (1989): 103–25.

108–9    Craig Bailey and Mary Chen of the Columbia *Aplysia* group describe the anatomical changes that *Aplysia* develops with long-term memory in "The Anatomy of Long-Term Sensitization in *Aplysia:* Morphological Insights into Learning and Memory," in L. R. Squire, N. M. Weinberger, G. Lynch, and J. L. McGaugh, eds., *Memory: Organization and Locus of Change* (New York: Oxford University Press, 1991).

On the Texas Health Science Center studies of cellular response to long-term memory, see J. H. Byrne, "Cellular Analysis of Associative Learning," *Physiological Review* 67 (1987): 329–439.

On larval memory through metamorphosis, see T. Tully, L. Kruse, and V. Cambiazo, "Memory Through Metamorphosis in Normal and Mutant *Drosophila melanogaster,*" *Journal of Neuroscience,* in press.

My clinical study of twenty preschoolers with documented traumas is "What Happens to the Memories of Early Trauma? A Study of Twenty Children Under Age Five at the Time of Documented Traumatic Events," *Journal of the American Academy of Child and Adolescent Psychiatry* 27 (1988): 96–104.

112      Richard Galdston's paper on "psychotic transference" in child abusers is "Observations on Children Who Have Been Physically Abused by Their Parents," *American Journal of Psychiatry* 122 (1965): 440–43. My own research on physical child abuse is published in two articles: L. Terr and A. Watson, "The Battered Child Rebrutalized: Ten Cases of Medical Legal Confusion," *American Journal of Psychiatry* 124 (1968): 126–33, and L. Terr, "A Family Study of Child Abuse," *American Journal of Psychiatry* 127 (1970): 665–71. For other studies on the reasons parents abuse their children, see L. Silver, C. Dubliner, and R. Lurie, "Does Violence Breed Violence? Contributions from a Study of the Child Abuse Syndrome," *American Journal of Psychiatry* 126 (1969): 404–7; and J. E. Oliver, "Intergenerational Transmission of Child Abuse," *American Journal of Psychiatry* 150 (1993): 1315–24.

113–14   Work on human and animal amnesia from Dr. Squire's lab includes L. R. Squire, "Memory and the Hippocampus: A Synthesis from Findings with Rats, Monkeys, and Humans," *Psychological Review* 99 (1992): 195–231; and L. R. Squire, F. Haist, and A. P. Shimamura, "The Neurology of Memory: Quantitative Assessment of Retrograde Amnesia in Two Groups of Amnesic Patients," *Journal of Neuroscience* 9 (1989): 828–39.

The idea that the hippocampus does not stay active over very long periods of time in storing memory is found in S. Zola-Morgan and L. R. Squire, "The Primate Hippocampal Formation: Evidence for a Time-Limited Role in Memory Storage," *Science* 250 (1990): 288–90.

117    D. Sylvester's *Magritte* (New York: Abrams, 1992) describes the aftermath of Madame Magritte's suicide, including the discovery of her drowned body, which washed up several days later onto a slag heap. For my understanding of the artist, I also rely on Suzi Gablik, *Magritte* (New York: Thames & Hudson, 1985); A. Hammacher, *Magritte* (New York: Abrams, 1973); and H. Torczyner, *Magritte* (France: Draeger, 1977). An interesting psychiatric paper on Magritte was written by Milton Viederman. It is "René Magritte," *Journal of the American Psychoanalytic Association* 35 (1987): 967–98. I wrote about Magritte in "Childhood Trauma and the Creative Product: Poe, Wharton, Magritte, Hitchcock, and Bergman," *Psychoanalytic Study of the Child* 42 (1987): 545–72.

My material on Munch comes from J. P. Hodin, *Edvard Munch* (London: Thames & Hudson, 1972); T. Messer, *Munch* (New York: Abrams, 1985); and R. Stang, *Edvard Munch: The Man and His Art* (New York: Abbeville Press, 1977).

Hayden Herrera's biography of Frida Kahlo, *Frida* (New York: Harper & Row, 1983) includes plates of many of her paintings and drawings. It is one of the best art biographies I have read and includes the material I refer to here.

### Chapter 5. The Two Miss Americas of 1958 and Her Sister

120    The newspaper photo I describe at the beginning and end of this chapter was originally printed in 1951 in the *Rocky Mountain News*. It is reprinted in an article by J. R. Moehringer, "Ex-Miss America Reveals Horror," *Rocky Mountain News,* May 10, 1991, p. 8.

121    The Bill McNichols quote comes from "Van Derburs Were Pillars of Denver Society," *Denver Post,* May 9, 1991, p. 14A.

Boots Van Derbur describes Van as an "Adonis" in *People,* June 10, 1991, p. 92. Her quote about their marriage, her quickened heartbeat at the sight of him, and the good things she tries to remember comes from the same article.

121    Francis S. Van Derbur's obituary appears in the *Denver Post,* Sep-

tember 17, 1984, p. 1, and the *Rocky Mountain News,* same date
and page no.

The Van Derbur graves and the neon cross on Mt. Lindo: see
"Van Derburs Were Pillars of Denver Society," *Denver Post,* May 9,
1991.

122 My source for Marilyn's scrapbook and the family's "initiative
slips" program is Gwen Van Derbur Mitchell, whom I interviewed on May 9, 1992.

For Marilyn's Miss America pageant history, see "Miss America
Crown Fits Like a Glass Slipper," *Denver Post,* May 9, 1991, p.
14A.

123 The classic paper on child abuse is C. H. Kempe, F. N. Silverman,
B. F. Steele, W. Droegmueller, and H. K. Silver, "The Battered-
Child Syndrome," *Journal of the American Medical Association* 81
(1962): 17–24.

123 I quote Marilyn Van Derbur Atler's Kempe Center benefit speech
from two sources: Kevin Simpson and Carol Kreck's article in the
*Denver Post,* "Beauty Queen's Ordeal: Incest," May 9, 1991, p. 1;
and Marilyn Van Derbur Atler's written version of the speech, a
copy of which was sent to me by a friend.

124 Freud described splitting in "Splitting of the Ego in the Process of
Defense" [1940], in *Standard Edition,* vol. 23, trans. and ed.
J. Strachey (London: Hogarth Press, 1964), pp. 275–78.

124 Marilyn's lunch with D. D. Harvey: see interview of D. D. Harvey
with religion writer Virginia Culver, in the *Denver Post,* "Minister's
'Miracle' Words Unlock Atler's Dark Secret," June 9, 1991, p. 1.
The minister reports that he told Marilyn at lunch that "there is
something deep inside you that needs to come out." She replied,
"There's nothing, D. D." Almost without thinking, Harvey said
the words "Father. Bedroom." And Marilyn burst into tears.

125 For Marilyn's three-month marriage in 1961 and her on-and-off
courtship with Larry Atler, see the June 10, 1991, article in *People.*

126 J. Christopher Perry differentiates between splitting of the self
and splitting of the object in his "Defense Mechanism Rating
Scale," in G. Vaillant, ed., *Ego Mechanisms of Defense: A Guide for
Clinicians and Researchers* (Washington, D.C.: American Psychiatric Press, 1992).

126–27 Extreme splitting and MPD in children are described in R. P.
Kluft, ed., *Childhood Antecedents of Multiple Personality* (Washington, D.C.: American Psychiatric Press, 1985); F. Putnam, "Dissociative Disorders in Children and Adolescents," *Psychiatric Clinics
of North America* 14 (1991): 519–33; and N. L. Hornstein and
S. Tyson, "Inpatient Treatment of Children with Multiple Person-

ality Dissociative Disorders and Their Families," *Psychiatric Clinics of North America* 14 (1991): 631–48.

128    In her Kempe Center benefit speech, Marilyn Van Derbur Atler said, "I was hospitalized [with paralysis] for the better part of 3 months."

The Kempe Center benefit speech is also a source for Marilyn's other symptoms and the increasing difficulties she experienced as Jennifer entered adolescence. Symptoms are also noted in M. Van Derbur Atler's "Say 'Incest' Out Loud," *McCall's,* September 1991, p. 78.

128    Marilyn told of "undertaking a wide range of specific therapies," including individual psychotherapy, hypnotherapy, rolfing, and incest support groups in the September 1991 issue of *McCall's.* In an article under her byline in *People,* June 10, 1991, Marilyn wrote that from 1984 to May 1991 she spent "many hours a week in various kinds of therapy." She told Carol Kreck, of the *Denver Post,* that she had also gone through acupuncture, acupressure, and self-defense classes: "She tried them all," Kreck says, in "The Decision to Speak Out," May 10, 1991, p. 1.

129    Freud began speaking of "denial of external reality"—without using those specific words—in 1894. In 1915, he wrote of it again. Finally, in 1924, he named the defense *Verleugnung.* His English translator, James Strachey, renders it as "disavowal." See *Standard Edition,* "The Neuro-psychoses of Defense," vol. 3 (1962); "The Unconscious," vol. 14 (1957); and "The Loss of Reality in Neurosis and Psychosis," vol. 19 (1961).

Marilyn alludes to negative reaction on Denver talk radio in "Marilyn Van Derbur Atler's Diary," *Rocky Mountain News,* April 26 and 27, 1992, pp. 32 and 8.

130    Gwen Mitchell's revelation of her own sexual abuse can be found in F. Germer, "Ex-Beauty Queen's Sister Acknowledges Father Molested Her, Too," *Rocky Mountain News,* May 11, 1991, p. 6.

131    Boots' 1984 denial, "It's in your fantasy," is quoted in a speech Marilyn Atler gave at Montview Boulevard Presbyterian Church, May 23, 1991: J. R. Moehringer, "Incest Victims Gather," *Rocky Mountain News,* May 24, 1991, p. 6. Gwen Mitchell told me, in a personal interview in May 1992, that after her mother responded to Marilyn this way, Gwen and her mother spoke by phone and Gwen came to visit her mother in Denver to tell her that she, too, had been abused by Francis S. Van Derbur.

131–32    "First Person with Maria Shriver" featured Marilyn Van Derbur Atler on November 12, 1991. Marilyn appeared again with Maria Shriver on August 26, 1993. In this interview it was clear that her ambivalence about her father had disappeared. She said she no longer loved him.

132     My paper on Stephen King is "Terror Writing by the Formerly Terrified: A Look at Stephen King," *Psychoanalytic Study of the Child* 44 (1989): 369–90.

I taped Marilyn's appearance on "Sally Jessy Raphaël." It was a month after her Kempe benefit speech (June 7, 1991) and the program was entitled, "The Beauty Queen with the Ugly Past."

*Newsweek* covered Marilyn Van Derbur Atler's story in N. Darnton (with K. Springen, L. Wright, and S. Keene-Osborn), "The Pain of the Last Taboo," October 7, 1991, p. 70.

133     Marilyn's twenty appointments a day as Miss America were mentioned in her article in *People,* p. 91.

133     "Good Afternoon, Colorado" televised Marilyn on May 9, 1991.

133–34  See Culver interview of D. D. Harvey, *Denver Post,* June 9, 1991.

Marilyn told Sally Jessy Raphaël's audience about the physical barriers she habitually kept between herself and D. D. Harvey.

134–35  Marilyn's refusal to write or authorize a book: see F. Germer, "Incest Revealed 'to Help Others,'" *Rocky Mountain News,* May 11, 1991. J. R. Moehringer also wrote about Marilyn Atler's distrust of the publishing industry in "Ex-Miss America Reveals Horror," *Rocky Mountain News,* May 10, 1991.

135     Marilyn's visit to her old house: see C. Kreck, "Sister Crucial in Van Derbur's Healing Process," *Denver Post,* May 13, 1991, p. 1.

136     On Marilyn's shyness, also see "Miss America Crown Fits Like a Glass Slipper," *Denver Post,* May 9, 1991. After she was named Miss America, Marilyn was quoted as saying, "I never expected to win the title. I was pudgy. I was horribly shy, and my biggest hope was that I wouldn't fall off the runway." The shame about her body is evident here.

136     Marilyn's allusion to her sexual problems is in a notation in her newspaper "diary" about a talk that Larry Atler gave on Nov. 19, 1991, in Fort Collins, Colorado: "He spoke about sexual dysfunction. Every survivor [of incest] knows about that. Every significant other knows about that. I had spent 13 years of my life trying not to FEEL ANYTHING."

137     The "screaming skin" is mentioned by Marilyn in her Kempe benefit speech.

137–38  Marilyn's erasure of the doll's mouth: see "Incest Victims Gather," *Rocky Mountain News,* May 24, 1991.

Marilyn describes her anal pain in the *Rocky Mountain News* "diary," April 26, 1992, p. 33.

139     The story of Sybil, who was an MPD sufferer and a patient of

the psychiatrist Cornelia Wilbur, is told in F. R. Schreiber, *Sybil* (Chicago: Henry Regnery, 1975). Eve, a famous multiple-personality patient, was described in C. Thigpen and H. Cleckley, *The Three Faces of Eve* (Augusta: Cleckley-Thigpen, 1955). "Eve" published her own story, taking exception to some of what Thigpen and Cleckley wrote about her, in C. Sizemore, *I'm Eve* (Garden City, N.Y.: Doubleday, 1977).

141   Marilyn's quote about her mind leaving her body comes from "Sister Crucial in Van Derbur's Healing Process," *Denver Post,* May 13, 1991.

142   Projective identification is a defense first described by the European psychoanalyst Melanie Klein. See her *Envy and Gratitude* (London: Tavistock, 1957). The American psychoanalyst Otto Kernberg expanded on this defense in "Borderline Personality Organization," *Journal of the American Psychoanalytic Association* 15 (1967): 641–85, and *Borderline Conditions and Pathological Narcissism* (New York: Jason Aronson, 1975).

145   Virginia Woolf's "A Sketch of the Past" is in J. Schulkind, ed., *Moments of Being* (San Diego: Harcourt Brace Jovanovich, 1985). See also L. Terr, "Who's Afraid in Virginia Woolf? Clues to Early Sexual Abuse in Literature," *Psychoanalytic Study of the Child* 45 (1990): 533–46.

146   On children's use of "denial in fantasy," see R. Pynoos and S. Eth, "The Child As Witness to Homicide," *Journal of Social Issues* 40 (1984): 87–108.

The *Challenger* study is L. Terr, D. Bloch, B. Michel, J. Reinhart, and S. Matayer, "Children's Responses to the *Challenger* Spacecraft Disaster," *New Research Program and Abstracts,* American Psychiatric Association, Annual Meeting, New York City, May 17, 1990, p. 269.

149   On Carol Kreck's statement in the *Denver Post* that other Van Derbur sisters were abused: In the spring of 1993, I phoned Ms. Kreck and asked her for her sources. She told me that the sisters' family members and coworkers had given her the material about these additional abuses. She also said that she considered it significant that well over a year after the release of Marilyn's and Gwen's incest stories the middle two Van Derbur sisters had still issued no denials of their own.

150   Intellectualization is defined by George Vaillant as "thinking about instinctual wishes in formal, bland terms that leaves the associated affect unconscious," in *Ego Mechanisms of Defense,* p. 246. J. Christopher Perry sees intellectualization as a defense against psychic trauma as well as instinctual wishes. ("The individual

deals with emotional conflicts, or internal or external stressors, by the excessive use of abstract thinking or generalizing to avoid experiencing disturbing feelings.") See *Ego Mechanisms of Defense,* p. 258.

## Chapter 6. The Child Star's Tale

154 For more information on attention-deficit/hyperactivity disorder and its treatment with Ritalin, see L. Silver, *The Misunderstood Child: A Guide for Parents of Learning Disabled Children* (New York: McGraw-Hill, 1984); and P. Wender, *The Hyperactive Child, Adolescent, and Adult: Attention Deficit Disorder Through the Lifespan* (New York: Oxford University Press, 1987).

155 On Elizabeth Loftus' work on misinformation, see particularly her *Memory* (Reading, Mass.: Addison-Wesley, 1980).

156 Baruch Fischhoff's study on hindsight and its effect on memory is in B. Fischoff and R. Beyth, "'I Knew It Would Happen'— Remembered Probabilities of Once-Future Things," *Organizational Behavior and Human Performance* 13 (1975): 1–16. Another interesting Fischhoff paper on this subject is "Hindsight≠Foresight: The Effect of Outcome Knowledge on Judgment Under Uncertainty," *Journal of Experimental Psychology: Human Perception and Performance* 104 (1975): 288–99.

An excellent review of the importance of cuing in helping children to remember is R. Fivush, "Developmental Perspectives on Autobiographical Recall," in G. S. Goodman and B. L. Bottoms, eds., *Child Victims, Child Witnesses: Understanding and Improving Testimony* (New York: Guilford, 1993).

My opinions on anatomically correct dolls were published in debate form, including a rebuttal, against the opinions and rebuttal of Dr. Alayne Yates, the chief of the Division of Child Psychiatry at the University of Arizona Medical School; see A. Yates and L. Terr, "Anatomically Correct Dolls: Should They Be Used as the Basis for Expert Testimony?" *Journal of the American Academy of Child and Adolescent Psychiatry* 27 (1988): 254–57 and 387–88. The California Court of Appeal has banned information from coming into court if it is obtained from a child's use of anatomically correct dolls. See *In re Amber B. and Teela C.* 191 Cal. App. 3rd 682 (1987).

156–57 Gail Goodman is a leading psychological researcher on children's credibility as witnesses. See K. J. Saywitz, G. S. Goodman, E. Nicholas, and S. Moan, "Children's Memories of Physical

Examinations Involving Genital Touch: Implications for Reports of Child Sexual Abuse," *Journal of Consulting and Clinical Psychology* 59 (1991): 682–91.

160    The study of fifty-three women's attempts to confirm incest memories is J. Herman and E. Schatzow, "Recovery and Verification of Memories of Childhood Sexual Trauma," *Psychoanalytic Psychology* 4 (1987): 1–14.

161    Lawrence Wright's article on Paul Ingram's confession and retraction appears in *The New Yorker,* May 17 and 24, 1993. A paper by the Berkeley sociologist Richard Ofshe also discusses the Ingram case; it is "Inadvertent Hypnosis During Interrogation," *International Journal of Clinical and Experimental Hypnosis* 40 (1992): 125–56. Paul Ingram's motion to withdraw his guilty plea was rejected by the Washington State appellate court in January 1992, and by the State Supreme Court in September 1992.

163    Jean Piaget told his story of false memory in *Play, Dreams, and Imitation in Childhood,* trans. L. Gattegno and F. M. Hodgson (New York: W. W. Norton, 1951). My friend Peter Tanguay, a psychiatric researcher at UCLA, heard Piaget tell the incident to a small group of visiting psychiatrists and psychologists in Switzerland. He said nothing at the time about having suffered any symptoms, but Peter also assures me that Piaget was particularly tight-lipped about himself.

163    I have referred to a number of Elizabeth Loftus's writings in my notes on chapter 2. Others include: E. Loftus, "Reconstructing Memory: The Incredible Eyewitness," *Psychology Today* 8 (1974): 116–18; and E. Loftus and J. Palmer, "Reconstruction of Automobile Destruction: An Example of the Interaction Between Language and Memory," *Journal of Verbal Learning and Verbal Behavior* 13 (1974): 585–89.

   On incorrectly remembered details in the Chowchilla schoolbus kidnapping, see L. Terr, "Children of Chowchilla: A Study of Psychic Trauma" *Psychoanalytic Study of the Child* 34 (1979): 547–623; and in the *Challenger* study, see: L. Terr, D. Bloch, B. Michel, J. Reinhart, and S. Matayer, "Children's Responses to the *Challenger* Spacecraft Disaster," *New Research Program and Abstracts,* American Psychiatric Association Annual Meeting, New York City, May 17, 1990, p. 269.

164    The study of eighteen children in custody battles is E. P. Benedek and D. H. Schetky, "Allegations of Sexual Abuse in Child Custody and Visitation Disputes," in D. H. Schetky and E. P. Benedek, eds., *Emerging Issues in Child Psychiatry and the Law* (New York: Brunner/Mazel, 1985).

In 1989, the psychologists Mark Everson and Barbara Boat surveyed workers from the Child Protective Service agencies in North Carolina, in an attempt to calculate the percentage of false reporting of sexual abuse by children and adolescents. Among preschool and kindergarten-age children, the percentage of false allegations appeared to be between 1.7% and 2.7%. Among adolescents, the percentage was substantially higher—between 8.0% and 12.7%. The overall false reporting rate was 4.7% to 7.6%. Everson and Boat's paper is "False Allegations of Sexual Abuse," *Journal of the American Academy of Child and Adolescent Psychiatry* 28 (1989): 230–35.

164          The False Memory Syndrome Foundation claims a membership of a few thousand people nationwide. It was founded in March 1992, and its headquarters are in Philadelphia.

168–70    Stephen Ceci's experiments through the 1980s are summarized in S. J. Ceci, D. Ross, and M. P. Toglia, *Children's Eyewitness Memory* (New York: Springer-Verlag, 1987) and in S. J. Ceci, M. P. Toglia, and D. Ross, *Perspectives on Children's Testimony* (New York: Springer-Verlag, 1989). The "Sam Stone" experiment appears in S. J. Ceci, M. Leichtman, and T. White, "Interviewing Preschoolers: Remembrance of Things Planted," in D. P. Peters, ed., *The Child Witness in Context: Cognitive, Social, and Legal Perspectives* (Holland: Kluwer, in press).

172          Re E. Bass and L. Davis, *The Courage to Heal* (New York: Harper & Row, 1988): There are many good things in this book, despite its suggestiveness. The idea of writing journal entries, poems, and stories related to personal pain is a good one and works well for a number of patients in therapy. This idea was popularized in the Bass and Davis book.

On the symptoms of childhood sex-abuse survivors, see J. L. Herman, *Father-Daughter Incest* (Cambridge: Harvard University Press, 1981), and her *Trauma and Recovery* (New York: Basic Books, 1992).

Another excellent source for understanding the symptoms and signs in adults of childhood sexual abuse is John Briere's *Child Abuse Trauma* (Newberry Park, Calif.: Sage Publications, 1992). My paper "Childhood Traumas: An Outline and Overview," *American Journal of Psychiatry* 148 (1991): 10–20, ties these symptoms to the findings in other kinds of childhood traumas.

175          On Münchhausen by proxy, see R. Meadow, "Münchhausen by Proxy: The Hinterland of Child Abuse," *Lancet* 2 (1977): 343–45; D. Rogers, J. Tripp, A. Bentovim, et al.; "Non-Accidental Poisoning: An Extended Syndrome of Child Abuse," *British Journal of*

*Medicine* 2 (1976): 793–96; and H. A. Schreier and J. A. Libow, *Hurting for Love: Münchhausen Syndrome by Proxy* (New York: Guilford, 1993).

## Chapter 7. The Black Dahlia's Son

187     J. Ellroy's first nine crime books are: *Brown's Requiem* (New York: Avon Books, 1981); *Clandestine* (New York: Avon Books, 1982); *Blood on the Moon* (New York: Mysterious Press, 1984); *Because the Night* (New York: Mysterious Press, 1984); *Suicide Hill* (New York: Mysterious Press, 1986); *Killer on the Road* (originally published as *Silent Terror*) (New York: Avon Books, 1986); *The Black Dahlia* (New York: Mysterious Press, 1987); *The Big Nowhere* (New York: Mysterious Press, 1988); *L.A. Confidential* (New York: Mysterious Press, 1990). A year after my interviews with Ellroy, *White Jazz* was published (New York: Knopf, 1992).

189     On multiple versions of the self, see R. Schafer, *Retelling a Life* (New York: Basic Books, 1992).

191–92   Donald Spence's book on therapeutic influences on memory— *Narrative Truth and Historical Truth* (New York: W. W. Norton, 1982)—is a psychoanalytic classic. It takes issue with Freud's metaphor of the analyst as archaeologist, suggesting that what "really happened" in a person's childhood is probably beyond reach of the ordinary psychoanalytic situation.

194–95   Studies on the amount, accuracy, and consistency of children's memories are reviewed in R. Fivush, "Developmental Perspectives on Autobiographical Recall," in G. S. Goodman and B. L. Bottoms, eds., *Child Victims, Child Witnesses: Understanding and Improving Testimony* (New York: Guilford, 1993). Two of Fivush's own studies of children's memories are N. R. Hamond and R. Fivush, "Memories of Mickey Mouse: Young Children Recount Their Trip to Disneyworld," *Cognitive Development* 6 (1990): 433–48; and J. A. Hudson and R. Fivush, "As Time Goes By: Sixth Graders Remember a Kindergarten Experience," *Emory Cognition Project Report #135* (Atlanta: Emory University, 1987).

196–97   On omens, see L. Terr, "Children of Chowchilla: A Study of Psychic Trauma," *Psychoanalytic Study of the Child* 34 (1979): 547–623.

197     For a review of Robert Pynoos' thinking on childhood trauma, including the idea of cognitive appraisals and reappraisals, see R. Pynoos, "Traumatic Stress and Developmental Psychopathology in Children," in J. M. Oldham, M. B. Riba, and A. Tasman,

eds., *Review of Psychiatry* 12 (Washington, D.C.: American Psychiatric Press, 1993).

The psychoanalyst Ernst Kris offers an oft-cited instance of condensation in a preschooler's memory in his paper "The Recovery of Childhood Memories in Psychoanalysis," *Psychoanalytic Study of the Child* 11 (1956): 54–88. This paper takes the position that the therapist should not expect to find the real truth in an early childhood memory.

200    Paranormal experiences connected with the *Challenger* explosion are in the yet unpublished portions of L. Terr, D. Bloch, B. Michel, J. Reinhart, and S. Matayer, "Children's Responses to the *Challenger* Spacecraft Disaster."

The occurrence of paranormal experience linked to trauma is explained and exemplified in L. Terr, "Remembered Images in Psychic Trauma: One Explanation for the Supernatural," *Psychoanalytic Study of the Child* 40 (1985): 493–533; and "Time and Trauma," *Psychoanalytic Study of the Child* 39 (1984): 633–66.

201    On time sense connected with traumatic events, see chapter 8 in L. Terr, *Too Scared to Cry* (New York: Harper & Row, 1990; paper ed., Basic Books, 1992).

201    The time problems that children exhibited four to five years after the Chowchilla kidnapping can be found in L. Terr, "Chowchilla Revisited," *American Journal of Psychiatry* 140 (1983): 1543–50; and L. Terr, "Time Sense Following Psychic Trauma: A Clinical Study of Ten Adults and Twenty Children," *American Journal of Orthopsychiatry* 53 (1983): 244–61.

203    On the gist of a real memory staying true while details go off, see L. Terr, "What Happens to the Memories of Early Trauma? A Study of Twenty Children Under Age Five at the Time of Documented Traumatic Events," *Journal of the American Academy of Child and Adolescent Psychiatry* 27 (1988): 96–104; and L. Terr, "Childhood Traumas: An Outline and Overview," *American Journal of Psychiatry* 148 (1991): 10–20. There is also considerable foundation for this statement in the Chowchilla studies.

207–8    On the railroad incident in Stephen King's childhood, see his *Danse Macabre* (New York: Everest House, 1981), pp. 84–85.

The study correlating children's closeness to violence with their free recollections of the violence is R. Pynoos and K. Nader, "Children's Memory and Proximity to Violence," *Journal of the American Academy of Child and Adolescent Psychiatry* 28 (1989): 236–41.

209    James Ellroy detailed his youthful career as a criminal for me in my second interview with him, in August 1991.

210    On all the defenses as means of forgetting, see G. Vaillant, ed., *Ego*

*Mechanisms of Defense: A Guide for Clinicians and Researchers* (Washington, D.C.: American Psychiatric Press, 1992).

211   On James Ellroy's trip with the *Rolling Stone* crew to the place his mother's body was found: the piece about Ellroy, by M. Gilmore, was published in *Men's Journal,* one of the publications affiliated with *Rolling Stone,* Fall 1992, p. 164.

On "passive into active," see S. Freud, "Beyond the Pleasure Principle" [1920], *Standard Edition,* vol. 18, trans. and ed. J. Strachey (London: Hogarth Press, 1955), pp. 15–17; and A. Freud, *The Ego and the Mechanisms of Defense* [1937] (New York: International Universities Press, 1946), pp. 121–22.

213   "The recall of the past is hostage to the transference": *Narrative Truth and Historical Truth,* p. 95.

215   Jonathan Kellerman's quote is taken from the front cover of the Avon paperback edition of *Because the Night.*

## Chapter 8. Searching for Corky

223   Freud's concept of infantile amnesia is postulated in "The Psychopathology of Everyday Life" [1901] and "Three Essays on the Theory of Sexuality" [1905], *Standard Edition,* vols. 6 and 7, trans. and ed. J. Strachey (London: Hogarth Press, 1960 and 1953). The theory of infantile amnesia is restated in "Introductory Lectures on Psychoanalysis" [1916–17], in *Standard Edition,* vols. 15–16, 1963.

Freud's concept of screen memories appears in the paper "Screen Memories" [1889], *Standard Edition,* vol. 3, 1962; and in "Leonardo da Vinci and a Memory of His Childhood" [1910], in *Standard Edition,* vol. 11, 1957.

224   The results of asking students for their earliest memories are given in G. J. Dudycha and M. M. Dudycha, "Adolescents' Memories of Preschool Experiences," *Journal of Genetic Psychology* 42 (1933): 468–80. The results of asking for all memories before age eight are found in S. Waldfogel's "The Frequency and Affective Character of Childhood Memories," *Psychological Monographs* 62, no. 291 (1948).

The study of memories of the birth of a sibling is K. Sheingold and Y. J. Tenney, "Memory for a Salient Childhood Event," in U. Neisser, ed., *Memory Observed* (San Francisco: W. H. Freeman, 1982).

The John F. Kennedy assassination memory study is G. Winograd and W. A. Killinger, Jr., "Relating Age at Encoding in Early

Childhood to Adult Recall: Development of Flashbulb Memories," *Journal of Experimental Psychology: General* 112 (1983): 413–22.

224 My study of documented preschool traumas is L. Terr, "What Happens to the Memories of Early Trauma? A Study of Twenty Children Under Age Five at the Time of Documented Traumatic Events," *Journal of the American Academy of Child and Adolescent Psychiatry* 27 (1988): 96–104. For a good review of the cognitive and developmental-psychology literature on early childhood memories, see D. Pillemer and S. White, "Childhood Events Recalled by Children and Adults," *Advances in Child Development and Behavior* 21 (1989): 297–340.

225–26 Daniel Stern's puppet experiments are found in P. A. Nachman and D. N. Stern, "Affective Reactions to Stimuli and Infants' Preferences for Novelty and Familiarity," *Journal of the American Academy of Child Psychiatry* 25 (1986): 801–4; and D. N. Stern, *The Interpersonal World of the Infant: A View from Psychoanalysis and Developmental Psychology* (New York: Basic Books, 1985).

Re memory pathways: Mortimer Mishkin's team at the National Institute of Mental Health has mapped out certain anatomical distributions for habit memories, as opposed to explicit memories, in monkeys. See M. Mishkin and T. Appenzeller, "The Anatomy of Memory," *Scientific American* 256 (June 1987): 80–89. These mappings help explain why things learned nonverbally by human infants remain nonverbal, though influential.

227–29 Dr. Marigold Linton's studies of her memories of world events are presented in two professional papers and one magazine article: "Memory for Real-World Events," in D. A. Norman and D. E. Runelhart, eds., *Exploration in Cognition* (San Francisco: W. H. Freeman, 1975); "Real-World Memory After Six Years: An In-Vivo Study of Very Long-Term Memory," in M. M. Gruneberg, P. E. Morris, and R. N. Sykes, eds., *Practical Aspects of Memory* (London: Academic Press, 1979); and "I Remember It Well," *Psychology Today,* July 1979. She discusses her retrievals of personal memory in "Transformations of Memory in Everyday Life," in U. Neisser, ed., *Memory Observed: Remembering in Natural Contexts* (San Francisco: W. H. Freeman, 1982); and "Ways of Searching and the Contents of Memory," in D. C. Rubin, ed., *Autobiographical Memory* (New York: Cambridge University Press, 1986).

232 On processing of spatial memories: B. Gustafsson and H. Wigström proposed coincident pre- and postsynaptic activity as essential to long-term potentiation in the hippocampus in "Physiological

Mechanisms Underlying Long-Term Potentiation," *Trends in Neuroscience* 11 (1988): 156–62. A recent review of their work and the work of others on the hippocampus and memory is B. Gustafsson and H. Wigström, "Long-term Potentiation in the Hippocampal CA1 Region," *Progress in Brain Research* 83 (1990): 223–32.

233      Frank Conroy spoke—along with the writers Diane Middlebrook, Linda Sexton, Robert Hass, and Tobias Wolff—at the American College of Psychiatrists Annual Meeting, in San Francisco, February 12–16, 1992. They spoke on their own memories, as they affect and are affected by their writings. For examples of their work, see Conroy's *Stop-Time* (New York: Viking-Penguin, 1977); Middlebrook's *Anne Sexton* (Boston: Houghton Mifflin, 1991); L. Sexton's *Mirror Images* (New York: Doubleday, 1985); Hass's *Human Wishes* (New York: Ecco Press, 1990), and *20th Century Pleasures* (New York: Ecco Press, 1984); and Wolff's *This Boy's Life: A Memoir* (New York: HarperCollins, 1990).

234      For the winter counts of the Plains Indians, "anchoring in memory an event to a particular winter," see W. E. Farr, *The Reservation Blackfeet, 1882–1945: A Photographic History of Cultural Survival* (Seattle: University of Washington Press, 1984), p. ix. See also the Kiowa and Sioux calendars in O. La Farge, *A Pictorial History of the American Indian* (New York: Crown, 1906), pp. 152 and 164.

237–39   The techniques of Marigold Linton's memory-retrieval experiments are discussed in M. Linton, "Ways of Searching and the Contents of Memory."

# INDEX